First published in 2023 by Wordville Press Ltd.
(info@wordville.net)

*Adventurer - Bernard Miles and the Mermaid
Theatre* © Alan Strachan, 2023

Cover image: Fourth birthday celebrations for
the Mermaid Theatre (1963) source: Mirrorpix

HB ISBN: 9781914228988
PB ISBN: 9781914228995

10 9 8 7 6 5 4 3 2 1

ADVENTURER

BERNARD MILES AND THE MERMAID THEATRE

Alan Strachan

with acknowledgments to Gerald Frow

ADVENTURER

BERNARD MILES AND THE MERMAID THEATRE

Wordville

performing arts in print

ACKNOWLEDGMENTS

With thanks to the London Library, the British Library, bb books, Heywood Hill Ltd, Alan Brodie, Jan Carey, Sir Michael Codron, the late Bill Freedman, Ben Frow, the late Derek Glynne, Lynn Haill, Jacki Harding, Andrew Hilton, Graham Jenkins, Ponnusamy Karunahan, Richard Mangan, Iain Mackintosh, Patricia Macnaughton, Jo Miles, Forbes Nelson, Biddy Noakes, the late Ron Pember, Damian Ramos and Penny Ryder.

For their support of this book, thanks to Sir Len Blavatnik, Simon Callow, Sir Michael Codron, Sir Richard Eyre, Andrew Hochhauser, KC, Sir Cameron Mackintosh, Sir Ian McKellen and Sir Howard Panter.

ALAN STRACHAN

Alan Strachan is a theatre director and biographer. Born in Scotland, his first theatrical job was as an ASM at the original Byre Theatre in St Andrews. He worked at the Mermaid Theatre for six years in the 1970s, directing new plays, revivals and co-devising and directing the long-running and internationally produced musical revues *Cowardly Custard* and *Cole*.

His biographical subjects include Michael Redgrave (*'Secret Dreams'*), *'Putting it On',* co-authored with its subject, leading London impresario Sir Michael Codron and Vivien Leigh (*'Dark Star'*) which won the 2020 Theatre Book Prize.

To the memory of Bernard and Josephine, with gratitude and love.

And for Jennifer.

Wot larks!

Table of Contents

List of Illustrations

Foreword

IN THE SUMMER OF 1969, I ran away from university to become an actor, but hadn't the least idea how to earn a living until such time as I could get into drama school. Cleaning seemed the only viable option. Appalled by this notion, a former colleague from the Old Vic box office who was then the No 2 at the Mermaid Theatre but about to return to the Vic, arranged for me to take over from him. I couldn't have been more delighted. I had known the Mermaid Theatre as a theatregoer from the mid 1960s. Going there always had the feeling of an adventure. Though it was a mere twenty minutes' walk from the West End, it seemed part of a different world altogether, on the cusp of the cities of Westminster and London, at the point where the street names suddenly ceased being nineteenth-century and became Elizabethan or Jacobean – Castle Baynard Street, White Lion Hill; the theatre itself sat in Puddle Dock. To reach it you walked past the delightfully mid-Victorian, faux-medieval, art-nouveau pub The Blackfriars, past Blackfriars Station with its impressive entrance, spelling out potential destinations – Dover, Calais, Paris, Brussels, Berlin, St Petersburg; opposite was the ugly 1960s mass of Printing House Square, out of which poured, at all hours of the day and night, waves of journalists, thirsty for news. Or just plain thirsty.

Turning right from the station, you were more or less at the theatre. There was something piratical about the place, this converted wharf abutting on the river, its great wide-open foyer, like a poop deck, kitted out with various nautical appurtenances, notably a great ship's bell which summoned the audience into the auditorium – that wonderfully bare and epic space bounded by the roughly cleaned brick walls of the old building, the seats sweeping straight down in a rake to the open stage where there was nowhere to hide: no wings, no flies, just lights, actors and carpentry. *Treasure Island* had been acted on one of these wooden structures: a great revolving disk, with trapdoors and masts and barrels ingeniously fashioned by the radically innovative Irish designer Sean Kenny. No wonder the theatre seemed piratical to me. Right at the centre of the show, as the ripest Long John Silver imaginable, giving Robert Newton a serious run for his money, was Bernard Miles, the onlie begetter of the Mermaid and all its works: scholar, playwright, actor, director, anarchist, otherwise known as the Uncrowned Hero of the Chiltern Hills, when, as not infrequently, he needed to raise a few bob for the theatre by doing a spot of moonlighting on a variety bill at the London Palladium.

Now I was a part of his kingdom. The box office manager, an elegant and warmly welcoming middle-aged woman named Joan Robinson was my guide to the Mermaid and its crazy ways; in her own fashion, pouring tea and supplying slices of cake to the public, she was quite as eccentric as everybody else employed by Bernard – of whom, I soon discovered, everyone despaired. The mere mention of his name was enough to provoke an automatic roll of the eyes, backstage, front of house, or in the dinky riverside restaurant at the back of theatre. If it was not his latest initiative – and the innovations came thick and fast – it was some terrible solecism committed; as far as the box office was concerned, we came to dread his visits, when he would wander in, live and rather vindictive parrot on shoulder, and answer the phone, offering a short history of Elizabethan theatre or his reflections on the failures of the current government or – horror! – free tickets for a sold-out show.

There was a remarkable turnover of general managers, for obvious reasons, occasional appearances of furtive and desperate men from the workshops who were finding it increasingly difficult to secure essential supplies on credit, a peppering of posh young chaps from the Arts Council, huge explosions from bewigged and ever so slightly squiffy Connie, who ran the bar, curses from Caroline and José, caterers and ex-acrobats, or a principled lament from Aggie, the distinguished elderly American in charge of the bookstall. Weaving through all this was the tiny figure of Sama Swaminathan, the House Manager, whose essential function was to pour oil, of which he appeared to have a limitless quantity, on troubled waters. It seemed as if Bernard rather than appointing staff, had cast them from a pool of character actors not unlike the RKO contract players of the 1930s: the little restaurant, for goodness sake, was run by the magnificently haughty Countess Wanda Krazynska. Cast in this way, the place seemed – and indeed was – in a state of perpetual crisis and turmoil, but because this was the normal state of affairs, no one seemed unduly perturbed. If you live under a volcano, evading oncoming lava is a routine matter.

All of this was radically different from the National Theatre at the Old Vic, my only other experience of professional theatre, which under the beady eyes of Sir Laurence Olivier and his House Manager, Rupert Rhymes, was run like a military operation. The Mermaid was, as I had rightly sensed even before I came to work there, altogether more nautical, more like being on a storm-tossed galleon, all hands on deck, the mate drunk, the captain on the fo'c'sle, roaring out instructions.

I saw all of this in action later. As it happens, when I arrived, things were somewhat becalmed. It was the theatre's tenth anniversary season, and Bernard had re-revived the theatre's very first production from 1959, *Lock Up Your Daughters*, a musical adapted by him from Henry Fielding's play *Rape Upon Rape*. Its bawdiness had lost some of its shock value by the late 1960s, but it was rollicking stuff, and packed them in, remaining in place for some months, during which life in the Box Office was uneventful. I filled the days with devising new operating systems, all of which were firmly discountenanced by Joannie, who had her own entirely original system, which was essentially no system at all. One particularly slow afternoon, I discovered somewhere in the recesses of the tiny Box Office a cache of programmes which she had been collecting over the years. I was astonished at the variety of the repertoire: the Ancient Greeks, Jacobean plays which had not been performed since the early 17th century, experimental Shakespeare (*Henry V in Battledress*), French and German plays of the 19th century (Sardou and Hauptmann), the plays of Henry James and Saki, all-but-forgotten early Shaw, Brecht – the British première of *Galileo* – and new plays, notably by Bill Naughton, among them the triumphant first production of *Alfie*. In Joannie's improvised archive there were, too, programme leaflets for the Mermaid's innovative theatre-in-education project, The Molecule Club, still going strong in 1969.

This was an astonishing repertory, to rival and even surpass that of any theatre in the country, even the heavily-subsidised National Theatre and Royal Shakespeare Company, both of which had started after the Mermaid. The mixture of popular and scholarly, of known and unknown, of exquisite and rough, was quintessential Bernard Miles, who, in addition to being the tireless motor of the organisation, frequently appeared on stage himself, with variable results, but he could often be superb when he hit the nail on the head, which he did famously as the father in *All in Good Time* – Olivier came backstage to tell him that he was jealous of his performance – and his Galileo, which

Brecht's widow proclaimed the equal of Ernst Busch, who created the part. To say nothing of Long John Silver.

I revised my view of Bernard. I had from the beginning been delighted by his antic spirit, his earthiness, his commitment to a neo-Elizabethan directness of communication between actors and audience, and his refusal to put on any managerial affectations. But now I saw that beyond that there was a radical intellect at work, and a vast ambition for the function of theatre within society.

All this time during that hot summer of '69, as I sat poring over the Mermaid's past, its future was ominously coming into existence. The constant accompaniment of our days was the sound of the wreckers' ball knocking down all the adjacent buildings while great concrete piles were driven – thump, thump, THUMP – into the riverbank to underpin the extension of the Embankment, so that when their work was done the sight of the lapping water and the swans drifting by the restaurant window, which had made eating there such a uniquely charming experience, could barely be glimpsed through the heavy traffic hurtling by. Soon Blackfriars station with all its promises of exotic travel would be gone, too, and in time the very walls of the Mermaid would be knocked down and expanded, to destroy the perfect natural symmetry of the original warehouse, the outline of the theatre itself invisible underneath the monstrous, shapeless, red-bricked new building piled on top of it.

At the launch of the newly-fashioned theatre with a musical version of *Eastward Ho!*, I was among the throng who filtered into the traduced new auditorium. As I descended the stairs, someone plucked at my sleeve. It was Bernard, looking much as he always had and completely at odds with the blingy opening night crowd. He looked like a gardener who had wandered in from deadheading the roses. "Simon," he said urgently, pulling me aside, "Simon. When all this" – he waved dismissively at the audience still piling in – "is behind us, we're going to get into our stride with a proper programme – the three great undeciders in dramatic history: Hamlet, the Prince of Homburg and Segismundo in *Life is a Dream*. You're ready for them now. What d'you say? What you say?" I said, shouting to be heard above the crowd, that of course I would do them. Could we speak tomorrow? "Very good, very good, very good," he said, and slipped into the crowd. I barely watched the feeble show, my brain teeming: they were three utterly thrilling plays and parts, two of them barely known in England. What was most thrilling was that the old the boy was still heroically trying to put the whole range of European theatre on to the Mermaid stage.

I called the office the next day – they told me that they didn't have a number for him; he was no longer part of the organisation. I never saw him again.

The Mermaid, fallen into the hands of unscrupulous and in some cases actually criminal developers, sputtered along for a few seasons under valiant actor-mangers like Roy Marsden and Marc Sinden, but both the surrounding area and the theatre itself had altogether lost their charm. In due course the theatre that had been a jewel in the crown of the City of London was declassified by one of its own planning committees – cashiered, stripped of its status as a theatre. It is now a conference centre.

I often think of Bernard, but always in the context of the Mermaid. When one day I came across Alan Strachan, whom I had known since those early days when we both worked there, he told me that he was writing a book about Bernard. I rejoiced: he's a superb biographer, as he has proved on many occasions, but as Bernard's sometime associate director, he knew the Mermaid's story and its glorious if idiosyncratic ways at first hand; he knows where the bodies are buried. I urged him on at all costs. Above all, I said, I wanted to know about Bernard before the Mermaid. Well, now I do. This full, rich and enthralling account of the making of one of the British theatre's great figures is long overdue. It fills in what has for far too long been a blank in the record of the great art at which this country has from at least the 16th century excelled. Bernard was one of its most important – and most original – standard bearers, for whom we have much to be grateful, as any reader of this riveting book will discover.

SIMON CALLOW, 2023

Prologue

FOR YEARS, ESPECIALLY after he was made only the second theatrical peer (Lord Miles of Blackfriars in the City of London), Bernard Miles promised he was shaping his autobiography (working title – '*The Hindsight Saga*'.) Often in the evening in his creation of the Mermaid Theatre on the north bank of the Thames at Blackfriars's Puddle Dock, he would say he was off to his office to get on with writing. But, after his death, only some scattered pages, in random order, were found. Similarly he planned a biography ('*Born to Sing*') of the great Norwegian soprano, Kirsten Flagstad, the outstanding female Wagnerian of the 20th century with whom he had a relationship in the 1950s but that too was never finished, with only a few loose pages surviving.

A biography of Bernard was written but never published. It was the work of Gerald Frow who had worked for several years from just before the opening of the Mermaid in 1959 as the theatre's press representative. Gerald was vital to the early success of the Mermaid; he was a superb publicist, universally popular with theatre journalists, arts editors and critics. His ebullient personality – he seemed always to be laughing – made an excellent foil to Bernard's more ironic character. He and Sally Miles, elder daughter of the three children of Bernard and his actress-director wife, Josephine Wilson, had a tempestuous affair and a frequently dramatic marriage but, for reasons unclear, Bernard fired Gerald (reason given – the theatre could not afford him – was hard to credit given the level of reward there) although their ties were never completely severed.

Gerald's book, begun not long after Bernard's death in 1991, had the incalculable benefit of being able to draw on conversations with and recollections of Bernard himself over the years, two of his sisters and his sister-in-law as well as school and Oxford friends together with colleagues from his early theatrical years. The book was never published; Biddy, Bernard's younger daughter explained that Gerald finished his book shortly before his own death and that the manuscript was unrevised, with some errors and unreliable chronology. Undoubtedly Gerald would have revised it had he lived, but as it was it remained unpublished.

But it should be stressed – strongly – that I would not have taken on this book had it not been for Gerald's work, especially the sections on his early life when so many who provided the material for that part of Bernard's life were now dead. I worked at the Mermaid for six years in the 1970s – latterly as associate director. I had always assumed subsequently that Bernard would finish his own book and, when that seemed unforthcoming, that another biographer would write of his life and of the Mermaid, an extraordinary episode in 20th century British theatrical history. I knew nothing of Gerald's book until much later when the leading literary agent, Alan Brodie, asked me if I would read it on behalf of Gerald's widow Jean (his third wife) with a view to getting it finally published. I enjoyed reading it although the MS was too long and needed substantial revision, but even with the promise of cuts and revisions no publisher seemed interested. Finally, a few of years ago, when I passed the Mermaid (all shuttered up) I decided to use Gerald's book as the basis for a new book. Sharing my feeling that the Mileses and the Mermaid deserved a book was Simon Callow who has been determined to help find a publisher and to drive a crowd-funding campaign to help publication. Simon felt, like me, that the book, while no hagiography, was a belated thank-you (Simon too was given an early break by Bernard). Without Simon's continued prompting I might well have abandoned the idea of writing Bernard's life.

ALAN STRACHAN, 2023

Part One

EVEN IN THE late 1950s London remained heavily scarred by wartime damage – an impoverished City of London was a particularly devastated area although somehow St. Paul's Cathedral, often targeted, remained unscathed. Down by the river the Blitz had devastated the area, with warehouses and offices lying in rubble. The south-west side of the Thames had seen the Festival of Britain bring some life with buildings such as the Skylon and eventually the whole South Bank was transformed.

On the opposite bank, some few hundred yards to the west, much of what had been a bustling Dickensian area was still mostly in ruins but, by the end of the decade, some changes were beginning the restoration of the whole of the City. Not least was the redevelopment of a blitzed warehouse of soot-covered brick (seven floors reduced to just the ground floor, a romantic ruin by night, depressing by day.) This stood by a tiny riverside creek – Puddle Dock. It seemed an unlikely space for a theatre, but actor/director Bernard Miles and his wife Josephine (also an actor) saw the potential of the site and somehow persuaded the City Fathers to allow them to develop the first theatre to be built in the City for 400 years.

Theatre, by its nature, is ephemeral (Caruso was the first to describe it as "sculpting in snow.") Both the Mileses were passionate about making theatre accessible and were equally passionate about the open stage; the Mermaid had an influence much bigger than its size, and virtually all the new theatres built in the 1960s boom incorporated aspects of the Mermaid's design – an open stage, a single raked block of seats with ample leg room, bars, restaurants, free programmes, informative and handsomely produced (until a more chilly financial climate prevailed.) Bernard and Josephine had already adapted two buildings as theatres – The Little Mermaid in the converted hall in the garden of their house in Acacia Road and another in the City's Royal Exchange (two seasons in each venue) for Coronation Year. Both were extremely successful – London, not just the City, welcomed these enterprises, antidotes to a still-austere landscape.

For Bernard, the whole area around Blackfriars up to St. Paul's, so strongly associated with the dramatists and poets of the late Elizabethan and earlier Jacobean theatre – and where Shakespeare had a house – was, in the words of theatrical historian W. MacQueen-Pope "theatrical holy ground." He was convinced, following the successful seasons at the converted hall and the Royal Exchange, it might be able to support a permanent theatre, even if none had been built there for 400 years. He poured all his formidable energy, and not a little of his income from films, into the project. There were some inevitable setbacks – by no means all the City Fathers approved of the plans and, at times, money was agonisingly tight. But the theatre box-office was open early in 1959 (a converted hut) with opening night scheduled for 28th May. Bernard was determined to open on schedule and to exploit the riverside position as much as possible; he and Gerald Frow were set on beginning with a bang; they took infinite pains to plan a gala occasion.

They had a balmy evening for the launch of the Mermaid with Bernard vowing a terrible vengeance on Gerald if the show did not start at precisely 6.10pm. Bernard and Josephine had just climbed into their glad rags to wait at the entrance to the auditorium just as the Mayoral limousine eased its way into Upper Thames Street. Meanwhile, carefully synchronised half a mile upstream aboard Scott's *Discovery*, preparations for a small boat manned by Westminster Sea Cadets and carrying a little mermaid had been completed and now put off from the pier and headed for Puddle Dock. The history of the Thames featured strongly when just before the boat arrived four watermen, all from the Phelps family, noted on the river for decades, took their places. All the Phelpses were holders of the Doggett Coat and Badge, initiated by the 18th century actor Thomas Doggett, clad in the orange livery of their order with, on their left arm, the prominent circular badge signifying Liberty. They made an impressive sight, with the cadets lined up alongside the Mermaid, timed precisely as the Lord Mayor with his party including the City Swordsman, the Common Cryer and the City Marshall processed with the Mileses down the cobbled lane on the other side of the theatre from Puddle Dock, leading to the riverside steps. The little mermaid (Caroline Hawkins, daughter of the actor Jack Hawkins) was carried ashore by Edward Phelps. As they joined the Lord Mayor's party, Harry Phelps addressed the Lord Mayor on a microphone relaying his words to the waiting audience asking Gillett to carry the little mermaid into the theatre, "its right and proper home." The Mayor replied in similar vein, bestowing her name upon the actors whose assembly "places all in the debt of Master Bernard Miles." Young Caroline was then transferred into the Mayor's arms and he led the procession through the theatre's dock doors on to the low stage. Exactly at that point the coup de théâtre carefully planned by Bernard and Gerald began. All traffic on the river ceased while the great bells of St. Paul's pealed out and the flotilla of tugs lying near the theatre sounded their sirens in salute. Joining the music from the river the onstage orchestra on the set's upper level joined in the glorious '*Lord Mayor's March*' from Handel's *Scipio* during which Gerald tried to control the throng of TV and press reporters while the Lord Mayor spoke eloquently over the music praising "a wonderful concept of theatre, of enormous courage and enterprise" adding "I think I can speak for all of the City when I say that we will do all we can to make this theatre a lasting success." To crown this the ribbon round the mermaid's waist fell away, there was a superbly confident trumpet flourish and thunderous applause. As the Lord Mayor commanded, "on with the Play", Gerald pushed the protesting media out of the theatre and, as the dock doors closed, the City chimes and the first chords of Johnson's score sounded the underscoring to the prologue of *Lock Up Your Daughters*.

The opening production, subject of much speculation, had been kept a secret for as long as possible ("I learned from General Horrocks's memoirs," said Bernard – "that surprise is the first element of any venture," adding, "well, our first production will be a surprise, I can tell you.") He had returned to the forgotten old Henry Fielding play, *Rape Upon Rape* (purchased for one shilling in a Scarborough second-hand bookshop). The title was, of course, unusable as were Fielding's own alternatives – *The Coffee-House Politician* or *The Justice Caught in His Own Trap*. Bernard and Josephine held informal lunches occasionally at Puddle Dock – sausages, English cheeses and stoneground bread, plus rosé wine. At one of those events a guest was musical director/composer Antony Hopkins. Offered a drink he refused, accepting only a soft drink, also refusing, as a non-smoker, a large cigar. Bernard was somewhat bewildered, having, he said, never met a teetotaller and non-smoker of a musician. Feeling he was letting Bernard down, Hopkins added: "But lock up your daughters!" Bernard had his title.

Bernard had slimmed down Fielding's text to create a lean, fast-moving book for the musical but the team would have a dangerously short period to come up with a text and score before rehearsals. Bernard asked his friend Laurie Johnson to write the score; an extremely versatile composer and arranger – he arranged for big bands – Ted Heath, Geraldo – before setting up as a freelance. He was intrigued by *Lock Up* and accepted at once; the lyricist was also his suggestion – a young Cockney called Lionel Bart who had recently received golden opinions for a musical for Theatre Workshop at E15 under Joan Littlewood – *Fings Ain't Wot They Used To Be*. It was an inspired suggestion – Bart had a casual, flip style, perfectly suited to the material. He was also a fast worker, just as well given the schedule. Bernard was delighted by the energy Bart brought to the show:

> "No fast cars then, no silk shirts, cashmere jerseys or suede shoes. He was just a simple working lad as keen as mustard to get his feet on the ladder of stardom."

Bart's lyrics for *Lock Up* were ceaselessly inventive, none more so than the opening number, cunningly introducing the main characters along with the City Crier's calling the hours, alongside powerful ballads, a very clever cha-cha and a strong first-act closer for Hy Hazell as a neglected but randy wife:

> "When does the ravishing begin?
> You could burst me with a pin,
> So much sin I'm holding in."

Another younger and iconoclastic member of the creative team was the designer, a 26 year-old Irishman called Sean Kenny. Often taciturn, even more often dismissive of most current theatre design, which was still essentially decorative and painterly. Change was on the way. Another bold young design talent was John Bury with several trail-blazing productions at Stratford East to his credit. Both explored the possibilities of materials such as concrete and steel, disdaining the purely decorative designs of which Lesley Hurry was a master. He bumped into Bury at the Stratford-upon-Avon stage door, elegantly suited and booted. Hurry regarded the boiler-suited Bury, before speaking "Go home, you fucking cement-mixer," to which Bury simply shrugged, just as Kenny would have done. Bernard, also something of an iconoclast and a designer himself, was able to appreciate Kenny's art. He shared with Kenny a passion for the work of Edward Gordon Craig and Bernard's admiration for that informed his appreciation of Bury and Kenny.

Sean's mantra was simple:

"Let us free the theatre from the cumbersome shackles of outmoded tradition."

Their temperaments were polarry different but Walter Hodges had to admit his admiration for Sean's work:

"I didn't like him at all because he appeared almost contemptuous of me – well, let's say cocky, no – let's say rude."

Nevertheless, he went on to say:

"Sean Kenny was one of Bernard's great discoveries (not great – greatest), a meteoric career which, in fact, was created by the Puddle Dock Mermaid style."

Hodges was not the old-fashioned figure Sean might suggest:

"How wonderful to see a new playhouse of fresh form rise up amid the confusion of our enfeebled theatre. The Mermaid is our empty room – let's use it – all of us – playwrights, directors, designer, actors, spectators – everyone."

Most critics were as voluble in praise for the Mermaid, the building itself and *Lock Up* rapidly became a 'hot ticket.'

There would be problems – there can be no doubt that the Mermaid was underfunded for most of its existence. Bernard was going to have to be extra careful as he planned the theatre's future repertoire.

THE MERMAID ENHANCED London's theatreland and London was where Bernard, after a peripatetic apprenticeship in provincial repertory and on tour, was based for the bulk of his life. But he remained at heart the countryman he was born. His most famous creation 'on the halls' in Variety was cradled in the Nonconformist soil of his childhood – 'The Uncrowned Hero of the Chiltern Hills', ruminating over his cartwheel or at his wagon and when just before the war in the late 1930s he and his family moved to an isolated cottage in the Chiltern foothills he said that there "I re-learned the language of my heart," claiming that "the country and all that belongs to it has run like a steel cord through everything I have done."

Gerald Frow was able to trace Bernard's ancestry back to the early 19th century and his great-grandfather James Miles who was, in common with many of Bernard's ancestors, a farm labourer. Mileses were plentiful in that border country where Hertfordshire, Buckinghamshire and Middlesex meet. James married the daughter of another farm worker, Mary Ford, but not long after the wedding they moved away, aiming to cross via the Grand Junction Canal into Middlesex. The area gradually became swallowed up by rapid urbanisation into Greater London but then was still heavily wooded with the same rolling hills and striking views. It looked initially a seductive scene but, while the canal meandered charmingly, closer inspection would reveal the many barges laden with agricultural produce and all kinds of raw materials destined for London and, beside the canal it was a less sylvan scene with a copper mine and the large kilns of the Harefield Lime Factory. James is described as a "lime labourer", still at work aged 79, in census returns. Like most of Bernard's ancestors he had a fierce nonconformist work ethic, as did Bernard himself.

Bernard's grandfather was another James, one of seven children born in Lime Works Road; five boys followed in the labouring tradition while the two girls entered domestic service. Emma, the elder, remained single and became a talented dressmaker (a gift to be passed down the line.) The family moved a few miles south to a stretch of the Uxbridge Road between Hillingdon Heath and Hayes End, then still recognisably 'country.'

Eliza married a gamekeeper, John Grey, and soon John Miles joined them in a cottage off the Uxbridge Road. At 17, he was by all accounts a cheerful chap working on several local farms. His bride, another Eliza, was a labourer's daughter and they moved to a small cottage near Hayes. They had no children; in 1871 Eliza died at which point James left the area and moved to the sharply contrasting world of London's East End, then a teeming, noisy area of family workshops, immigrant workers and artisans. Now working as a gardener, James married again, to Marian, daughter of a Middlesex farm labourer. The couple moved soon afterwards back to the Uxbridge Road to set up a small general store and it was there that Bernard's father, Edwin James Miles, the first of three children, was born in 1875, to be followed by two daughters.

James was struck by tragedy once more in the late summer of 1885. Aged 10, Edwin and his sister Louisa were in the living-room with both front and back doors open. A paraffin lamp stood on the table at which Edwin was reading. Somehow the lamp exploded and, although a policeman ran to extinguish the fire, the two children were badly burnt. His other sister Emma later told Gerald

Frow: "I well remember the dreadful sight of them being attended to and I dread the thoughts of it." Louisa's injuries were so severe that she died. There was a family suggestion that the lamp somehow was overturned by James, who was drunk at the time; Edwin later confided to his sister that was the case. He was less scarred "but he was in Hayes Cottage Hospital for a very long time and had to wear a handkerchief around his face to keep the bottom lip up."

Edwin never returned to school but started his long working life as soon as possible and soon after his 16th birthday he began work as a labourer at a garden nursery in Hillingdon Heath (he loved flowers and plants from a very young age.) He moved to a new, adventurous flower nursery at nearby Cowley where he stayed for the rest of his working life. Started by a young man from a long-established family of printers and publishers of local newspapers, Milton Hutchings, who also had a passion for plants and realised too what a find he had in Edwin who was soon working as the firm's salesman, travelling regularly to Covent Garden. He was discovered to be a first-class salesman (his son dubbed him "The King of Covent Garden.")

Edwin met his wife, Barbara Hooper, a cook in a Hayes household, outside the Methodist Chapel off to Uxbridge Road. Devout but not a regular churchgoer, he was charmed by Barbara's lovely voice and began courting her on Sundays. In August 1901 they married. Bernard never knew the full story of his mother's background. Her family originally came from Scotland – the Deeside area with villages such as Glenlochar Bridge. Bernard's parents owned an old family Bible belonging to his maternal grandfather and always could remember the oddly spelled verse on the fly-leaf:

"John Fletcher is my name,
Scotland is my nashen,
Glenlochar is my dwelling-place
And Christ is my salvashen"

From his two marriages John Fletcher fathered eight daughters and a son, occasionally visiting Stockport to visit his daughter Jane, respectably married as Mrs John Griffiths. However, nine years previously she had given birth to an illegitimate daughter Barbara. She was Bernard's mother.

The marriage of Edwin and Barbara Miller was happy. They made their home in a relatively new house in a row of small brick buildings in what was still open country near Hillingdon Heath, of which Bernard retained some vivid early memories:

"At the time there were working farms all around us and one of the first things I remember is sitting on top of a load of hay piled five or six feet, pulled by a great Shire horse named Dobbin. But the swallowing up process had already begun and with oddly designed houses springing up on either side of the main Uxbridge road, the seeds of ribbon development were already seen."

Four children were born to Edwin and Barbara - Leonard (1902), Kathleen (1904), Enid (1906) and Bernard (1907). Barbara was an attractive, capable, busy woman who brought her children up very well, while Edwin was a seemingly gentle, undemonstrative man (Kathleen said that although he was scarred, children loved him.) Their beliefs, critical to the children's rearing, consisted of simple agricultural and Nonconformist values; according to Bernard one must be honest, punctual, industrious, orderly, truthful even to bluntness, generous according to one's means and, last but not least, one should not show off. It might be said that Bernard met most of those basic requirements although he had, too, an occasional wayward streak. It was a musical household; there was a gramophone (an early party piece of Bernard's, learnt from Harry Lauder's recording, was '*I Love a Lassie.*') Kathleen recalled:

"On Sunday afternoon when we came home from Sunday school we'd sit round the piano... my mother would play hymns and we'd sing. And at nights when we were abed, my mother would play the piano and my father would play the violin – he played beautifully. They'd have a little concert on their own."

Nobody could ever recall the reason but soon the family changed their religious alliance from the Methodists to the Baptists and now worshipped at the Salem Baptist Chapel in the Uxbridge Road –

"...where I learned I was a fearful sinner and I had already done a lot of wicked things (I was only three years old) but that Jesus loved me and would forgive me and that, if I agreed to be forgiven, I would go to heaven when I died, which was a great comfort to me."

He learned to sing hymns such as '*Dare to be a Daniel*'; these simple songs were never forgotten, not least the verse inspired by St. Mathew's gospel, sung at his funeral –

Jesus bids us shine with a clear, pure light,
Like a little candle burning in the night;
In this world of darkness we must shine,
You in your small corner and I in mine.

Bernard's recollections of his early childhood recall the Laurie Lee of '*Cider with Rosie*', especially the social highlights of the Sunday School year, the summer and winter special occasions. The former saw two farm carts drawn by shire horses Daisy and Dobbin, carry children through country roads to a field with trestle tables laden with sandwiches and big urns of tea, followed by races and a tug-of-war, while the winter treat was held in the Sunday schoolroom near Christmas-time, with Magic Lantern shows which Bernard adored:

"Little did those good folk realise that they were leading one small soul towards Satan's chosen ground, the theatre and towards the music hall, to the basest part of it!"

He also recited at the winter occasions, never forgetting the sound of the whole chapel bursting into applause:

"And, as our critic William Hazlitt says: "One thunder of applause from the pit and gallery is worth a century of posthumous fame." In other words, I was hooked – for exhibiting myself, for being the centre of an assembly of which I would be the one they were looking at and praising and applauding."

By this time the Miles family had moved, just some few hundred yards closer to Uxbridge to "a house of some quality and certainly a step up in the world." As a special treat occasionally he was permitted to accompany his father on the overnight journey with the plants and flowers to Covent Garden, leaving the nursery late in the evening, Bernard wrapped up in the back of the firm's new van, arriving after dawn to hear rival salesmen setting up their stalls. These were magic trips for the boy, now old enough for his first schooldays.

Bernard never was one of Shakespeare's "Seven Ages of Man" schoolboys, "creeping like snail unwillingly to school": From his earliest schools – the Infant School in Hillingdon and then, aged eight, the Heath Boys' School – he was blissfully happy, eager for learning, excellent at games and always ready for fun, his talent for mimicry, his streak of comedy, making him popular with his schoolmates. From the outset he was, to use his sister Kathleen's word, "adventurey"; he climbed trees, often falling out of them, and rode bicycles, often falling off them. On more than a few occasions he spent time, often in plaster, in Hayes Cottage Hospital with broken bones, concussion or dislocated shoulders. 'Adventurey' came to describe his whole life. He had a similarly venturesome schoolfriend, Sydney Rutherford, son of the Baptist Chapel's minister, with whom he got up to all sorts of mischief. Sydney's nephew Tony Rutherford, reported later that the nearest pillar box to Bernard's home was inconveniently remote:

"So Bernard and Syd moved it – to outside Bernard's house."

The impression of Bernard and Syd then recalls the 'adventurey' escapades of William Brown and his chum Ginger in Richmal Crompton's '*Just William*' books.

Serious schooling began in the autumn of 1918 at Uxbridge County School where his brother Leonard was already a pupil. This was an ideal school for a precocious boy avid for knowledge. The school was established under the 1902 Education Act which put education primarily into the care of local councils empowered to provide secondary education. It had opened in 1907 under an enlightened headmaster, the Reverend Walter Sawfell, strict but kind who remained head throughout Bernard's time. There were sceptics – not everyone approved of boys and girls in their teens being educated together – and it was not free (both Leonard and Bernard had scholarships) but Mr. Miles had to find the fee (£2.2s.6d) for Enid.

Bernard thoroughly enjoyed his eight years at Uxbridge County where young people were treated as intelligent human beings and encouraged to have interests not simply academic. Bernard was described as "precociously bright" academically, quickly excelling at Latin and mathematics, sailing through exams with ease. But by far the most enduring influence on him was the senior English teacher, Miss Cecilia Hill, his first theatrical mentor. Ken Pearce, a teacher at UCS and later the school archivist, wondered, "Would Bernard have ever embarked on an acting career if it had not been for the remarkable lady?" Herself a schoolmaster's daughter, Miss Hill had been partly educated at Cheltenham Ladies' College and had taught at various private schools. Even seventy years later many UCS former pupils remember her magnetic personality, always strikingly well dressed, something of a Jean Brodie figure. A group of her brightest Sixth Formers would be invited back to her house near the school; Bernard, in time, would be frequently found among the chosen ones treated to "tea and vigorous conversation."

Bernard made his acting debut with his brother in a 1920 'entertainment' in aid of the school library, performing the *King John* episode in which the boy Prince pleads with Hubert to "spare his eyes" ("B. Miles deserves special praise" wrote the school magazine.) The first complete play in which Bernard acted for Miss Hill was one which she had written herself as part of 1923's 'Christmas Entertainment'. Titled *The Guest* it was set in Uxbridge's King's Head Inn "a few days before Christmas, 1600." A kind of Elizabethan miscellany of music and verse with Bernard in a major role as The Poet, this was described as a great success. He also appeared in some of the *Little Plays of St. Francis*, Laurence Housman's cycle of plays on the life of St. Francis of Assisi. Other productions under Miss Hill in which Bernard appeared included *Twelfth Night* (his Malvolio described as "especially good in the Dark Room") and the melancholy Jacques in *As You Like It*. Intriguingly in the light of Bernard's explorations of the stage space in various Mermaids of the 1950s, Miss Hill's productions are described in the school magazine as being given on "an open stage" with a minimum of scenery and furniture, colour being supplied by splendidly vivid costumes.

By far the most influential venture nudging Bernard to the stage was his final appearance in the school play when he played the title role in *Richard III*, by far Cecilia Hill's most ambitious production to date. With more than thirty speaking parts, she dragooned even old boys like Leonard and Sydney into appearing while she played the Duchess of York herself. As a bonus Cecilia, who was known to have London theatrical friends, had invited to the second performance a major classical star, Baliol Holloway, who for several years had led the Stratford Memorial Theatre company and would soon head the Old Vic where he would star in a new production of *Richard III*. Then 43, tall and lean, he had been on the stage since he was 16 and had a mesmeric stage presence (photographs of his Richard III, lank-haired with piercing blue eyes, resemble Olivier in the role). Cecilia had arranged with "Ba" to show Bernard round the Old Vic one Saturday morning and Bernard, who had never been inside a theatre before, was thrilled to stand on the historic stage, be taken backstage and to hear the actor's theatrical tales. "Ba" even produced the mighty sword which he always used as Richard and presented it to Bernard to use in Cecilia's production. This experience surely spurred Bernard on to give his very best and, according to the *Middlesex Advertiser and Gazette* which printed a long review under a two-decker headline ("Richard III – brilliant acting by B. Miles"), he seemed to have succeeded:

> "He made the man live before us in all his pride of intellect, his ruthlessness and cruelty. From his first speech, in which he muses on his deformity and determines to be revenged on the world, we see him greedily ministering to that pride... he meets his death with pride unbroken."

After this, Bernard was set on a theatrical career. He was leaving UCS as one of its most popular pupils. He had shone at sports as well as academically – on the football field as Captain of the First XI following Leonard and on the cricket field. Although gifted in team sports his greatest sporting fulfilment was on the athletic track, running – alone. As he put it:

> "I was moderately good at games and always did my best. But I loved running... Nothing expresses the ego like running. You're on your own, totally isolated, fighting yourself all the time, exquisite pain, misery and joy too."

Bernard never totally lost touch with UCS. Grateful for the grounding there, he occasionally visited old teachers in later life and attended the funerals of his favourites. But now he was ready for University. His parents had already decided that he, like Leonard, would be a teacher and that he would go to Oxford. He always acknowledged that his father raised the money for Oxford (no scholarship this time) by "Thrift. Massive thrift!" Also, both Leonard, now a teacher, and Cecilia Hill are said to have contributed in some measure to his University education.

There was some time after leaving UCS before he would "go up." He earned some cash that summer working at the horticultural nursery ("I was a great disbudder.") Then he had a brief holiday. He and Cecilia Hill visited Belgium. Together.

BERNARD HAD BEEN a star at UCS. At Pembroke College, Oxford however, his lustre dimmed, so much so that he failed to get a degree.

He often said throughout his life that he felt something of an outsider and indeed, at that time, students from his background were comparatively few at Oxford. He made surprisingly little impact; looking into his early life Gerald Frow was taken aback when so few of his contemporaries could even remember him although Pembroke was one of Oxford's smaller colleges. Partly this was because his parents had insisted he spend his first year in lodgings rather than in college rooms. This was an unusual arrangement; possibly his parents were over-protective and wanted to keep him away from the gilded Bright Young Things whose pranks often filled the gossip-columns. And, of course, money was tight (Bernard had a lifelong dread of debt.) So for most of his three Oxford years Bernard was a loner. Fellow 'Pemmy' undergraduate Sydney Linton recalled "a quiet looker-on" while Hugh Willatt, who later worked for the Arts Council, described him as:

"without any particular friend of group of friends… He seemed to live his own life, somewhat eccentric, amiable and a little baffling."

He did become friends with Tom Hopkinson, later editor of *Picture Post*, but he went down at the end of Bernard's first year. Very surprisingly Bernard did no acting at Oxford – the OUDS records have no mention of his membership – apart from a few Pembroke playreadings. When Leonard visited they saw Sir John Martin-Harvey in Shaw's *The Shewing-Up of Blanco Posnet* (later part of the Mermaid's Shavian rediscoveries.) In a letter home mentioning this theatre visit he added, "Miss Hill is coming down tomorrow night – we are going to hear a great Polish pianist."

Company of course was not essential for Bernard; his early theatrical life on tour in 'digs' meant often considerable solitude, but as he once wrote to his manager Derek Glynne: "I like being alone. What I mean is I can be quite happy alone!" He was also solitary on the Iffley Road running track, doing well in competition; his personal best for the mile of 4 minutes, 35 seconds was impressive for those days. Bad luck prevented further distinction when a knee injury scuppered hopes of becoming a running 'Blue' although he carried on running in the University second team, nicknamed "The Centipedes" (membership was restricted originally to 50 people – 100 feet) and was elected to the famous Achilles Club, its membership made up of past and present members of the Oxford and Cambridge Athletic Clubs, entry by election only

(later in reference books Bernard listed his clubs as "Savile and Achilles" – he never joined the Garrick which he thought was too exclusive.)

One organisation he did join was Oxford's John Bunyan Society which had links with New Road's Baptist Church. Founded in 1905 it was formed to enable Baptist members "for discussion of matter of a religious and literary nature." He was a regular attendee and, in 1928, was elected president. His name appears in the records of one other Oxford society, the Philosophical Society, which was to prove his academic downfall. The President of that Society was a notable Oxford figure, the philosophy tutor R. G. Collingwood. An affable, chubby and balding figure, always in tweeds, Collingwood had an international reputation, publishing his *Religion and Philosophy* in 1916. His scrutiny of empirical psychology and analysis of religion as a form of knowledge was part of his continuing attempt to reconcile philosophy and history and Bernard was highly impressed by it and Collingwood's lectures which he began to attend perhaps too frequently. The philosopher, also a noted archaeologist (an authority on Roman Britain), was one of those Renaissance men by whom Bernard was always fascinated. Had Collingwood been Bernard's tutor and his subject philosophy he might well have achieved a First Class Degree. Unfortunately he was meant to be studying Modern History.

One further thing occupied Bernard's Oxford spare time. Leonard's future wife Winnie, then studying at Cambridge, visited Bernard occasionally, summing up his extracurricular interest smartly – "Women!" Winnie said she had an old schoolfriend who became "very friendly with him." In later years he would talk fondly of assignations with girls from St. Hugh's or St. Hilda's. He concealed the name of one regular squeeze by calling her "Daphne", treating her soon after they had met to a recital by the great guitarist Segovia and another by the Russian pianist Vladimir de Pachman and it would seem that his outlay on concert tickets brought the desired results: "A mutual love of music naturally begat an even closer harmony."

An Oxford female undergraduate who would become a friend (with no romantic interest) was Marjorie Clayton, daughter of an ex-actor now part of the management Waller and Clayton who had produced the London version of *No, No Nanette!* Subsequently a chance meeting with Marjorie would lead to a vital turning point in Bernard's career.

His long vacation from Oxford in 1928 was somewhat eventful. Once again he acted as a member of the Old Uxonians' Dramatic Club, playing (very amusingly) the pedantic schoolmaster Holofernes in Cecilia's production of *Love's Labour's Lost* while he also took part, as did Sydney Rutherford, in the Past & Present Pupils' cricket match. A week later he attended the fifth birthday party of Joan Marguerite Waterhouse, sister of Katherine Waterhouse, one of Bernard's UCS friends, bringing the presents of a Japanese doll and an A.A. Milne-ish poem. Over the years sporadically, he would correspond with Joan in a kind of epistolary amitié amoureuse.

The Mileses had moved into a new house, "Glenlochar", further up the Uxbridge Road and, during that vacation, Bernard's secret affair with Cecilia Hill was rumbled. His mother found a letter from Cecilia to Bernard indicating strongly that they were lovers. His aghast mother and sisters turned to the Lord ("All of us prayed that nothing would come of it and Bernard might be saved from this older woman's wiles.") Edwin eschewed prayers typically bluntly announcing "She will never put her foot in our gateway." And, as far as can be discovered, she never did. In any event his relationship with Cecilia seems to have dwindled into a warm friendship which continued until her death in 1968.

Returning to Oxford to begin his final year, Robin Collingwood's lectures remained his principal focus. Hugh Willatt drily commented later that "As to history, his proper subject, he was, I suppose, an erratic student." Bernard had done well academically to date, having passed his Mods, (his intermediate exams) in Latin, French, English and Political Economy in 1927. But as his Finals approached he began to realise with a rather sickening clarity that he had a huge amount of cramming still to do. His future-sister-in-law Winnie recalled sitting in the Glenlochar garden with him (Winnie was also approaching her Finals) as he said:

"Winnie, I think I've left it too late. I thought I could do it in four months. And I've only got three."

He was, uncharacteristically, panicking: He had applied successfully for a teaching post to begin in the autumn term at a preparatory school in Yorkshire (he had glowing references from UCS teachers, including Cecilia) but he suspected there might be none from Oxford and dreaded disappointing the family and all who had believed in him. And he had, indeed, left it too late. When the results were posted on July 31st, he had to read that he had "failed to satisfy the examiners." The family row when he returned, tail very much between his legs, to Glenlochar, was never forgotten. Winnie was there and recalled:

> "I never heard Mr. Miles raise his voice except that one time with Bernard. He properly let fly at him."

Edwin flatly refused to allow Bernard to omit news of his failure to the school to which he should soon be travelling, while Bernard tried to claim blithely that it was only a prep school so a degree was not essential. Edwin furiously insisted, demanding Bernard write to the head with news of his results and to ask if he could still come (he could.) But the temperature at home climbed further when, somewhat unwisely, Bernard mentioned the possibility of an acting career, at which his father became incandescent, thundering, "Be a teacher! And stay a teacher!" Bernard's sister Kathleen also witnessed this fiery scene with father and son "going at each other hammer and tongs" until in his rage Bernard snatched a book from the shelf and hurled it across the room ("It was a book I loved," said Kathleen).

SO IT WAS a decidedly subdued Bernard who set out for Filey, just south of Scarborough, in 1929, still harbouring theatrical dreams which would persist in the austere and chilly climate of the North Yorkshire coast.

Filey in the 1920s was still a quiet seaside town with a large fishing fleet, busier in summer when holidaymakers filled the B&Bs and the town's many cafés. Out of season it could be bleak with North Sea winds lashing the coast and the cliffs.

Never one to be downcast for long, after his Oxford disappointment Bernard rather took to Filey. Undoubtedly by now, despite the paternal opposition, he was set on a professional stage career, looking on his schoolmaster days purely as a stopgap – and a bit of a lark – regularly telling his pupils that he would set off for London and life upon the stage at the end of the school year.

Southcliff Preparatory School, perched on the cliff tops, a redbrick, tall-chimneyed building (built 1901) was comparatively enlightened, certainly nothing like Evelyn Waugh's Llanabba in '*Decline and Fall*' although there was the standard emphasis on sports (the prospectus boasted "pure air and water, a bracing atmosphere and playing fields"), run by the Reverend Gaskell with another four masters (about 40 boys boarded). Bernard had been engaged to teach 'General Subjects' – English, History and Art – plus taking the boys for cricket and football. Soon he became a popular teacher, easy going ("I never taught them anything much, except maybe to laugh"); having settled in he decided to enjoy this dutiful year. He played loud dance music (Jack Hylton's Kit-Kat Band) in his bedsit on the attic floor, went for long runs along the cliff-tops in even the wettest, windiest weather. And there were jolly weekends when his old chum Syd Rutherford from UCS came up to Yorkshire, bunking in Bernard's room and joining him in Scarborough's Spa Ballroom for the Saturday dances. Bernard introduced Syd to his "rich widder-woman"; how he hooked up with Kathleen Crabbe, "a very smart lady", around forty and sounding not unlike Cecilia Hill, remains a mystery. He may well have had a dalliance with her but when he introduced her to Syd, clearly sparks were struck and soon she and Syd were married despite the 15 years age gap.

Bernard's sister-in-law Winnie, now a teacher herself, always insisted he would have been an excellent teacher; he liked recommending books and composers to younger friends like Joan Waterhouse and, at Puddle Dock, contemplated a morning assembly with staff and casts before starting work. He retained throughout his life something of the air of a tall, lean and bespectacled schoolmaster starting each day with a notepad, finely-honed pencils, a penknife for sharpening them and an india-rubber eraser. But, by the summer of 1930, he was keen to be off to London to do what he wanted to do.

Bypassing Glenlochar, Bernard headed for the capital having already fixed to share a flat with Tom Hopkinson at the very up-market address of Great Smith Street, Westminster in the heart of division-bell area. Hopkinson then worked for an advertising agency and had been offered the apartment in the 18th century house belonging to his uncle, an Independent MP who used the ground and first floors, letting the upper floor to Tom. There was an attic room for Bernard's bedroom and they paid the princely sum of £1 a week each for rent.

In those days, with a booming touring circuit and an increasingly flourishing repertory system alongside London theatre, it was much easier in pre-TV days to find work in the theatre. At that stage Bernard was still somewhat green, not entirely sure of what kind of actor he wanted to be, but with his drive towards hard work he was prepared to start at the bottom, to stage-manage or paint scenery – even design and build it – if necessary. A constant was his conviction that the theatre was much more than just entertainment but that it had a vital moral purpose. When he was more experienced he wrote of his feeling about acting in a piece included in the souvenir brochure for the 1959 Mermaid's opening. Satirically he creates the persona of a Mrs. Worthington's daughter, of minimal talent but rich and famous as an 'influencer' avant le jour who is taken up by a TV producer for a mindless game show which makes her a star with her own series, a newspaper column and a new brand of lipstick (this was written long before reality programmes like *Love Island*). He goes on to say that this must surely discourage any hard-working aspirant while failing to answer the question, "Why do we go on doing it?"

For Bernard, the answer is that it offers unique opportunities for self-expression, laughter, applause, intense and loving companionship. "The sensation of holding an audience spellbound, of being utterly in control of them, is deeply satisfying… what is there to compare with unexpected success in a barn? Or for that first love on tour, in a provincial bedsitting room? But the actor in turn scatters blessings, he passes the benediction on. He is part of the healing fraternity. For even at its worst the stage is a solace, a cure for loneliness, a gathering together in the name of mankind. More and more frequently there steals over one the suspicion that the whole human story is a kind of play, a tragi-comedy in many episodes with the script still being written."

On the subject of acting Bernard was quite prepared to take up the cudgels with James Agate of *The Sunday Times*, by far the most powerful critic of his era. Bernard totally disagreed with Agate who claimed, as a lecturer and after-dinner speaker, that he got nothing back from any audience ("It is my job as an artist not to get but to give") to which Bernard responded, "Nonsense":

> "You depend upon the attention of your audience. You know when you have them where you want them… a theatrical performance is an act of faith between actors and audience. Each goes out towards the other. The collaboration of audience with the artist is the sine qua non of all art and, most of all, the dramatic art."

And when Agate continued to argue that the actor's work is done before the curtain goes up, Bernard continued:

> "You make the simple confusion of performance with preparation. An actor's preparation is complete before he meets an audience but not his performance… My performance before I meet the first audience is ready but not complete. And each fresh audience creates a fresh performance."

No reply from Agate is recorded to that salvo. Even when a beginner these were Bernard's views on acting although he knew he would have to work hard ("watch and learn" were lifelong watchwords.)

HIS FIRST PROFESSIONAL engagement came soon after his arrival in London, courtesy of the man he always would call his "theatrical godfather", Baliol Holloway. Ba always wanted to form his own London company dedicated to Shakespeare with the highest acting and scenic standards; he had grown tired of the often lower-than-low budget operations at Stratford and The Old Vic ("Oh God," the devout Lilian Baylis would pray at Waterloo Road; "send me some good actors – cheap") and aimed to restore the high scenic standards, if less lavishly, of the Irving/Tree era. Finally, in 1930, he had funding and Baliol Holloway Productions opened at The New Theatre (now the Noël Coward) with Ba once more in the title role in *Richard III*. It was a strong company with several ex-'Bensonians', actors schooled in those companies under Sir Frank Benson; they included the formidable Nancy Price as Queen Margaret and the extraordinary Hubert Carter who had acted with Tree, a massive man with a mighty voice (Brian Blessed-cubed) who drank, before each performance, a pint of ox blood brought directly from the butcher.

Bernard was contracted (£4.10 per week) to play Second Messenger "and to assist the Property Master" which he was happy to do, having made and painted banners and shields for UCS ventures. Rehearsals – fascinating for Bernard – went well but technical and dress rehearsals were sticky; the production aimed to be fleet without complicated scene-changes. It was well-reviewed; the production, with specially-composed music by both Vaughan Williams and Gustav Holst, was praised for being free from "both the reverential dullness and the studied eccentricities that are alternate blights on Shakespeare."

Now in his own mind a legitimate, professional actor this experience also made Bernard realise that he could always have a career behind the scenes, loving as he did "timber, canvas, cleats, stage-screws, counterweights and the smell of boiling size."

That got him his next job when Nancy Price decided to go into management with her People's National Theatre, where he stage-managed, made furniture and scene-painted. The little Fortune Theatre opposite the stage-door of Drury Lane was the organisation's first house (it never had a permanent home during its decade of existence). Price was an indomitable woman, tall and commanding with a deep-rooted commitment to popular theatre with the policy of "Good Plays at Popular Prices", producing Euripides, Pirandello and the occasional 'commercial' success such as the Chinese-set *Lady Precious Stream*. She was a countrywoman by nature. She and Bernard had that and more in common; many of her ideas of forming links with her audience he would later incorporate at the Mermaid. She, in turn, was impressed by Bernard's hard work and his stage management skills. The Frederick Anstey comedy *The Man from Blakeney's* required an enormous table for a full-course dinner and for that Bernard provided, in less than 24 hours, a table 31` in circumference (there could have been little room left on the Fortune stage.) He remained for *A Christmas Carol*, the costumes for which were made by Doris Paul "hungry for love" as Bernard later described her, who also played "Scrooge's sweetheart." She remains an elusive figure – Bernard lodged with her and possibly there was an affair – little can be established about her except that she owned the properties in which she lived and that, following a pattern in Bernard's life, she was older than him.

With no opportunities for acting, Bernard left the People's Theatre. Again it was Ba Holloway who helped him, steering him towards Sybil Thorndike and her husband Lewis Casson who were readying the first revival of their great success, Bernard Shaw's 1924 *Saint Joan* for a West End season and a tour. Not exactly hopeful after Casson's first remark to him when auditioning ("Well, you're not exactly an Adonis, are you?") Bernard was booked to 'walk on' amongst the monks in the Trial scene and to understudy the Dauphin as well as to paint the props. Bernard was in his element. Ba's third *Richard III* was hailed as his best, charged with a mesmeric power, enhanced by the specially-composed music, different sections scored by Vaughan Williams and Gustav Holst.

The production moved to the Prince of Wales's with Bernard now as First Messenger (no salary increase) and some cast changes including the young Rex Harrison. He was put under Bernard's tuition for his first few lines. Harrison wrote later that he had difficulties with the line "Upon the stroke of four" when asked the time, which he claims to have delivered in such a naturalistic contemporary manner that it was taken from him and given to Bernard. Harrison never appeared in Shakespeare again.

Towards the end of the tour, in Glasgow, he bumped into Marjorie Clayton, also on tour in the city with *The Student Prince*. It transpired that her husband, actor-director, Neil Porter, also in the cast, had just been appointed director of the Sheffield Repertory Theatre and was beginning to marshal his staff. When

Marjorie mentioned that Neil was looking for a scene painter, Bernard at once replied, "I can paint scenery and do anything else off the stage." Marjorie swiftly sent him to see Neil and Bernard was hired, the contract making it clear that he would also be doing some acting.

Sheffield in 1931 was still a dirty, sooty chimneyed factory-city with a peculiar sulphurous air, all smoke and steam. In what had been a Temperance Hall, the Sheffield Rep would be soon opening with new support (much publicised) from Sheffield University, with members of staff including B. Ifor Evans of the English Department. At the end of 1931 there were many features in the local press reporting Neil Porter's arrival as the director (a Lilian Baylis recommendation). He and Bernard were well-matched; Porter was three years older, also an admirer of Ba Holloway (with whom he had acted at the Old Vic) a passionate cricketer and, like Bernard, holding strongly progressive views about the theatre and theatre design. Virtually all the programmes for Sheffield productions over the next year carried the credit: "Settings designed by Bernard Miles." More crucially, it was clear that Porter would cast him regularly ("From him I learned most of the pure craft of acting that I have managed to assimilate," said Bernard.)

Plunged at once into the deep end, Bernard's first appearance on the Sheffield stage was in Anstey's 1910 comedy, *Vice Versa* (a kind of precursor of *Freaky Friday*) in which a pompous father and his shy, retiring schoolboy son, are switched into each other's body. Bernard was happily cast in the strong supporting role of Blinkhorn, receiving an excellent *Sheffield Telegraph* review ("Mr. B. Miles was capital as a priggish assistant master.") *Vice Versa* was so successful it warranted an extra week's run which was providential for Porter who had to replace a stricken leading lady for his first season. Providential for Bernard too; Porter cast a young redheaded beauty with a career to date rather more impressive than Bernard's and the stage name of Josephine Wilson. Her real name was Nellie Hinchcliffe. Born in Leeds, another sooty mill town then, her father's career was rising rapidly in the employment of one of Leeds's many mills. Her mother, Sarah, was a vivacious young woman with smiling eyes while she had two brothers, both with an adventurous streak and both later engineers. The elder, George, when retired from the oil business in the Middle East, returned to England to 'muck in' at the Mermaid, determined – as Bernard put it – "to save his beloved sister from going down the insolvency drain."

Even in early childhood Nellie showed performing and artistic talent – she became a first-rate sculptor. Sarah was no stage mother out of *Gypsy* but she saw her daughter's talent and tried to help her. By the time her high school education was complete, Sarah was making moves, arranging for Nellie to meet Henry Ainley when he played Leeds Grand. There was a tenuous family link – Ainley's mother was a Hinchcliffe and Henry had been born in Leeds. He had started with Benson but rocketed to stardom under Sir George Alexander at the prestigious St. James's Theatre in London, notably in the verse tragedy of *Paolo and Francesca*. His dazzling good looks and silver voice also helped another verse play, James Elroy Flecker's *Hassan* to another major success. He was most encouraging to Nellie and gave her a letter of introduction to the actor-manager Henry Baynton. He too had begun under Benson. The recently-formed Baynton company was highly respected and, when it visited Leeds in June 1920, Sarah and Nellie called on him backstage where Nellie's audition and looks landed her a place in Baynton's company to begin the autumn tour.

Nellie made her first appearance with the company in November 1920 as Donalbain in *Macbeth* (men's parts were not unusually played by young women – Sybil Thorndike was a memorable Prince Hal at the Old Vic in wartime). Baynton gave Nellie vital experience in an extremely wide range of roles – the company had a repertoire of some twenty plays including Irving's warhorse of *The Bells*, Sheridan, Shakespeare and Pinero. Josephine remained with Baynton when his company joined forces with Robert Courtneidge, prominent author (*The Arcadians*) and manager, a Scot who enjoyed his reputation as a demanding taskmaster not unlike Baylis in his imprecations, also assuming he had a hotline to God, prone to sink to his knees during rehearsals to plead, "Lord, have mercy on them, for they know not what they do!"

Bernard was impressed by Josephine's experience. With little time for conventional West End frivols, she was a stalwart of what was then the London Fringe circuit – the Everyman in Hampstead, the Q Theatre, the Barnes Theatre – often in trail-blazing work involving some impressive talent. At the Everyman, where Sybil Thorndike, Claude Rains, Mrs. Patrick Campbell, Noël Coward and Peggy Ashcroft were happy to appear in its whitewashed, coconut-matting floored austerity – Josephine played in Ibsen's *Pillars of Society*, alongside a youthful Charles Laughton. Both were Yorkshire-born and bred and they struck up a firm friendship. Laughton also appeared with her in two Chekhov plays at the little Barnes Theatre (converted from a Public Hall) directed by the charismatic émigré figure of Theodore Komisarjevsky (nicknamed "Come and

Seduce me" by John Gielgud.) Most successful of the Chekhov sequence was *Three Sisters*, a revival of a revelatory previous production, with Josephine as the youngest sister Irina and Laughton outstanding in the tricky role of Solyony, given an edge of real and frightening tension in this production. In the middle of all this Fringe work, by contrast, Josephine enjoyed a sunny break on an Australian tour playing Strindberg and Ostrovsky's *The Storm*.

At this point in her career Josephine was somewhat riven. Her sculpture was praised at various London Galleries. For a time she had a flat just off the Strand near the avant-garde Twenty-One Gallery, run by the dynamic Molly Bernard-Smith who encouraged her. Joseph Maillol had offered her a place in his Paris studio and acting offers had not dried up because of her Australian trip. Finally she decided that the theatre had first claim on her; she had liked Neil Porter when they met and signed up for Sheffield when Porter outlined some of his likely plays. The local press gave her quite a build-up ("An actress of experience and proved reputation.") Bernard fell very heavily for her ("I'd say that's for me!") he said and Josephine was similarly taken ("He's charming!" she said to Marjorie Clayton.) Nobody would ever call him stunningly handsome but, at that time, when he still had all his hair with eyes, always glinting and full of mischief, and with a ready sense of humour (often a more effective aphrodisiac than looks) he did have the charm of which Josephine spoke.

Bernard wasted little time before pitching woo:

"Where's the sense of paying for two bedsitting rooms," I said. And she agreed. Well, she was Yorkshire… And before I knew where I was, I was in Paradise Square. Right next to the bookshop."

Paradise Square was a delightful Georgian enclave near the theatre, a very mixed quarter of small businesses, estate agents and bookshops: Josephine had her modelling stand and he had an orange box for his books. "We were as happy as larks," said Josephine. The only cloud over this idyllic time was Josephine's mother's poor health. Bernard and Josephine (who never forgot his care for her mother) moved her into a private nursing home closer to the theatre but she died aged 56 from her heart problems.

Their work at Sheffield was satisfying; they appeared in a wide range of plays from J.M. Barrie's *The Admirable Crichton*, Frederick Lonsdale's society comedy *Aren't We All?* to, a favourite for Josephine, Charlotte in *The Brontes*. When the theatre closed for a summer break they returned to London, staying with Doris

Paul in Earl's Court Square. Doris and Josephine became good friends; the trio even came up with the idea for a small company of their own (The Players) aiming to take Shakespeare into schools. Intriguingly the presentation stressed simplicity and little cumbersome scenery. This notion never properly got off the ground, largely because the trio was rarely in London at the same time.

Back in Sheffield some of the autumn season's work was rather safe: the melodrama of *The Green Goddess*, a piece of exotic pish-tushery by the so-called radical drama critic William Archer. But it also included the venture of most interest to Bernard – *Othello* in which he would play Iago to Neil Porter's Moor. Bernard also designed a much-praised set with only essential furniture, clever use of screens and sharply-angled lighting. The notice from the *Sheffield Telegraph*'s critic, Charles Cameron, was long, considered and laudatory for both main performances. Of Bernard's Iago he said:

"He did not fall into the trap of insidiousness. The essence of Iago is that he is a rough, honest fellow suspected by nobody."

The respected B. Ifor Evans of the University, also enthused:

"I have never seen the essential feature of the Elizabethan stage so efficiently adapted to the modern picture-frame stage. I found this *Othello* one of the most exciting and moving performances that I have seen for years."

There were few parts for Josephine that season and she returned to London, with Bernard following when *Othello* ended its successful run. His time in Sheffield had tempered his acting, charging it with a fully assimilated technique inside which he could experiment. He and Josephine were popular company members although a few 'tut-tutted' about their living together. Bernard, without telling Josephine, seems to have got *The Telegraph* to carry a piece announcing their engagement (the date and place of the wedding to be 8th December at Chelsea Registry Office). His parents were not told either. Actually they did not marry until 12th January 1933 at the Registry Office in Kensington's Marloes Road. Tom Hopkinson witnessed the brief ceremony and joined the newlyweds for a snatched wedding breakfast at a nearby ABC Café. Then Bernard high-tailed it to the London rehearsals for a Birmingham Rep. production to open very soon.

Birmingham Rep. was then one of the most prestigious in the country, cushioned by the family money (the Maypole Dairy Company) of Sir Barry

Jackson, the theatre's director. It was supremely well run and attracted top flight casts (Olivier, Paul Scofield, Ralph Richardson and Margaret Leighton were just some who had played there.) Few reps. had the resources to mount the Kaufman/Hart Hollywood satire, *Once in a Lifetime* with a vast cast and several lavish sets, but Bernard had no fat role in this high-octane play. He played a portrait-painter with a handful of lines and one of the studio moguls (the Schlepfin Brother.) The play sold out at Birmingham and then moved to the West End where there were some cast changes – Josephine took over as one of the glamorous Cigarette Girls ("Cigars! Cigarettes") in the opulent Gold Room of the Los Angeles Stilton Hotel. These small parts were barely fulfilling but the money was better than most rep. salaries, Josephine was pregnant and they gained useful West End credit. After *Once in a Lifetime* closed Bernard was quite happy to accept an offer for a new company, Theatre Ways, again to act and design, for a seaside summer season in the Pier Theatre in Hastings. The magnificent Marguerite Dumont figure of Sybil Arundale ran a weekly rep., mostly of recent undemanding West End light comedies which asked from Bernard mainly a variety of French-windowed Home Counties drawing-rooms. As designer he was somewhat startled when set fit-ups brought in unusual crews:

> "I had no idea that the stage hands doubled up as fishermen and so used nautical language in the theatre. During the first set-up I asked one of them to move a flat two feet further on the stage and to take it a bit further up. I got a bit of a surprise when he called to his mate 'Bring her bows nor' nor' east, Jack, and shove her arse windward.'"

Bernard used this period as a chance to hone his comedy playing. He had a big success opposite the redoubtable Sybil in the West End hit, *The Limpet*, which she had written, and another in a favourite play, R.C. Sherriff's *Badger's Green*, centred round a village cricket-match. The summer heat was difficult for Josephine; she returned to stay with Doris in London while Bernard saw out the season as a firebrand communist in a J.B. Priestley rarity *The Roundabout*.

Using a great deal of crepe hair and make-up, his valedictory appearance was as the wispily abstracted old Caraway Pim in A.A. Milne's *Mr. Pim Passes By*. Just before leaving Hastings Bernard heard that his mentor Ba Holloway was appearing just along the coast at Eastbourne. Ba told him that the young stage manager, John Counsell, who had come to the rescue on *Richard III*, had decided to go into management at The Theatre Royal, Windsor, and needed a scenic artist. Never one to enjoy being out of work for long Bernard at once contacted Counsell and was hired.

Counsell had admirable intentions within the restrictions of weekly rep. but his first period there was short-lived with thin audiences and rapidly-mounting debts. Bernard and Counsell most of the time got on although the urbane, ex-public schoolboy, OUDS star was from a very different background but they had similar theatrical ambitions. As Counsell recalled:

"He was a great individualist with very emphatic and usually heretical views about everything. He had a staunch faith in our cause and was never tired of impressing upon me that it was the big conceptions that mattered, not silly details."

Counsell thought Bernard's designs first rate ("he could have had a very successful career as a designer"; he echoed quite a few others in saying "though on occasions he drove me mad, I was very fond of him.")

THE WINDSOR VENTURE folded after eight months and the following period was a difficult time. His first daughter, Sally, was born during the Windsor time, most summer shows were already cast and West End work was scarce. Bernard must have, at times, been deeply worried but his nonconformist background had steeled him to take on hardship and struggle. In a letter written in old age he said:

"That's what life is all about – TAKING PUNISHMENT – in every way – mental, spiritual, and fighting back and knowing that you have landed some bloody good punches."

But with Josephine and a baby – Sally, her fiery temperament evident early, was quite a handful from the start – to support he simply had to work. Always resourceful, Josephine had found a cheap little brick cottage, cheek-by-jowl with the posh houses of Upper Mall, with the wonderful address of Hog Cottage, Hampshire Hog Lane, Hammersmith (it would have made an ideal vocal exercise for Eliza Doolittle). It was his father who came to his rescue, suggesting that he would pay him a carpenter's daily rate for work on Leonard's new Gloucestershire home. Bernard spent his time there doing whatever maintenance work was required and putting up bookcases and kitchen shelves, a period enlivened by the arrival in Chipping Norton of "The Strollers" to which Winnie and Bernard went every night. Bernard always had a high regard for strolling players, keeping going in all weathers and in all conditions.

He always stoutly believed that acorns could grow into oaks. Some radio work came his way (eventually he would do a great deal of radio work), both he and Josephine were occasionally cast in productions for the various Sunday drama societies, which rehearsed for a few weeks and gave a couple of performances, which paid a few guineas.

And, most crucial of all, he made his first excursion into the film world when he landed a small role (3 days' work for £6 per day) in *The Love Test*, a bubble of a romantic comedy set in a research laboratory. This was directed by a rising film name – Michael Powell – who described it as "a desperate attempt by me to imitate an American B-Feature." *The Love Test* led to no trips to the film studios in the immediate aftermath but Bernard had, as always, squirreled away and absorbed as much as he could about a medium which fascinated him ("watch and learn!")

With money tight soon afterwards, with London proving barren ground and the new rep. seasons already under way, Bernard and Josephine decided to return to the provinces. They gave up Hog Cottage, took Sally to stay with Bernard's parents at Glenlochar and went separate ways – Josephine to Hull, Bernard joining a new York Repertory Company which aimed to revitalise the Theatre Royal, playing twice–nightly (Bernard was always keen on this practice.) It opened with undemanding fare – Joyce Carey's *Sweet Aloes* while Josephine had equally lightweight material in Ivor Novello's *The Truth Game*. They both made enduring friendships in their respective companies – at Hull, Maurice Denham, the sharp comedienne Ambrosine Phillpotts – and a young James Stewart who changed his name to Stewart Granger, while Bernard made a lifelong friend in York's musical director Edgar Matthews, an ebullient personality famous for the way in which he discussed great music and musicians:

> "Matthews talked of the great composers as if they were old friends. His conversation was peppered with references to "Old Mozart" and "Old Haydn" and "this cunning sod Bach." He was particularly fond of Bach's Grand Fugue – "Bloody marvellous counterpoint, Miles old man! Bloody marvellous!"

Matthew would provide rich material before long, in some of the characters Bernard created for the 1930s revues which would help change his fortunes. After the York season Bernard returned to London, again staying with Doris Paul, now in Royal Crescent in Holland Park (another 'posh' address.) He hired an au pair for Sally while Josephine was finishing her Hull contract and then decided to have another attempt to break into films. He knew that he would be most unlikely to be cast in even supporting roles and that he would have work his way up but he was quite prepared to do so. Also he sensed that the British film industry was on the cusp of major change.

Actors then could be snooty about film work, a common attitude being Ralph Richardson's: "The Cinema is where you sell what you have learnt in the theatre." And, in the early days of British talkies, directors and actors were hired because of their ability to handle dialogue – a leading director of the era was the choleric Basil Dean, a major theatre figure but whose films, while beautifully enunciated, were as animated as Sherman tanks, basically filmed plays. One or two names were more interesting – Alfred Hitchcock, Carol Reed – and the industry generally gradually acquired new vigour when a whole wave of European film talent began to come to Britain as émigrés – actors (Conrad Veidt, Frederick Valk, Elisabeth Bergner, Anton Walbrook), directors and producers (most notable the three Korda brothers), many of whom had worked in the glory days of Berlin's Ufa Studios.

Most British studios then were mainly involved in churning out 'Quota Quickies' to satisfy the percentage of domestic screen footage demanded by the government in return for permitting the lion's share to Hollywood product. These films – usually about an hour long – were looked down on at the time, and indeed many were lazily scripted and technically clumsy, but although the 1930s are often portrayed as the Dark Ages of British film, the poor relation of Hollywood and not only in competitive terms, it was a hugely popular medium with 18 million tickets sold each week in the late 1930s with an average of three 'Dream Palaces' opening each week. And the scorned Quickies nurtured talent; Carol Reed, David Lean and Michael Balcon all cut their creative teeth in that fast turnaround world (one week was the usually scheduled period for a 'Quickie' film.)

Some Hollywood studios established production units in the UK, financing supposedly 'British' films and there were many independent producers turning out B-Features cheaply and, above all, quickly. Michael Powell wrote: "The going rate for the intrepid producers of these quote-quickies was one pound sterling per foot of film, cash on the table."

In the late 1930s Bernard's main source of income was from the many small parts (even as an uncredited extra) in these films but as he "watched, listened and learnt" that hack-work still gave him a priceless grounding in movie-making. It was often a tricky and tiring time with Josephine still in Hull; they wrote often (sadly only a few letters from them have survived). He described how he had to "do the rounds" of agents and studios, writing in early 1936:

"Sweet – great news. Warner Bros. rang this morning and want me to play the chief detective in a new picture directed by Ralph Ince (a well-respected director.) So out I trailed to Elstree... I am to have £8.8s a day! And it will last for 8 or 10 days. So, you see you will be well-dressed and turned out. And soon away from Hull."

After the Ince film – *Twelve Good Men* – in which he played a dogged Inspector Pine, he was cast in a smaller role as the Chief Modeller in *Night at Madame Tussaud's*, a creepy film with an unsettling performance from Bernard as the waxworks-maker. With Josephine finally back from Hull, Bernard found new digs, a small basement flat in Shepherd's Bush owned by the noted British soprano Eva Turner who willingly gave Bernard a good deal of material on his latest 'enthusiasm', opera. He had also been talking singing lessons from the Scottish teacher Robert Bruce Lockhart, "wildly Bohemian, of scrupulous courtesy and recklessly generous," according to Bernard.

On her return, Josephine found some film work too – a downtrodden wife in *East Riding* for Alexander Korda and, although a small part she played the enigmatic nun with high heels under her habit in Hitchcock's *The Lady Vanishes*. A second pregnancy meant she would again have to give up work for a time and a small basement flat would be difficult for a growing family. That, together with increasing European unease (Mussolini crushing Abyssinia and Hitler reoccupying the Rhineland) informed Bernard's decision to move the family to the country.

IN THE 1920S Josephine had at times spent weekends in the Buckinghamshire cottage belonging to the family of a fellow-actor in the Baynton Company ("the only piece of country Nellie knew," said Bernard.) Crabtree Cottage, near the village of Ivinghoe, was surrounded by fields and trees on the slopes of Beacon Hill. Stone built, it had two rooms and a kitchen downstairs and three small bedrooms above. It had no mains electricity, no running water (there was a well) and an earth closet beside the back door (it was to Bernard "absolute primitive – a rural paradise!") The only shop in nearby Ivinghoe sold paraffin for lamps and the stove and, in Ivinghoe Aston, there was one pub, the Swan, and the Wesleyan chapel.

Bernard's only transport until he learnt to drive (appallingly) many years later was a bicycle borrowed from Leonard (according to Winnie: "We never saw it again!") Four miles away was Tring, from where he could catch the train to London and, if money was tight, he could ride to Denham Studios and back (40 miles) for a small film role. He would take any work going, putting his artistic talents to work helping to restore the astonishing backcloths for *Le Coq d'Or*, originally for Diaghilev's Ballets Russes, for a Covent Garden revival. Although nearing 30 he had to take such casual jobs without self-pity ("You never know where it might lead.") He loved the peace of Crabtree Cottage but idleness was alien to him; he restored the outbuildings or gathered logs for the wood-burning stove.

An old friend Milton Rosmer, who had moved into films, found a small part for him in *The Challenge*, based on the adventure of the competition between Edward Whymper and the Italians to climb the Matterhorn. He hugely enjoyed his brief time on *Convict 99* playing a warden opposite the great Will Hay. But it was often exhausting work:

> "I cycle to Denham for a day's work in *The Rebel Son* for Adrian Brunel – get home after riding 40 miles there and back when the telephone rings: "Can I go next day to do a close-up?" I struggle out and earn an extra 8 guineas."

THE HARD GRAFT and dogged application would eventually pay off. Living near Crabtree was a young filmmaker, one of twins, who met Bernard often on the 8:15 from Tring to London. Then working for an independent company Roy Boulting and his brother John were keen to make films which might reflect contemporary British society. Roy was intrigued by Bernard, always if possible in a corner seat, with a book or notebook and pencil:

"Most impressive of all were those ever probing, ever lively, deep-set, dark-brown eyes, glinting, sparkling whenever the summer light fell upon them."

The two men took to each other ("We both recognised in each other an inherent distrust and dislike of conformity," said Roy) and Roy was touched when Bernard turned up at his house with a table he had made for the Boultings, having noticed that the one in their house was virtually falling apart, for which he refused any payment. As Boulting said:

"Bernard, I believe, exacted great satisfaction and took a certain pride in exercising gifts that he felt helped him to maintain contact and a continuing understanding of the practical everyday life of the English working man."

Against an increasingly tense international situation, the theatre carried on. Bernard appeared at the delightful 'Theatre on the Green' in Richmond, in May 1938 in Marson Bowers's play *The Ditch at Varennes* and stayed on to direct Alec Guinness and Carol Goodner in *The Doctor's Dilemma*. He had an excellent role in Robert Gore-Browne's *Can We Tell?* in the West End at the New. This traced a man's rise to a captain of industry and a baronetcy between 1878 and 1938 with Bernard doing well as a workplace agitator. It had excellent notices but the febrile atmosphere surrounding Neville Chamberlain's first flight to meet Hitler saw the box-office collapse; it closed after only three weeks. This was an unhappy time: Bernard's mother died in October, aged only 62. Bernard was able to get home and attend the funeral at the Salem Baptist Church.

FAMILY SADNESS TURNED to professional joy as Bernard's fortunes began to change after his long apprenticeship. The Players' Theatre then had its premises in King Street, Covent Garden under two actors, Peter Ridgeway and South-African born Leonard Sachs. Originally presenting mainly plays they experimented with a late-night programme of Victorian cabaret; this referred back to the past of 42 King Street when its basement housed W.C. Evans and his "Song and Supper Room," a cosy firelit room smelling of gin, baked potatoes and mutton chops. Literary and Bohemian London had flocked – Dickens, Thackeray etc. – and now Philip Ridgeway devised evenings of Victorian entertainment (recitations, songs, parlour-room ballads and sketches) with performances of a play at 8:15 with "The Joys" following at 11:30.

Some acts would appear "by popular demand" including a teenage Peter Ustinov as the crumbling ancient "The Bishop of Limpopoland", or Robert Eddison as the Hon. Maud Eddison giving lantern-lectures. Bernard made his first Players appearance in *The Joys* with Leonard Sachs as Chairman (a role he would repeat for television's *Good Old Days*), making a big impression as his invention of "The Cockney Bandsman", definitely having its inspiration in his York colleague Edgar Matthews, always talking of "old Haydn" and "that proper old caution Bach":

"Good evening all! Back in harness! Tonight I want to talk to you for a little while about fundamentals. Now, as most of you are no doubt aware – and I expect those that are not aware won't mind being told – music, like all the rest of us, had to begin in a small way. I don't know if you've ever heard of Pan, the Greek God of – er, we'll just say the famous Greek God and leave it at that! Well, this Pan was one day sitting under a tree having a quiet think, and he sees a nymph named Syrinx bathing, and you see he wanted her. And when I say wanted I'm not being platonic, I might tell you!

Anyway she gave him the slip and she went to complain to Jupiter. So she said "Jupiter," she said, "this Pan wants me." And he said "Oh!" he said, "Really? Has he declared himself yet?" And she said, "In his own way, yes."

So he went "Well, what do you want me to do about it?" And she said "I'd like you to turn me into a bull-rush." He said "Yes, that's a rather good idea," he said. "That ought to be safe enough." So he said "Come here, Syrinx." And he goes "Oooooo! Boooump!" and there she was – a bull-rush, you see. And he planted her out. But when this Pan saw her he evidently thought she was just as charming as she was before because he plucked her. No! Honestly…

And he made her into his pan pipes as Syrinx. And so we got the first musical instrument and forerunner of the harmonica – which is derived from two Greek words – harm meaning "mouth" and "onica" meaning "organ"

And so on until –

"In conclusion, ladies and gentlemen I want play you a little tenor euphonium rendering of '*The Hunt Music*' from the overture to William Tell by Rossini. This is the fastest thing I play. The result of many years of patient application, regular practice, a little natural ability, clean living and a refusal to admit defeat!"

Of course the pianist did all the hard work for this piece, with Bernard providing an emphatic 'Toot! Toot!' at suitable intervals.

The *Late Joys* built up a regular following, including Vivian Cox, in 1938 a young Cambridge graduate who later worked at the Mermaid. Of more immediate significance was another visitor, Herbert Farjeon, the reigning figure of London's intimate revue. His most recent production had been *Nine Sharp* at the Little Theatre in John Street just off the Strand. He was preparing a new revue to follow it and Bernard was invited to join a stellar company – Hermione Baddeley, Cyril Ritchard, George Benson along with a newcomer spotted by Farjeon called Joyce Grenfell. It received unanimously glowing notices, *The Daily Telegraph*'s W.A. Darlington acknowledging that:

"The best treatment I can pay to this entertainment is to say that I have not heard so much loud laughter from dramatic critics for many months, if ever."

Bernard, singled out in the notices, at last was making a metropolitan name for himself and could see employment for some time ahead and with daytimes free (the Little played no matinees) to fit in filming or radio.

But, once more, it seemed as if his luck might not hold. On September 1st Hitler invaded Poland and that night several London theatres closed. With Chamberlain's declaration of war two days later the others did too. The movie world was also swift to adapt. At Denham the shooting of *The Thief of Baghdad* was halted while Korda poured all the resources of London Films into a propaganda full-length feature, *The Lion Has Wings*, giving it no less and three directors (Michael Powell, Brian Desmond Hurst and Adrian Brunel) with a Rolls Royce cast including Ralph Richardson and Merle Oberon with Bernard in a small role as one of an Observer Corps with a few lines. Powell understood the brief – to build the case against Hitler as "a warmonger and butcher", to show Britain's potential for men and munitions in the coming conflict and to star the RAF. Mixing documentary and newsreel footage with dramatic scenes, Powell described it as "an outrageous piece of propaganda with some stagey episodes."

Before it was completed London theatres once more began to open, led by the indomitable Windmill. *The Little Revue* gleefully sent up the Windmill

("Voila! Les Non-Stop Nudes – They grin and bare it!") while some new material included one of Bernard's Wagnerian numbers, "The Race for the Rheingold Stakes":

"Well, here we are on the lovely racecourse up at Valhalla with Nibelheim on our right and the Hall of the Gibichung on our left. All set for the race of the day, the Rheingold Stakes or the Ride of the Valkyries as it's commonly known. As always in these Wagner events, the going's very heavy so we mustn't expect fast time. As you know there are nine riders, all sisters. All one litter as a matter of fact, by Wotan out of Erda. Out of wedlock too but none the worse for that."

The Little Revue was immensely successful; it ran through the first winter of the war until 9th March 1940 with regular new material.

Then a really strong film role came his way, the first major production from the Boulting's Charter Films, a powerful story based on events involving the Lutherean Pastor Niemöller who resisted the Nazification of the church. Arrested by the Gestapo, he is sent to a concentration camp. Titled *Pastor Hall*, the title role was played by Wilfred Lawson with an impressive list of British character actors including Bernard as Heinrich Degan, a storm trooper whose loyalty to a friend proves stronger than his allegiance to the Nazis. In the last reel the pastor goes back into his church to preach a final sermon but is shot as he returns outside. Bernard's performance is excellent and he greatly admired the Boultings' work. In turn Roy Boulting enjoyed working with Bernard:

"Make no mistake: Bernard was good – never less than interesting and mostly, hugely rewarding. Particularly striking was his passionate need, his unremitting searching of his role… It was Bernard who fully awakened me to the fact that every actor, intelligent as he was or otherwise, was a living, walking, talking problem in search of a solution."

Following the surrender of Holland to the Nazis, Anthony Eden, the War Minister, made a radio appeal for men to join the new local Defence and Volunteers (L.D.V.), later renamed The Home Guard. Both Bernard and Roy Boulting were among the first to come forward; Boulting, who was expecting imminent call-up to the army, joined "The Pitmen Patrolmen" while Bernard enlisted in "The Ivinghoe Invincibles." Both took their posts seriously. Apart from their hessian LDV armbands no equipment seemed to be forthcoming.

Roy and Bernard smartly took themselves off to the firm of Bapty & Co. near Leicester Square which specialised in hiring weapons for film and theatre and arrived back as "the two most heavily-armed recruits in the Chiltern Hills." When official equipment did arrive they found 80 mackintosh capes, 25 tins of anti-gas ointment, 150 army boots, all size 6, and all for the left foot. Still Bernard felt that he and Roy did "yeoman service" in the Home Guard and had happy memories of cycling home in moonlight after training sessions "through those wonderful summer nights fully armed with rifle across handlebars and revolver strapped over shoulder."

The German sweep through Belgium to the French coast marked the worst threat to the British forces to date, with the majority of British troops seemingly cornered in Dunkirk. Against this nervous background Bernard was about to open in one of the most significant theatrical enterprises of the war.

A new London "little theatre" opened its doors when Herbert Marshall, who had worked in Moscow with Stanislavski and Meyerhold and co-founded London's left-wing Unity Theatre off the Euston Road, took over the old London Academy of Music building opposite South Kensington Tube station as The Neighbourhood Playhouse. Seating around 250 it had a partial glass ceiling – perilous at a time of Luftwaffe air raids. It promised "an international repertory, its method that of Stanislavski adapted to our particular material and conditions." Its first production was *Thunder Rock*, first produced in New York by the trail-blazing Group Theatre and directed by Elia Kazan, just beginning his career as Broadway's wunderkind director. The play's strong anti-isolationism tone and a less than totally committed Kazan production made little impact on the New York stage at the time.

In London, the play found its moment. Michael Redgrave jumped at the central role of Charleson, a John Reed figure who has withdrawn from the world to a remote Lake Michigan lighthouse, baffled by man's inability to learn from history ("I've rejected a world that I can't help.") His imagination brings to life the shipwrecked 'Forty-Niners' drowned in the lake in 1849, reflections of his defeatism, moving and talking together with only their Captain, Joshua, aware that they are dead. It is Joshua who challenges Charleson to allow them to live as they wish they were in actuality with their own problems from their own time. From their courage he finds again his faith in the knowledge of his own finite mind and he can return to the world reactivated. Baldly outlined the play can sound portentously allegorical but its elements of Pirandello – the coup de théâtre of the Forty-Niners' appearance is as striking as that of his *Six Characters* – giving it a potent theatrical charge. The play seemed something of a crystallisation of the time; and the London critics, reviewing it on a night which might be followed by national disaster at Dunkirk, had only the highest praise for the palpable quality of Charleson's tracing of a character at war with himself. Redgrave excelled in creating riven characters, "men in invisible chains," he said, and Charleson was a stunning example of his ability to inhabit such roles. The supporting cast excelled – the powerful Frederick Valk immeasurably moving as a Viennese doctor escaping from fear and prejudice, Bernard's unerring refusal to play for sympathy as a North Country Jew dying of consumption. Indeed all the performances helped to clothe a nervous audience with courage; they entered the theatre despondent and left in silence but with hope.

Thunder Rock immediately sold out for its limited run in Kensington. At the Ministry of Information, Duff Cooper was only one of those bowled over by the play and determined to help it find a wider public. Redgrave was summoned to the Treasury where he was discreetly grilled by officials deputed to establish a way of arranging government subsidy to the production, who added, "Mind you, if this comes up in the house, we should simply deny it."

Finally, co-produced by H.M. Tennent under Hugh Beaumont, the leading commercial management of the era, *Thunder Rock* transferred to The Globe on Shaftesbury Avenue. A glamorous first night saw notices surpassing those at the Neighbourhood Playhouse even if the *Evening Standard* reviewed the audience (Somerset Maugham, Lady Diana Cooper "in black lace.") George Orwell in *Time and Tide* insisted, "This play ought not to be missed, especially in a time of drought." The ministry actually pocketed a not inconsiderable profit; in the ensuing months public money increasingly was pumped into the theatre (the Old Vic included) through the recently-created CEMA (Council for the Encouragement of Music and Arts), forerunner of The Arts Council.

In early September, the Luftwaffe launched "the winter of the bombs" on London and theatres (excepting the Windmill) again closed. *Thunder Rock*, with Alec Guinness as Charleson, went out on tour before it could return to London in early 1941. Bernard would be heavily involved in the subsequent screen version but, for the time being, he spent as much time as possible with his young family at Crabtree and with the Home Guard as well as working on his "country act", collecting material – some drawn from the local Rose and Crown – which could be used for the creation of his most famous 'stand-up' character, "The Clod", later dubbed "The Uncrowned King of the Chiltern Hills."

Films – with more significant roles – became more frequent. For Two Cities Films, directed by Anthony Asquith, he played with subtly understated menace, Captain Müller, head of the Gestapo Detection Unit in *Freedom Radio*, centred round the establishment of an underground radio transmitter aimed at stirring up an anti-Nazi uprising. Also for Asquith he was splendidly droll in the part of a rigidly by-the-book village copper in his first sizeable film comedy role in *Quiet Wedding*, the adaptation of Esther McCracken's long-running West End hit with a screenplay by Terence Rattigan and an exceptionally starry cast including Margaret Lockwood, Roland Culver and Peggy Ashcroft. This was a major popular success.

He also managed to fit in several 'shorts', often for the Ministry of Information – *The Dawn Guard* for the Boultings and *Home Guard*, set in a country pub with Bernard the only professional actor among a group of recent local recruits to the Home Guard, sharing information on the making of Molotov Cocktails and the digging of tank traps, described by Edgar Anstey in *The Spectator* as "a beautifully made film with a number of shrewd yet unforced liberal comments to give the conversation the vitality of men for themselves."

Bernard had acquired a new 'prop' – a large wheel (off an old farm-cart), too big for a taxi, so he bowled it from Euston to Piccadilly into the basement of 13 Albemarle Street, formerly a nightclub and now, 'for the duration', the home of The Players Theatre. Introduced by Leonard Sachs as "positively reeking of the soil," he explained:

"I just 'ad this wheel given me – orf an old dung cart. I'm going to take 'im home and make a ladder out of 'im."

In his countryman persona he would ruminate with an earthy wit and regale the gossip of his Hertfordshire village:

"Willie Franklin – he's bin married five times. Three times intentional and twice catched. He would 'ave married again only he got caught in a self-binding machine in such a manner as he weren't a marriageable proposition no more. Of course he tried to hush it up but I knowed about it. Well, I could tell by the way he was walking."

After a stint at The Players, one of the few London theatres still open, he appeared in a new Farjeon review, *Diversion*, playing matinées only at Wyndham's Theatre. This had one of Farjeon's most distinguished casts – alongside Bernard were Edith Evans, Peter Ustinov and Joyce Grenfell with among the six supporting 'Chorus', the young Dirk Bogarde. Bernard had recently rented a tiny pied-à-terre in Malvern Court, South Kensington, and later moved to similar lodgings in James Street beside Selfridges where he would stay during rehearsals. Some nights were spent in the affable Savile Club where he had many friends. He was there with writer friends Walter Greenwood and Moray McLaren on 29th December 1940 when a member rushed in with the news that the City was ablaze and St. Paul's itself a possible hit. He enjoyed for years telling of how he and his friends decided to hire a taxi to the City; when they approached Ludgate Hill the driver dropped them to see "all Hell was let loose" amid the ack-ack fire, the roar of the flames and collapsing buildings, the background to the famous photograph taken at the height of the raid with St. Paul's still standing amidst the flames, as *The Times* reported:

"The dome seemed to ride the sea of fire like a great ship lifting above smoke and flame the inevitable ensign of the golden cross."

The driver too got out and all stood gazing up Ludgate Hill to the Cathedral and it was he who spoke first:

"There it is, then! The fucking old cross! What about that? Can't get the fucking old cross, can 'e? Makes you think, don't it? Can't get the fucking old cross!"

Whereupon he got back in his cab and drove away. Bernard added:

"It was the most powerful affirmation of Christian faith I heard in my lifetime. And I had a vision. I thought I saw the hand of God reach from Heaven and point at the vanishing cab. And I thought I heard a voice which said 'There goes my faithful taxi-driver, in whom I am fucking well pleased.'"

Diversion No.2 opened on New Year's Day, 1941, to ecstatic notices. The Village Clod, with much new material, was especially praised, some comparing his farm labourer to Will Rogers's study of the Cowboy. The revue ran until April. Throughout the run Bernard spent a good deal of time at the British Film

Institute studying documentary films; he had become increasingly absorbed in the technique of the documentary and the relative merits of professional and amateur actors writing in the *Documentary News Letter* – and coming down on the side of professionals:

> "The actor assimilates reality and proceeds to generalise upon it, to quintessentialise it… The actor's task is to exhibit the "-ness" of a particular phase of life, the youthfulness of youth, the motherliness of a mother etc. Thus Chaplin shows us, not just a downtrodden little man but the downtroddeness itself in its most distilled form."

Clearly Bernard was ambitious to try being on the other side of the camera, often pitching ideas for documentary films to Roy Boulting, who advised patience. He was aware of Bernard's ambition and said he was secretly hoping that a chair with Bernard's name on the back would appear soon – "But I should hate to see you go before you are ready."

Michael Powell was reunited with Bernard in the summer of 1941 when the new Michael Powell | Emeric Pressburger company, The Archers, went into production with *One of Our Aircraft is Missing*. It had an impressive production team – two future directors, Ronald Neame and David Lean as cinematographer and editor respectively – and a strong cast made up of the crew of Wellington Bomber B for Bertie – Eric Portman, Godfrey Tearle alongside Bernard as Front Gunner Sergeant Geoff Hickman. Bertie flies out on a summer evening, the target being the Mercedes-Benz Stuttgart factory, but on its return journey the plane is struck by ack-ack fire which puts one engine out of action. Then, over Holland, the second engine fails; the crew manage to bail out but they are 38 miles from the North Sea. The Holland scenes were, in fact, shot on that section of the Lincolnshire coast known as "Dutch England" as the film traces the men's journey, aided by the Dutch Resistance, across German-occupied territory to the sea where they can row out to one of the new 'lobster-pots', buoys giving shelter to the shot-down air crews.

During the Denham Studios filming Bernard did a good deal of entertaining, keeping his UCS connections with visits from Cecilia Hill who had brought some sixth-formers and Katherine and Marguerite (now 19) Waterhouse. It was a happy film and very successful commercially ("The best non-documentary film that the war has inspired," said *The New Statesman*), but later Michael Powell took some snide swipes at Bernard:

"Bernard Miles was not an actor, he was a preacher. He absorbed culture in large sticky slabs. He played small parts in some of my early films and was always trying to educate me."

Powell seemed to want to belittle Bernard's work, writing very much de haut en bas:

"Bernard had made a bit of a name for himself with a couple of comic monologues at the little Players' Theatre but this was the first time he had worked on equal terms with leading West End actors."

This verdict seems decidedly and inaccurately mean-spirited but Powell, although later venerated by Martin Scorsese, could be unpleasantly acerbic. He arrived on set each day immaculately dressed ("a distinguished ferret in a tweed suit and a bow tie" according to Anna Massey who made *Peeping Tom* for him, adding, "He thrived on tension.") Bernard could certainly be stubborn, at times "obstinate to the point of idiocy" according to Roy Boulting, but Powell's view seems somewhat at odds with the fact that after *One of Our Aircraft is Missing* was finished he was most anxious to work with Bernard again, this time in the theatre. With his friend Julius Gellner, Bernard had conceived the idea of a *Henry V* in a contemporary wartime setting, costumed in battledress. Powell was drawn to the concept:

"It was the perfect propaganda piece for wartime and there would be a part for our regulars. I would direct it. Bernard suggested we sell the idea to Larry Olivier."

They travelled together to Worthy Down near Winchester where Olivier was in the Fleet Air Arm to persuade him to play the King. Politely, Olivier passed – of course soon he would direct and star (in armour) in his own screen version.

At this stage of the war Bernard was assuming that his call-up into the Navy was still imminent. Sally and Biddy were safe at the co-educational prep. school Springfield Grange near Great Missenden, rather like Bedales with its relaxed atmosphere. Sally, whose temperament resembled her father's – their relationship could often be fiery – said of boarding school, "One needs a holiday from one's parents!" With the children at school in termtime Josephine could take on more work; she made several films at this time, including a circus-set drama, *The Dark Tower* and *We Dive at Dawn* playing the estranged wife of Eric Portman, a favourite actor with whom she had worked in the Baynton Company.

Bernard, prepared for call-up, could not take on contracts of any length but contentedly played a small part in a stirring film about the Spitfire's creation, *The First of the Few*, directed by Leslie Howard. Soon afterwards he had a call from the producer of *The Home Guard*, somewhat mysteriously asking him to come to a Wardour Street viewing theatre. This would be a life-changing meeting. On arrival, Taylor simply told Bernard to sit down at the back and keep quiet. Very soon three smartly-dressed figures came in, recognised at once by Bernard as Noël Coward, Lord Louis Mountbatten and Coward's friend, novelist and playwright Clemence Dane:

> "They gave us a brief 'good morning' and seated themselves at some distance away at the front. The lights were duly lowered and the projectionist was told to run the film. *Home Guard* was shown twice. When it was over the lights went up and our distinguished visits prepared to leave. As they passed me Dickie Mountbatten said "You'll do!" and Noël added "High praise indeed!" I still had no idea what it was about."

So began Bernard's involvement in what remains his outstanding film, *In Which We Serve*, Coward had seen Bernard at work when he visited the set of *One of Our Aircraft is Missing*; Powell said "he watched us stage and wrap up a sequence which was quite complicated in about five minutes" (he also took David Lean as his co-director and Ronald Neame as his director of photography for this new film.)

Following the *Home Guard* screening Bernard was told that a reservation from his scheduled Naval service had been applied for and that he was to play a part in a propaganda film about the Royal Navy. He had another meeting with Coward and David Lean at the Savoy Hotel and formally was offered the role of Chief Petty Officer (or Chief Buffer) in the film based on the story of Mountbatten's ship, H.M.S. Kelly which would go before the cameras early in the New Year for Two Cities Films.

The Boulting brothers had been pulled out of the services by the Ministry of Information – now keenly aware of the value of screen propaganda and morale-boosting – and given six months to shoot the screen version of *Thunder Rock*. The intention was to stress its anti-isolationist theme to help jolt America into entering the war, but of course the December 1941 attack on

Pearl Harbour by the Japanese achieved that beforehand. The Boultings hired Bernard to collaborate on the screenplay – they knew of his screen ambitions and of course he knew the play inside-out – alongside Jeffrey Dell, a regular screenwriter for Korda, and Anna Reiner, an Austrian émigré who had worked on *Pastor Hall*. It was a disparate group but in Roy Boulting's view "they turned in a superb screenplay for a film which would be described as strikingly bold in theme and treatment" and "more interesting technically than anything since *Citizen Kane*." This is something of an exaggeration; some of the innovations including 'opening-out' sequences with flashbacks to Charleson's Spanish Civil War experiences are indeed highly imaginative but Boulting was then inexperienced as a director of feature-length film ("Roy is apt to think the third rehearsal is the finished offering," noted Michael Redgrave) while some of the flashbacks are clumsy. But Mutz Greenbaum's superb photography eerily suggests the misty, dual dimension of the lighthouse and the sparingly-used close-ups powerfully convey the brooding internal confusions of Redgrave's Charleson. The film version was very well received at home and its American reception was superb.

In Which We Serve began shooting at Denham in January 1942 after a somewhat circuitous path from conception to finished film. During the previous July Coward had a visit from the ebullient émigré Filippo del Giudice and Anthony Havelock Allen, directors of "Del"'s Two Cities operation. He knew what they wanted from him – a film – and unusually, especially considering he had only acted in one film and directed none, he would have total control of casting and creative personnel. Next evening he dined with his old friend Mountbatten who related the saga of the sinking of his ship, H.M.S. Kelly off Crete. "Profoundly moved and impressed", Coward immediately felt that this was a story to tell "if only I could tell it without sentimentality and with truth." He worked on the film over the next few weeks, initially with the title *White Ensign* and received the Navy's permission although he had many obstacles to surmount. There were problems over the financing, with the Beaverbrook newspapers, less than cordial to Coward and somewhat snobbily unconvinced that he was to play Mountbatten (the film's Captain is the portrayal of an average naval officer, not a glamorous figure like Mountbatten.) Then the Ministry of Information told the Lords of the Admiralty that such a film might be poor propaganda, depicting as it did the sinking of a British ship by the enemy. Mountbatten's support and del Giudice's unswerving loyalty kept the venture on course until finally *In Which We Serve* went before the cameras.

An ambitious story, even after Coward streamlined his originally overlong first draft, the film uses montage and flashbacks to the domestic lives of its chief characters. Coward absorbed quite a lot from viewing *Citizen Kane* at Lean's suggestion. His basic story was of the H.M.S. Torrin and those who serve in her when she is bombed off Crete and goes down fighting. Survivors include the Captain (Coward), Chief Petty Officer Walter Hardy (Bernard) and Ordinary Seaman Shorty Blake (John Mills.) As they hang on to a Carley float, exhausted and wounded, their memories of home and family are interwoven with the scenes at sea. It took three months to film, mostly meticulously planned and organised. John Mills wrote in his diary:

"This is the only way to make pictures – efficiency, drive, enthusiasm and a perfect script!"

Less enjoyable were the long days spent doing take after take of those scenes set in an enormous tank of warm but oily water. Richard Attenborough, in his film debut as a frightened seaman, recalled it:

"We were in that tank for something like two to three weeks. The rest of us would hold our noses and lower ourselves into the water but The Master (Coward) – he would dive in – a little flat perhaps – but in he would dive. On the last day he came to the surface, covered in oil and filth, and said in that distinctive voice – 'There's dysentery in every ripple.'"

Much of *In Which We Serve* follows a fairly standard format for wartime films – a group of men linked as part of a crew or regiment and their experiences. Like several British films of the period the montage footage alternates vividly realistic action scenes with telling close-ups and reaction shots of individuals, usually shot with great economy. In *In Which We Serve* Coward and Lean, plus Neame, took this technique to new heights, creating a special tension, occasionally relaxed by some lighter touches, which builds inexorably throughout. The passage of time, of course, alters the lens through which an audience now views it; Coward's offbeat casting (he took immense pains to modify his characteristic clipped delivery) now teeters at times perilously close to the kind of gleeful parodies of 'Noël and Gertie' in *Round the Horne*. But Bernard and John Mills remain consistently true and touching, at their best in the scene in which Shorty has to tell the CPO that he has received a letter from his young wife, just delivered of a baby and that Bernard's wife had been killed in a Plymouth air-raid. The writing is spare, freighted with unvoiced emotion and both actors play it superbly without sentimentality, with no unearned emotion. That and many other scenes retain their impact.

Press and public reactions were unequivocally positive. Dilys Powell, doyenne of British film critics, minced no words, pronouncing it "the best film about the war yet made in this country or America." Most echoed this; even the *Daily Express*, rarely kind to Coward, approved:

> "This is Hollywood beaten to its knees by Noël Coward and the young men he has gathered to make a film which will surely triumph as entertainment wherever it is shown."

The American notices were similarly enthusiastic. And Coward was delighted when Churchill, originally opposed to the project, now watched the film several times, readily conceding that he had been wrong, admitting that it brought tears to his eyes each time. Bernard's career was significantly boosted by his appearance in a major British film and in a major role. He wrote to a now teenage Joan Waterhouse:

> "I had a wonderful birthday. Premiere of my film and afterwards to the Savoy Hotel to a party given by Noël Coward – had supper with a huge collection of celebrities – I was positively fêted. They all think the film is wonderful – all the papers have given me wonderful notices and have had lots of exciting offers for films in the New Year."

John Mills and his wife Mary Hayley Bell became good friends with the Mileses during the making of *In Which We Serve*. Mills wrote: "Mary and I loved Bernard – a tremendous enthusiast who lived for the theatre, he was a stimulating companion."

Mary's first play was completed by the end of filming. It was a tense story of the French resistance and, when Mills gave it to Bernard to read, he was as keen as Mills; they agreed that assuming they could find a management they would co-direct it in the West End with Mills starring. The only problem was the title – *To Stall the Grey Rat* ("good play, piss-poor title," was Coward's verdict, immediately coming up with the alternative which was used – *Men in Shadow*.)

Almost simultaneously Bernard, also keen to act on stage again, accepted Iago in *Othello* for the Old Vic on tour and then in London. This crystallised a dream of Bernard's originating during the run of *Thunder Rock* in which

Frederick Valk had impressed so much. He suggested Valk as Othello to Tyrone Guthrie who had taken over the Old Vic after Baylis's death. Guthrie agreed and also accepted Bernard's suggestion of Julius Gellner as director.

Gellner had an impressive theatrical history. Born in Prague he had worked in many German theatres before becoming head of Munich's Kammerspiele. To a keen student of modern European theatre like Bernard, the roll-call of Gellner's colleagues was glittering – Max Reinhardt, Bertolt Brecht, Erwin Piscator – and actors Alfred Bassermann, Werner Krauss and Elisabeth Bergner. As Hitler's rise began, Gellner returned to Prague but had to flee again when Hitler invaded Czechoslovakia. In London he knew Valk and other émigrés. "He was," said Bernard "to become one of the great influences on my life."

During *Othello* rehearsals John Mills had placed *Men in Shadow* with the West End management Linnit and Dunfee and wanted to know if Bernard could juggle his production with Mary's play. The schedule was tight – he would be on tour with *Othello* during some *Men in Shadow* rehearsals – but he blithely took it on.

On 17th June *Othello* opened for a three-week run at the Victoria Theatre in Burnley; the Old Vic was based there in wartime while Sadler's Wells and the Old Vic were damaged, and *Othello* would play The New Theatre in London. Both leading actors triumphed. Guthrie had been somewhat anxious about Valk, realising that "the language was a major difficulty," but he could see too that "Valk's voice matched his physique – a warm, velvety baritone with an upper register of extraordinary brilliance and power." Bernard's Iago was quieter, gently insinuating. The Othello / Iago scenes had wonderful vocal contrast ("A truly magnificent performance," said *The Burnley Express* of Bernard's Iago.)

Occasionally when the company played *The Merry Wives of Windsor* in rep. Bernard had been able to nip to London for casting meetings on Mills's play (ex-servicemen who had been discharged on medical grounds) and then John Mills directed alone when Bernard was occupied with technical and dress rehearsals at the New. It was a glorious London return for the Old Vic Company, with *The Times* describing *Othello* as "the most satisfying Shakespearean performance offered us for a long time", adding "Mr. Valk is extremely fortunate in his Iago. Mr. Bernard Miles contrives somehow to suggest a combination of earthy mischief with symbolic malignancy" while Agate judged this Iago to be "a fine performance, earthy and mercurial." Bernard should have been happy but this production was troubled by his moods and some surprisingly undisciplined behaviour. He may have been tired – acting in one theatre and directing in another (*Men in Shadow* was rated a moderate success.) Also he was most vexed by the Old Vic's late decision to drop *Merry Wives* and run *Othello* alone for the final weeks of the season which meant he could not monitor the Mills play. He made sure the Old Vic management was aware of his mood and could give everyone a hard time (the Old Vic archives has a two-page-long list of his "acts of misconduct.") One night he added five lines which had been cut in rehearsal and agreed with the stage director not to include them again. But, at the next performance, they were again included – and at this performance the curtain had had to be held while the management found a seat for Josephine. Next night was worse. Summoned to the production office he was soundly rebuked by the manager Donald Albery (a man who relished power – the later leading commercial producer Michael Codron said Albery always made him feel like "an inky schoolboy" and his air of patrician privilege inevitably rankled within Bernard.) Bernard broke the rules by leaving the theatre (forbidden after 'the half' – 30 minutes to curtain-up) and wandered in costume (breaking another Equity rule) through the courtyard between the New and Wyndham's stage doors, even going into the front of house sitting on the stairs up into the Dress Circle and being rude to the acting manager. The following evening he was late for his first entrance and the Old Vic suspended him. This, in fact, lasted for only the few days before the season closed and he was back in the company for the subsequent tour.

Possibly his recent workload, aggravated when John Mills developed mumps and Bernard 'went on' with the script of *Men in Shadow*, was partly responsible for his behaviour and it is true that as well as his antipathy to authority he could on occasion decline into a depressive spell, a series of 'black dogs' which rarely lasted long but which could be disconcerting for family and colleagues.

The *Othello* tour was without similar incidents. Bernard enjoyed touring, especially to congenial places such as Oxford or Bath, scouring the many second-hand bookshops and writing regularly to Josephine. He also returned to the on / off correspondence with Joan Waterhouse, recommending books and music. He went directly from *Othello* to the film studios to make a 40-minute training film at Wembley for the Army Kinematograph Service, a unit described by Peter Ustinov as one "composed of film-makers passing as soldiers." This script was the joint work of Ustinov and Eric Ambler and tracks how five markedly dissimilar recruits are moulded into an efficient team. Titled *The New Lot* Bernard played one of the recruits alongside a pre-*Dad's Army*

John Laurie, Ustinov and Bernard Lee. Later it became a full-length feature, *The Way Ahead*.

This was a useful reminder of the practicalities of film. At last Bernard was about to realise his ambition to direct a film, to write the screenplay and act in it; as he said: "Well, if Noël Coward could write and direct a film, why couldn't I?" He took his idea to the producer he most admired – Filippo del Giudice (known as "Del"), something of a power in the land after producing Olivier's *Henry V* and *In Which We Serve*. He and Bernard were kindred "adventurey" spirits, although Bernard never cared for the high life of a country estate and mogul-length cigars which Del so relished. Del had been a successful lawyer in Italy but detested Mussolini's fascists who, in 1932, had given him just four hours to leave the country. Briefly interred on the Isle of Man he took his Two Cities Company to initially big success. Exuberant and an eternal optimist he was popular with actors and creatives but somewhat distrusted by other producers and film companies. He was an encourager – always suggesting projects, as he did to Ernest Bevin who, as a passionate trade unionist wanted to make a film about the Tolpuddle Martyrs (Bevin and Bernard discussed the idea but nothing came of it.) And when Bernard said how much he wanted to create a film, Del's response was simple: "If you can think of a good story, go ahead and write it. Direct it. If you like, act in it. I give you a free hand."

In 1940 Bernard and Josephine had been struck by a newspaper item about a pair of Ringed Plovers spotted nesting in the countryside. Now he realised that the story could make a striking allegory of England at war and the country's inborn sense of friendship and hospitality towards refugees from other countries –

"Why not a story about a very rare bird finding its way to England, nesting here and running the many hazards that such a course would involve?"

What kind of bird, however? Characteristically Bernard went to the top, contacting Professor Julian Huxley, Secretary of the Royal Zoological Society and it was Huxley who suggested one of the pipit family – Anthus Campestris or the Tawny Pipit.

A synopsis was soon ready. Bernard set his story in a sleepy West Country village, Lipsbury Lea, with the Pipit news travelling to the Royal Ornithological Society. The news is already round the village leading to a public meeting on the village green at which a pillar of the community, Colonel Barton-Barrington warns that the visitors must be welcomed and protected. This proves tricky – the Ministry of Agriculture is planning to plough the fields for food production and the War Office wants it for tank manoeuvres. Plus it transpires that a traitor in the Royal Ornithological Society recruits two villagers to steal the eggs for sale. Despite everything against them, the village scores a big success when the mother bird is seen feeding five hungry fledglings.

Bernard and Josephine went to meet Del in Bournemouth but were crestfallen when he flicked through the story treatment before dinner, without comment.

At 2:30am the telephone rang: "Bernie? Allo, 'isa Del 'ere. I 'avea bin reading. I am so excited. I can no sleep. We make 'im at once!"

So Bernard struggled out of bed and stumbled along to Del's room where they began to lay plans for shooting *Tawny Pipit*. The shooting script was ready by April, ("The infectious enthusiasm, the blaze of leadership, all were there in full measure", said Bernard). Locations were to be in Lower Slaughter but Josephine, heavily pregnant with John, her third child, stayed at home. Filming took up most of the summer and it made for a happy shoot with a willing cast including the English rose Rosamund John and a host of top-flight British character actors alongside relative newcomer Kenneth More.

The film stands up well in the main with predominantly gentle comedy scenes (a highlight is set in the Church with the Vicar and the shy lady organist debating whether the word "breed" is suitable for a celebratory anthem.) In its day the late entry of the Russian visiting lady sniper who has killed over a hundred Nazis and who makes a fervent speech urging destruction of "the Fascist invaders" fitted well although it was a different story after the war. Nevertheless, with its tone anticipating several of the Ealing comedies, it remains a mainly charming film. One drawback is Bernard's own performance – this is a decidedly clichéd Colonel, somewhat overpitched, too alike his Players' Theatre crusty veterans. The film did only average business when it went on general release for Rank, who chose it to support a terrible Dorothy Lamour vehicle, *Her Jungle Love*. Bernard had taken up the cudgels previously with Rank, his fellow-Methodist, a mogul of the flour industry who had bought film studios and cinemas (Del was tied to Rank for distribution.)

Hearing a speech by Spyros Skouras, President of 20th Century Fox make when he was in England and complaining that British films could be hard to understand in America, he wrote to Rank in near-Messianic terms, arguing against watering down English accents and that the British should stick to the glorious variety of the English language:

"Mr. Skouras delighted us all by saying that the function of the cinema is to serve mankind. But he went on to say that the best films are those which gross the most money."

Possibly it did not occur to Bernard that Rank might be more likely to agree with Skouras.

AFTER HIS BLOODING on film, Bernard had a busy time, initially when moving house. Crabtree Cottage was no longer large enough for three children. They did not move far – to the delightful village of Bierton, close to Aylesbury where they rented an old but refurbished house, The Old Forge. Bernard liked it more than Josephine; there was no garden and with their latest child, John, she found that a disadvantage. Still, it was less than two miles from Aylesbury which had a direct train service to London. There was also a direct train to Great Missenden but visits to the girls' school there were intermittent at best; Biddy claimed that when her parents turned up one Parents' Day, she failed to recognise them and Sally, increasingly outspoken, had regular disagreements with Bernard.

He and Josephine would soon be at different ends of the UK. At a Players' performance Bernard met up again with Vivian Cox, then on leave from the Navy; he was serving on the battleship H.M.S Duke of York as a lieutenant on the staff of the C-in-C Home Fleet, Admiral Sir Bruce Fraser. According to Cox, on that leave Bernard constantly begged him to arrange for Bernard to see over the ship and a visit was soon fixed. There was a quid pro quo – Bernard would have to sing for his supper, entertaining men on all the ships. Bernard took to life at sea immediately, so enthusiastic that he would wander off various ships at Scapa Flow and search parties would have to be sent out to find him. His solo concerts were hugely successful ("he went down like wildfire," said Cox) and the Admiral came twice to a performance ("Dear Bernard! Everything was an adventure to him," said Cox when Bernard asked if he could sail with the fleet into battle.)

In early April, following the British sinking of the pride of the German Navy, the Scharnhorst (Vivien Cox became almost obsessed by the Scharnhorst episode, working on a play about it for ages), it was announced that Bernard would be returning to Scapa Flow with a new show under the banner of ENSA (the acronym for the forces' entertainment unit, known better as "Every Night Something Awful"), touring the islands for five weeks with a revue called

All Adrift. It proved a hectic time, travelling from island to island, ship to ship – "The war brought strolling playing back with a bang," said Bernard. The company included John Mills and Bernard, Josephine and the ballerina Natasha Sokolova. Bernard's showstopper was a self-composed song, poking fun at Navy hierarchy:

"You're in Whitehall, you're all right,
Home to the missus and the kids each night,
Lunch with an Admiral, supper with a Wren,
But don't forget the bleedin' ships are full of bleedin' men!"

One performance remained impaled on Bernard's memory for some time. The company gave a memorable show on an improvised stage erected between the twin fo'c'sles of two destroyers lying beside each other in Gutter Sound with the turrets and bridges packed with sailors. Bernard said later, "I remember saying to Josephine: 'This is what the Elizabethan theatre must have been like.'" It was no Damascene conversion but it remained a key element in his thinking as the eventual Mermaid Theatre went through its various incarnations and designs.

With peace looking increasingly likely, even with the danger of the V.E. bombs, the Nazis' final desperate weapons, pummelling London, Bernard decided that since Josephine still disliked Bierton, they should look for a house in London. He was about to go on tour again, in a Home Guard comedy he had written, *They Also Serve*, but in his absence Josephine could look out for a likely new home. During *Tawny Pipit*'s filming Bernard had got to know the architect Ernst Freud (Sigmund's son) who had a house in St. John's Wood, an area the Mileses liked. Freud and Josephine had little initial success searching in St. John's Wood but finally Bernard heard from Josephine:

"Nellie rings me. She and Freud have found a delightful house in Acacia Road. It's badly battered but she thinks I should have a look at it."

THE ACACIA ROAD house was indeed battered; the roof was in decent condition but a few near-misses during the Blitz had blown off doors and damaged ceilings while the garden was a jungle of saplings and couch grass. Restoring it would take some effort, not least with the restrictions on materials. It took most of a year before it was properly habitable but the result was ideal for the Miles family. There were several outbuildings – the house stood in an acre of ground – including a small cottage and, most crucially, a large hall (the Assembly Hall during its time as a school.) It was called Duff House from its incarnation as a dressmaker's business run by Lady Juliet Duff. That Assembly Hall would become the first Mermaid Theatre. Both Sally and Biddy were still at Springfield Grange while the Mileses were comfortable enough now to employ a nanny for John. It was never a grand house; the large dining-room was decorated not with paintings but with Bernard's extensive collection of farming implements and tools, including a large cartwheel hung on the wall.

Bernard joined Michael Wilding and Sally Gray on the film of *Carnival*, from a 1912 novel by Compton Mackenzie in which a dour Cornish farmer (Bernard) jealous of his wife's past lover, takes a drastic revenge. Bernard's cold, brooding power as Zachary Trewhella is a strong element in a film which never lived up to the hopes he had for it. He took up his pen again to write to Rank, initially flattering him by praising his "delightful freedom to speak our minds." He then goes on the attack, entreating Rank to make truly British films "rather than a sort of synthetic bastard product whose only virtue would be that it is easily digested which is what some of us fear the Americans would like us to make." No reply from Rank is recorded but Bernard's next film was for Rank with David Lean as director and it gave him a splendid opportunity. Lean came of age with this film of *Great Expectations*, greatly aided by Ronald Neame's monochrome photograph, using shadows, chiaroscuro and deep focus to superb effect. Goodness is a quality difficult to convey on screen but Bernard's Joe Gargery, utterly honest, trusting and loyal without a scruple of sentimentality, is a major asset in a film with many outstanding performances, including his friend John Mills as Pip. The film and Bernard's performance easily stand the test of time.

Progressive good intentions were behind the Group Theatre 46, which included Bernard and his manager Derek Glynne who looked after the business side of the venture. The policy was one of "basing a contemporary repertory on the new audience that has come into being during the past six years." The season comprised three plays – *Century for George* by Montagu Slater, tracing the development of the Amalgamated Engineering Union, *The Face of Coal*, a documentary play on mining by Bernard's friend Jack Lindsay and Bernard's own Home Guard play, unwisely retitled *Let Tyrants Tremble!* Julius Gellner directed all three, perhaps too much of a stretch. The theatre was the somewhat out-of-the-way Scala Theatre. A name from Bernard's past, Doris Paul, supervised the costumes. The budgets were, to say the least, tight. Some money came from the Arts Council (as CEMA had become) and, echoing the government's share in funding *Thunder Rock*, the Amalgamated Engineering Union, invested £3,500 in the opening play. B. Ifor Evans, so supportive of the Leeds *Othello*, viewed this as similar to the Middle Ages craft guilds in *The Mystery Plays*. The play traced the story of the AEU over a century with Bernard playing the engineer, Watkins, over the three different periods covered. Critics respected its ambition and theme but most echoed *The Times*:

> "It is scarcely the height of theatrical wisdom for a new theatre which is not a political organisation to introduce itself to the general public with a piece of political propaganda."

Bernard's Home Guard Play, *Let Tyrants Tremble!* – with Bernard as the veteran of the Zulu Wars – fared better although the fun of the early scenes was taken over by the cruder propaganda in the later sections. *Face of Coal* was openly propagandist in a kind of documentary style which featured in most of the work from the Army Bureau of Current Affairs (Jack Lindsay had been a regular writer for ABCA) received some respectful reviews although Julius Gellner's production was criticised as being too slow. All together the Scala season was respected more than it was admired. Losses were low given the minimal production costs. However there would be no further Theatre 46 seasons.

"Making another film to pull up" and replenish the coffers saw Bernard in another screen Dickens, *Nicholas Nickleby*, made for Ealing Studios, produced by Michael Balcon. Bernard was impressed by its director, Alberto Cavalcanti, born in Rio de Janeiro and a prominent figure in French 1920s cinema before settling in London and working for the documentary trail-blazer John Grierson. He had a deluxe cast for *Nicholas Nickleby* including Cedric Hardwicke as the cheating moneylender Ralph Nickleby, Stanley Holloway as Crummles and Sybil Thorndike as Mrs. Squeers. Again Bernard shines in Dickens – his Newman Noggs, ruined by Ralph Nickleby, "watches and learns" until finally he can meet his nemesis face to face. The final confrontation between Noggs and Ralph Nickleby is stirring stuff, fuelled by two superb performances.

Bernard had strong opportunities in *Fame is the Spur*, a Two Cities/Charter Films co-production with Ray Boulting directing and Del in charge of the production. Based on a bestseller by Howard Spring, Nigel Balchin's screenplay, not entirely happily, had to trim a long, multi-narrative novel for the screen. The story traces the career and compromises of Hamer Radshaw, a radical idealist who rises in the Labour party but is prepared to accommodate to political expediency, contrasted with the career of Hamer's childhood friend Tom Hannaway, who cleverly moves from a street barrow to a chain of grocer's shops. Whole episodes of Spring's novel are axed, including a meeting between Hamer and Friedrich Engels in a Manchester bookshop, but the performances are top-flight – Michael Redgrave, usually at his best playing conflicted men such as Radshaw and Bernard, wily and pragmatic, as the profiteer. Much to the disappointment of both leading actors, the film did poor business, possibly because of similarities between Hamer and Ramsay MacDonald and implicit criticism of Clement Attlee's 1945 Labour government coinciding with a mood of post-war disillusion.

At this stage Bernard was extremely busy; he recorded many productions for the fledgeling BBC Third Programmes, appearing with Frederick Valk in Laurie Lee's *Voyage of Magellan* and a much-praised Herbert Reed version of *Moby Dick* with a score by Antony Hopkins and a cast including Ralph Richardson and Cyril Cusack.

He also took pleasure in writing his first book, commissioned by William Collins as one of the '*Britain in Pictures*' series, illustrating in words and pictures the life, art and achievements. Undaunted by the restrictions (maximum of 20,000 words) to cover the entire history of the British theatre, he came up with a fresh and lively scrutiny of his subject. Unsurprisingly a major focus in the development of the British playhouse – the Elizabethan stage, the proscenium 'picture-frame' (he calls this 'a most unhappy innovation') and the modern challenge to the actor of trying to bridge a large gap before his or her voice can begin to register. His rapid kaleidoscopic view of British acting, moving from the anonymous *Mystery Plays* actors through Burbage, Garrick and Irving to Olivier and Richardson is something of a tour-de-force, ending with a rallying cry:

> "Finally, we all need to remember that actors used to be rogues and vagabonds and that an adherence to the more boring forms of society, dress and behaviour is only a recent growth and that it has nothing to do with the theatre."

THIS BATTLE BETWEEN the staid and the nonconformist would be only too graphically illustrated when Bernard decided to return to the theatre for two years, even if it meant radically cutting his income. Once again he joined the Old Vic which, during repairs to the Waterloo Road theatre, was based at the New for its London appearances. He was delighted, forgetting the trouble on *Othello* which the management certainly remembered. The Old Vic now had at its head the director John Burrell who survived the coup which saw the departure of Olivier and Richardson, dismissed by the chairman of the Old Vic governors, the very proper Lord Esher (the reasons remain murky but most insiders saw the hand of Guthrie, always distrustful of "stars.") Burrell was a somewhat reserved man, on occasion a fine director (Olivier's *Richard III*) but prone to vacillation (he had to be replaced on the West End production of *The Heiress* with Ashcroft and Richardson) when it was perilously adrift with only a week to go before opening. Burrell had a meeting with Derek Glynne to negotiate a new contract for Bernard and "the terms of an oral contract" were agreed in July 1947. Bernard was to play in two seasons (1946-7 and 1948-9). In the first season he would play Christopher Sly in *The Taming of the Shrew*, Face in Jonson's *The Alchemist* (on tour only), the intriguingly contrasted double of Robert de Baudricourt and the Inquisitor in *Saint Joan*, the small part of the Bishop of Carlisle in *Richard II* ("showing myself willingly as not all Old Vic leading actors have done, to accept the give-and-take of classical repertory") and (not to the company's delight) Beaumont and Fletcher's *Night of the Burning Pestle*, known irreverently backstage as "Knight of the Burning Pisshole". It was also clearly understood that there would be one further play and this issue was to become crucial to future events. Bernard and Derek Glynne both had "a very clear understanding" that the last play would be for Bernard, not necessarily a star role "but that it should be chosen in consultation with me and that it should contain such a part as I wish to play – i.e. not one of the proletarian roles from which I have been trying for years to escape!" At this stage the second season then was simply touched on but it was agreed that Bernard should play Macbeth and have an opportunity to direct.

The Old Vic had caveats; Bernard had to promise "not to repeat acts of misconduct similar to those which led to his suspension from the part of Iago" and, prior to anything put in writing, Derek Glynne was asked to vouch that Bernard "would assuredly give no excuse for complaint again."

"In the highest and happiest of spirits at being back with the Old Vic" he was amongst actors he admired – Alec Guinness, Trevor Howard, Harry Andrews, Peter Copley (Ralph Richardson would direct *Richard II*) and everything seemed set fair. The pre-London tour of *The Taming of the Shrew* opened in Edinburgh as the first dramatic offering of the first Festival and from the outset, despite some 'tut-tuts' from purists, was a major success. Josephine never saw it; she was also on the road as Donald Wolfit's leading lady.

In Belfast on the tour, Bernard received a cable, typically epic in length, from Del announcing that he was leaving Rank to set up another company, Pilgrim Pictures, and ending with the "news that will make you proud." This was the New York reaction to *Tawny Pipit*; originally the Little Carnegie Cinema had programmed *Nicholas Nickleby* but when that was withdrawn at the eleventh hour the cinema chose to programme the one copy of *Tawny Pipit* where it scored a surprise success. Opening cold with next to no publicity it seemed to catch the public mood; soon there were lines at the box-office and the film eventually ran for over 60 weeks at the Carnegie and, when more prints were available, did strong business in selected cinemas in other cities. With one exception the notices were glowing – "the most heart-warming comedy ever to come out of England" was the *World-Telegram*'s verdict. The dissenter was a very sour *New York Sun* which cordially disliked the film, arguing that it was dated and the dialogue "sprinkled with anti-Nazi speeches and laudation of Soviet Russia." Once more Bernard argued with Rank, sending a long letter to the magnate's home address. It was a proper telling-off, remarking that American critics gave *Tawny Pipit* an outstanding press, adding "a new feather to the cap of the Rank Organisation." He added that this "reflects little credit on your salesman colleagues", acidly pointing out that the Carnegie advertising copy was three years old and there was no stand-by print. Particularly strongly he laid into Rank for not giving him and Del the chance to make any revisions; in the light of the changed international situation he would have wanted to cut those sequences late in the film when the Russian sniper visits the village – "your people were well aware that the picture was made when a tribute to the USRR was fitting at the time when the war between Russia and the Wehrmacht was at its height." But, post-war anti-Soviet feeling was very high in America. "The picture may belong to you but don't you think you still have a responsibility to me?" Old wounds are re-opened when he rails again at the film's twinning on release with *Her Jungle Love*. He ends with stinging rebukes, charging Rank's representatives with an inability to distinguish between quantity and quality, closing by saying that if Rank finds the letter "bitter and unfriendly" it is because he is bitter and unfriendly. Rank's belated reply, very de haut en bas, made little reference to Bernard's main complaints.

Just before Old Vic rehearsals began Bernard, clearly in high good humour, had written to Burrell quoting Hazlitt's dictum that almost the first requirement for a comedian was to have "a strong spirit of enjoyment within himself." He added that he hoped Burrell would find his "energy, vitality and mad keenness of my work of great value in the coming months."

These thoughts perhaps did not strike a responsive chord in Burrell, rarely an especially joyous character. *The Shrew*, in a Liquorice Allsorts-ish design, fast and frenetic, had opened successfully on tour and then in London, where Bernard's Sly, on stage throughout, was highly praised. Shortly into the run he had a major shock; leaving the theatre after a performance he found a letter from Burrell containing something of an outburst against what he saw as Bernard's lack of self-discipline – "It is because you lack this to such an alarming degree that I am forced to speak to you about your performance and to make continual requests that you should not rock the boat by making yourself a centre of interest when it is unjustified by the play." He added that he had had "complaints" from some of the cast.

Now Bernard indeed could at times enjoy himself somewhat too much on the stage although in *The Shrew* he had been cast to enjoy the onstage antics and to communicate some of that joy to the audience. Later, in the 1970s I worked with Peter Copley at the Mermaid; he told me that at times Bernard could be overenthusiastic but that as far as he was aware, only one particular (and pedantic) actor complained. There was, it should be pointed out, not a single mention of any complaint about his performances in *Richard II*, *Saint Joan* or *The Government Inspector*.

During rehearsals for *The Government Inspector* things turned awkward. Burrell told Bernard he thought his performance as the fawning Mayor was promising to be very fine, also suggesting that Bernard might consider the Mayor in lieu of the final promised play or even accept a film offer from the Boultings for the same period. Bernard was careful to give no definite answer. He had described his first five months of this season as "the happiest and most fruitful months of my life – up to now!" Just after Christmas with an audience in holiday mood *The Shrew* went down especially well, with Bernard responding quite naturally to the warmth and liveliness. The atmosphere was ebullient. But in the interval Burrell appeared in his dressing-room to say he had received a complaint from a company member that Bernard was "interfering" with the cast. Bernard was puzzled, not recalling any "interference" but that "I would be careful."

Murmurs of trouble from another direction surfaced with the unexpected announcement that "because of a disagreement with the management" Petruchio in *The Shrew* would be taken over by John Clements who would also play Dunois in *Saint Joan*. The reasons for Trevor Howard's departure remain hazy but there was talk that his drinking had upset the management. The news rang alarm bells for Bernard and Glynne.

Clements was an established star and an actor of his status would not have agreed to take over supporting roles, however good. Bernard guessed (correctly as it transpired) that in order to lure him he had been promised the final play of the season which was already promised to Bernard. Glynne swiftly wrote to then telephoned Burrell to remind him that the last play of the season was promised to Bernard. Burrell and Glynne met and discussed the issue (there was no admission that Clements had been offered the play) and Burrell listened to Glynne's list of Bernard's possible plays of which *Measure for Measure*, unseen in the capital for a decade, was favourite. But time went by without a decision; despite the "clear understanding" of the oral contract with Burrell, both Bernard and Glynne had a feeling he was "going to be tricked out of it."

In the meantime, *Saint Joan* opened with Celia Johnson as the Maid and Alec Guinness outstanding as a whey-faced Dauphin. Bernard's unusual double of the choleric garrison commander Robert de Baudricourt and the Inquisitor, played with what one critic called "a sort of withdrawn gravity". This made a deep impression.

At home, assisted by a nanny, Bernard was trying to cope with life as a single parent (Josephine sailed just after Christmas for a Canadian tour with Wolfit.) Just before Christmas Bernard learned from Trevor Howard on the eve of his leaving the company, that Clements had definitely been offered *Coriolanus* as the final play of the season. Simultaneously the Boultings were pressing Bernard for an answer to the offer to appear in and collaborate on the screenplay of the West End success, *The Guinea Pig*. Yet again Glynne wrote to Burrell asking for the issue of the final play to be resolved speedily as there was a film offer on the table, although Bernard would prefer to remain with the company, depending on the choice of play.

Another shock awaited Bernard just before dress rehearsals for *The Government Inspector* when he found a letter in his pigeon-hole from Gordon Sandison, General Secretary of the actor's union Equity. This was totally unexpected and extremely serious. The letter said that the Old Vic had lodged "a formal complaint against him." He found Burrell sitting in the stalls and showed the letter to him. Burrell's reaction was that "it was all a mistake" although he admitted that he and Lovat Fraser, the Old Vic's general manager, had talked to Sandison but that he would call him at once to restore calm, later finding Bernard backstage during rehearsals to tell him he had made the call and "the whole matter could now be forgotten." *The Government Inspector* dazzled critics and audiences with witty designs from Felix Topolski and delightful performances from Guinness as the young pretender and Bernard as the rantipole Mayor.

But the matter was far from settled. Increasingly Bernard (as he told Sandison) felt that the Old Vic was deliberately making a case against him to wriggle out of the verbal agreement about the season's closing play. When *Coriolanus* was announced Bernard was offered the small role of Sicinius Velutus which – as the Old Vic must have anticipated – he turned down. Glynne, deeply shocked by the management's behaviour, wrote to Lovat Fraser expressing his disquiet and that he and his client felt "the management were not honouring the spirit of the contract."

The whole saga crushed Bernard. He did not have Josephine to console him but, in a letter from Canada, she tried to cheer him ("what a miserably mean lot they are!") adding "Oh, darling, we must have that theatre!" – the first suggestion on paper that she and Bernard were pondering a future in which they might manage their own careers. In their own theatre.

At the same time Bernard accepted the Boultings' offer of *The Guinea Pig* and to collaborate on the screenplay with the playwright Warren Chetham Strode. Covering the years 1942-6, it was for the time an angry play about a clever boy, played – as on stage – by Richard Attenborough (who was 24), plucked from an elementary school into the hothouse world of a famous public school. Produced by Del and with the Boultings steering an enjoyable set, it was a relief for Bernard to sink into the part of Frank Read, the boy's gentle tobacconist father and try to put the sorry Old Vic saga behind him. But the Vic's vindictiveness continued. Burrell's sidekick Lovat Fraser – exactly the sort of suited bureaucrat to rub Bernard up the wrong way – continued with what seemed a vendetta, ticking Bernard off for a piece of business throwing himself down on a bed. Bernard was furious – "Quite untrue – as I had often done this particular piece of business before." Fraser seemed to think that an actor must stick always to the text but, of course, after the induction, Sly has no text and the actor playing Sly should be skilled at improvising (as Bernard was) and able to quickly respond to audience reaction. Bernard complained to Burrell of this and he agreed that it was a "ridiculous" note and that he would speak to Fraser.

Of course, there remained the question of Bernard's contract for a second Old Vic season for which he had a legally binding contract with no "oral agreements" complications. Gordon Sandison agreed that the management was "under a contractual obligation to put on *Macbeth* and to give you an opportunity to play the lead." He was also to be given a production – to be mutually agreed – to direct. Derek Glynne had written to Burrell suggesting *Cymbeline* or *Troilus and Cressida* and also to suggest Julius Gellner as director for *Macbeth* and suggested they all meet. This received a troubling response: "I have been hesitating," wrote Burrell, "I regret to say the Governors have been very disturbed by the record of Bernard Miles this season." He agreed to meet Glynne and Bernard but there was no mention of a second season as Burrell simply repeated all his old accusations before weakly admitting that it was all in the court of the Old Vic Governors. A few days later Bernard and Glynne were granted a meeting with the Governors led by the arch-bureaucrat Lord Esher as chairman who brusquely insisted that Bernard had broken his agreement and that they intended to inform Equity forthwith. Bernard was dejected: "I have never been subjected to such confidence-shattering treatment as this." A week later he received a letter from the Old Vic's legal representatives revoking Bernard's contract for a second season because of "stage indiscipline" after "repeated remonstrances."

While agreeing to continue in the one play still in the repertoire involving him, *Saint Joan*, Bernard wrote tersely to Esher, "rejecting all accusations of having broken his contract." Legal wars seemed likely.

Yet through all this later *sturm und drang* with Bernard's personal life as complex as his professional career, he seemed oddly upbeat. He was in love.

THE MERMAID STAFF were aware of the self-mythist element in Bernard's nature; most of us took Bernard's autobiographical recollections of his grandfather as the truth. And, whenever Bernard alluded to a love affair with the great operatic soprano Kirsten Flagstad, he was surely embellishing the truth. But as it transpired he never knew his grandfather and the romantic involvement with Flagstad, although fairly brief, was true. Her career had progressed from light operas and operettas before gradually moving into more taxing roles – in Verdi

(Desdemona in *Othello*) and the title roles in *Aida* and *Tosca*. Her triumphs were predominantly in Wagner – Brünnhilde in *The Ring Cycle* and Isolde in *Tristan and Isolde*.

Bernard had seen Kirsten before he met her; one night when he was walking along Floral Street she emerged, swathed in white furs, from the Opera House stage door into a waiting car. He recognised her instantly – he had seen her in *The Flying Dutchman* not long before. The Opera House had only recently opened its doors again for opera but the 1947-8 season had the coup of Kirsten, acclaimed internationally as the Wagnerian soprano of the century booked to sing her greatest role, Isolde in *Tristan and Isolde*. Money was tight and so the production had to compromise, with decidedly moth-eaten sets from the stores but the vocal side of the evening under Karl Rankl, another émigré from Hitler's Germany who had worked under Otto Klemperer, was judged supreme.

Despite a horrible day on 10th March, outlining the Old Vic saga, Bernard would always remember the evening. His appointments diary for that day has only one pencilled entry: "Meet K.F. at R.B.L.'s". The latter was Robert Bruce Lockhart, an exuberant Scot from a predominantly military background with a reputation as a fine vocal coach (he had given Bernard some tuition previously.) He and his wife were then renting the old assistant master's cottage in the grounds of Duff House. So it was on a kind of home ground that Bernard and Kirsten first met. Subsequently, when working on a biography of Kirsten, never completed and unpublished, Bernard wrote:

> "It was hard to believe that the homely and rather severe-looking woman sitting in an upright chair at the Lockhart fireside with a pair of horn-rimmed spectacles perched rather shakily on her nose knitting a dark blue pullover and taking an occasional sip of black coffee could possibly be the youthful, radiant being who had sung Senta's ballad so gloriously at the Albert Hall."

A few days later they met again, this time at the Rankl's who lived nearby:

> "I had eyes for one person only. She was standing in the middle of the room in a dress of dull gold which glowed against the rich plum-coloured curtains."

After a convivial dinner more people, colleagues from Covent Garden, arrived and the conversation turned to Wagner and the Norse legends.

Somebody spoke of Bernard's *Tristan and Isolde* revue skit and the company insisted he perform it for them, describing the second act –

"As soon as the coast is clear this Isolde comes into the garden in her night-dress if you please. She's a big fine girl, mind you. Fifteen or sixteen stone, all nicely distributed. Anyhow she suddenly lets out a top A and a top B, fully supported on either side. 'Tris-tan!' 'Be-lov-ed!' she sings. And old Tristan comes out from behind a bush and… well, we're not children here are we? Look, I'll give you a line or two from the actual libretto. It says 'Tristan takes Isolde by the hand and pushes her gently back on to a little flowery bank where they lie back enraptured.' Well, just look at him! Then Old King Mark comes back and catches them *in flagrante delicto* (or 'in delicious fragrance as we say!')"

Bernard throughout kept half an eye on Kirsten and was relieved to see that she laughed longest of all. In his unfinished account of Kirsten's life, he wrote:

"I fell in love with her the moment I met her… I could see and think of nothing else for four or five years – it was of all pre-ordained."

This was a love story even after their relatively brief physical affair was over, ending only with Kirsten's death in 1962. For years the facts were unknown except to Bernard, Kirsten and Josephine, gifted with that rare quality of forgiveness. Some details appear in the few surviving pages of his unfinished biography, provisionally titled *Born to Sing*. Sadly the letters from her to Bernard were destroyed at Kirsten's insistence before she died.

In 1948, Kirsten was nearing 53. Her second husband, a controversial figure, had died 18 months previously having been accused of collaborating with the Nazis. Since the end of the war she had been tarred by the same brush in a sustained campaign of accusations as a collaborator. Money and property belonging to her in Norway had been confiscated. She married, at 24, a businessman in ironware but they divorced nine years later. After the divorce she married Henry Johansen who ran a plywood company and was happy for her to continue her career. By 1940 she was world-famous and on an American tour when the news came that Denmark and Norway had been invaded by the Nazis. Johansen told her to stay in America and she signed, reluctantly, for a second Metropolitan Opera season, but insisting she must return to Norway despite the danger. Bernard wrote: "She simply felt she ought to be at home when home was in trouble: she retreated to her country house in Kristiansand, remaining there throughout the war, refusing to sing for any German-arranged event, limiting professional engagements to a few appearances in Sweden or Switzerland, both neutral. As the war neared its end Johansen, who at Kirsten's urging resigned from Quisling's extreme-Right Wing Party of National Unity, was arrested by the Norwegian police and taken to an ex-Nazi death camp, but he died of cancer before he could be tried for collaboration with the Nazis. The anti-Flagstad campaign was fanned by pre-war enemies of Johansen and some American newspapers. Her first post-war concert in America in 1947 was marred by noisy protests and she was not employed by the Metropolitan Opera. Later she would write "England is the only country in which I never had a single unhappy moment."

So, when she met Bernard she was both lonely and somewhat vulnerable. "The worst thing about losing a husband is you are suddenly left without someone to lean on. You don't quite know what to do. You stand alone."

She and Bernard spent most of the next day together. He called her at the Waldorf Hotel the morning after the Rankl party: "The next few days," he wrote "were like a dream." They walked in London parks, visited the National Gallery and then Kew: "all very gay and light-hearted as we walked along between the crocus-spears in this springtime of the year." They were like young lovers.

Josephine then was in Canada but Bernard and Kirsten met several times to dine after the theatre. She saw him in *Saint Joan* and he would speedily change out of costume to run the short distance between the New and Covent Garden to catch the last act of *Tristan*, climaxing in Kristen's matchless '*Liebestod*':

> "Standing in the wings with that voice singing, singing. It's one thing to listen from the auditorium but, close at hand, my God! That '*Tristan Geliebte*' – it was a woman using every bit of herself, pouring the breath of life into those torrents of song. And as we sat in her dressing room afterwards – 'Tonight I sang it all for you.'"

After the theatre one night, again like young lovers, they walked down to the Embankment as far as Blackfriars Bridge to sit in one of the bridge recesses when she recounted the difficulties of her return to Norway. Bernard advised her to use her sole but formidable weapon and simply sing her enemies into submission. Only two years later her accompanist Edwin McArthur wrote to

Bernard from New York: "Her success has been phenomenal… she has come out on top."

She recalled that from that period her Covent Garden season was most treasured, naming Bernard as "the closest" of the friends she made then, describing him as "phenomenally musical." As for Bernard:

"She liked me because, like herself (1) I come from the soil, (2) I knew a lot about timber and Viking ships… and was very musical."

He might have added that he was able to make her laugh, which she loved. He was well aware that laughter can be a potent aphrodisiac (although they had not yet become lovers.) Shortly before the Opera House season ended she asked if he might be able to come to Holland when she performed there, possibly while *Coriolanus* was having technical and dress rehearsals. In an early draft of his projected book on Kirsten, Bernard implies that his visit to The Hague was before Josephine returned from Canada ("Nellie's trip had set me free," said Bernard.) But, in fact, she returned on 30th March while *Coriolanus* opened on 31st March with Kirsten's final performance on 2nd April. Bernard's visit was between 30th April and 5th May as is clear from his appointments diary.

Before Kirsten left England they visited Kew again when Kirsten mentioned she would like to sing one of the *bel canto* roles she had sung when young – perhaps Gluck's 'Alceste'. Bernard suggested a less familiar work, one of his favourites, Purcell's *Dido and Aeneas*, less taxing in length. He gave her a recording of Nancy Evans singing the famous aria from Dido, "*When I am Laid in Earth*."

Kirsten wrote to him on her European tour; she had been listening to the recording ("too lovely for words") and requested a piano score of the entire piece ("I do love you for liking such music and Gluck too.") She was performing in The Hague when Bernard arrived in Holland on 30th March from where they went on to the North Sea resort of Scheveningen. She had booked the Bridal Suite on the second floor of a charming hotel called Wittebrug "and I found myself in a luxurious single bedroom with a little pass door leading into hers, usually kept locked but now wide open. Here I spent five delicious days as her prisoner, retiring from the toil of the Old Vic and acting the unaccustomed (!!) role of lover, the claims of home, work, family and duty quite forgotten."

In 1963, shortly after her death, Bernard wrote to an old Norwegian friend of Kristen's –

"This lovely, exceedingly proper, orderly correct and regular woman, supreme singer of her day, responded for once in her life to an Isolde-like impulse and threw all her Norwegian provincialness to the wind."

Together they went to concerts – his first hearing of the Kreutzer Sonata during which she held his hand and whispered, "It's wonderful not to be alone any more." However, there was one fly in the ointment. "I hadn't yet told her I was married to an enchanting wife and had three beautiful children." When precisely he did tell her is unclear but he describes her as "understandably shocked," insisting, "I don't go with married men. I have seen too much unhappiness for that." In what Frow thinks was a final draft for a section of *Born to Sing*, Bernard writes:

"Indeed I think Kirsten might have resolved to give me up but Nellie, like a good wife, as always, wanted me to have what was good for me. Nellie constructed the working triangle and, when the frenzy was over, Kirsten settled in as part of the family. Josephine was happy to have loaned me out for a while."

John Miles told Frow that he was certain his mother would have handled the whole affair "with steely correctness – polite, charm, gracious she would not have made a drama out of it." Perhaps so – and she definitely comprehended the depth of feeling between her husband and Kirsten. Yet, on the page covering 30th April in Bernard's appointments diary, Bernard simply wrote 'Hague' but had added in the margin: "Kirsten" and eight exclamation marks. On the next page, covering 3-4 May, Josephine had written, in bold capitals – "NO, NO, A THOUSAND TIMES NO."

It would seem that Josephine, like some other remarkable wives of troubled actors of the time – Rachel Kempson, Angela Baddeley, Helen Cherry included – had that rare human quality of forgiveness. From all the evidence it seems that the physical affair ("the frenzy") between Bernard and Kirsten was brief but when Kirsten returned to England she counted the whole Miles family as among her closest friends. "We adopted her," said Bernard, and as "Tante K" she became part of the family. Later, Bernard was to write:

"How do you fall in love with a married man and in the end manage to embrace the whole family, shedding the one relationship to embrace a wider one? Having fallen in love with a fourteen stone dramatic soprano of surpassing beauty how do you keep the soprano without losing the wife? How, having fallen in love with a rustic comedian already married, do you manage to embrace the whole family for a lifetime? I think the answer is that love is very hard work."

Returning from The Hague Bernard still had his final Old Vic performances to face. He played in *Saint Joan* again but received no call for *The Shrew* on Friday and Saturday; the management put the understudy on as Sly. Lawyers' letters and letters between lawyers came thick and fast, the Vic's team bluntly saying that "if Mr. Miles wants to go to arbitration it remains for him to take the necessary steps." Arbitration would involve two arbitrators, one appointed by Equity, the other for the management with a legal chairman with Bernard claiming unfair dismissal. A twelve-point list of "breaches of contract" came from the Old Vic with Bernard's annotations dismissing them. He scribbled down some notes in response to the charges of "deviations from the production", rightly pointing out (again) that he had been engaged to play Sly because of his skill as an inventive comedian – "engaged to invent – a chorus or commentary upon the play with the play", adding that the accusation of "deviations" was meaningless as after the induction there was nothing laid down or fixed from which he could deviate. The wretched business dragged on until 1950 when it was reported to the Governors that the administrator had a personal interview with Bernard resulting in "an amicable settlement." It was agreed that the Old Vic Governors would not ask Bernard to pay for their legal expenses and that each party would pay their own. Bernard had joined the Old Vic "in the highest and happiest of spirits." Three years passed before he could write in his appointments diary: "Old Vic Season Finished (Thank God)." The events were common knowledge within the theatrical profession with many actors supporting Bernard against what they saw as an unbending and aloof management and Board; Esher led the Board and it was he who had written previously to Olivier and Richardson, both out of the country, to terminate their contracts as directors (Burrell, the other triumvirate member, was also sacked but soon returned.)

THE OLD VIC saga hurt Bernard deeply. He and Glynne remained convinced that the management's charges were contrived to force him out of the company. Certainly it remains suspicious that no complaint was made by the management over Bernard's performance until the problems caused by Trevor Howard's departure arose and also that no other play involving Bernard gave rise to similar accusations. However, as always he was determined to "rise above" and very soon he was absorbed in another project which he felt was just up his street – another film for Del. The new company formed by Del, Pilgrim Pictures, had *The Guinea Pig* nearing completion and Ustinov's *Private Angelo* about to shoot. His suggestion to Bernard had come from Ernest Bevin, a film on industrial relations, a novel subject for the British screen, which would bring him together on the screenplay with an old friend, Walter Greenwood.

Before work started he and Josephine flew to Zurich where Kirsten was performing. The trio had several meals together and Kirsten joined them in England for several concerts with Bernard as her unofficial manager. She then left for a long South African tour. The many letters Bernard wrote to her then sadly have not survived:

> "I fed her with letters, with jokes, fantasies, dreams in English, broken German, broken Scandinavian, broken Italian. Often I wrote as many as five letters a day."

The few surviving scraps of her letters, addressing him as "Dear Bestfriend" reveal that she was keen to meet again: ("I want very much to laugh again.")

The film for Del – *Chance of a Lifetime* – now took up most of Bernard's time. His collaboration on the script with Walter Greenwood was happy. They were friends already and had worked together before on an idea suggested by Ernest Bevin based on the Tolpuddle Martyrs, never made. Famous for his first published novel, '*Love on the Dole*', Salford-born Greenwood worked with Bernard to develop Bernard's ideas for the story (somewhat different from Del's.) The film would centre round a small independent engineering company which hits trouble when a troublesome workman is sacked, leading to the workforce, after an angry meeting, taking up the boss's challenge that if they think the can manage the operation better than he does, they are welcome to try. The film follows the successes and tribulations of the venture when the men take on a new works manager (Kenneth More.) Bernard was able to cast the film strongly – Basil Radford as the boss, Geoffrey Keen as the bolshie worker, Hattie Jacques as the Canteen Manageress. A 'guest star', Compton Mackenzie as a banker, was persuaded one evening in the Savile when Greenwood told him the part was a posh bank director who refuses the co-operative an overdraft, to which the novelist's reply was "I ought to be able to do that, Walter. I have a lot of experience in being denied overdrafts."

A possible major problem arose in early 1949 when one of Del's former associates wrote to Bernard that Pilgrim Pictures' finances were precarious, largely because of Del's extravagance. Bernard's reply did not deny that there was "a large debit side" to Del's account but he preferred to detail "the credit side":

> "When one is working for a person one wants to give all the loyalty one has. But at the same time I am not such a fool as to be unaware of the weaknesses of the set-up! I agree entirely with all you say and I am sure you are right in your diagnosis of the financial situation but when all is said I want to ask you how you can assess the value of a man who fought for such films as *Hamlet* and *Henry V* against the most bitter opposition."

He conceded that probably he might be disappointed over "promises of reward and clauses in my contract etc. etc." but stressed he knew of "nobody in Hollywood or Britain who would dream of letting me make this film."

As if on cue, a few days later Del wrote from New York asking him to "make sacrifices" in his fee in order to persuade ABC to supply more capitalisation. Bernard told Derek Glynne to agree.

On a tight budget (£150,000) *Chance of a Lifetime* was filmed entirely on location near Stroud in Gloucestershire. It was, said Kenneth More:

> "an extremely happy picture. We had glorious weather letting us work seven days a week, nights and all. There was no quibbling about overtime… Bernard is a remarkable man. He has a knack of getting the best out of everyone."

With filming over Bernard, Josephine and Sally flew to catch Kirsten in *Fidelio* at the Salzburg Festival, followed by a trip to Norway after Josephine and Sally flew home. There is no way of knowing for certain if Kirsten and Bernard were still occasional lovers but the bond of friendship was even more strong. Kirsten had by now recovered all her Norwegian properties and most of this visit was spent at her country home of Kristiansand, set in dense woodland of larch and fir. Later they drove through much of Norway in her chauffeured Lincoln Convertible visiting Oslo and her birthplace at Hamar.

Everything had gone so well on *Chance of a Lifetime* but trouble awaited Bernard's return for post-production work. It seemed possible that none of the three big circuits – Odeon, Gaumont and ABC – would book it. Reasons were vague but it was assumed the film was deemed "too political."

Bernard and Sir Arthur Jarratt (managing director of British Lion, the distributors), decided to find a way through the seeming impasse. Section 5 of the Cinematograph Act (1948) clearly states that if an independent producer felt that a film had been "unfairly refused a booking" he or she could request to have it viewed by the Board of Trade. Should that Committee judge the film to be good entertainment and should be shown, then the Board of Trade had the power to order one of the circuits to show it (each circuit had a limit of six such films a year). Yet again the film establishment seemed somewhat hostile to Del and Bernard.

Kirsten flew from Los Angeles to spend Christmas with the Mileses, laden with presents and singing Norwegian carols around the piano. On Christmas Eve Bernard took Kristen and the children to see Ivor Novello in his most recent romantic musical, *King's Rhapsody*. Novello had become a friend and was involved with the early meetings – often held at Novello's flat above the Strand (now Novello) Theatre – to lay plans for creating a theatre in the building which had once been the school hall at Duff House. "It looked like an abandoned barn," said Kristen when Bernard showed it to her. As they looked around Bernard had suddenly said, "Kristen, believe it or not, this is going to be my own theatre some day," which she took as one of Bernard's practical jokes. Then he asked her to sing a few notes, saying when she asked why:

"I'd like you to sing here when I've made it into a theatre, would you?"

And Kirsten replied:

"Yes, of course. Just like that."

i. Original brochure for the Mermaid Theatre, Duff House.

ii. Bernard Miles and his wife, Josephine Wilson.

iii. Duff House, St John's Wood, London, the location of Bernard Miles's first theatre, the Little Mermaid.

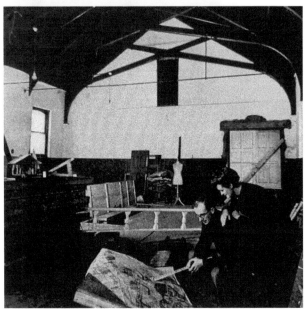

iv. The interior of the spacious hall at the back of the house where the Little Mermaid was built.

v. Kirsten Flagstad,
Norwegian opera
singer, the outstanding
Wagnerian soprano of
her era.

"I fell in love with her the
moment I met her..."
- Bernard Miles

vi. Baliol 'Ba' Holloway
as Richard III.

Bernard Miles's
"theatrical godfather"

vii. Bernard Miles (left) and John Mills sharing bad news in Noël Coward's In Which We Serve *(1942).*

vii. The poster for Miles's surprise US hit Tawny Pipit *(1944).*

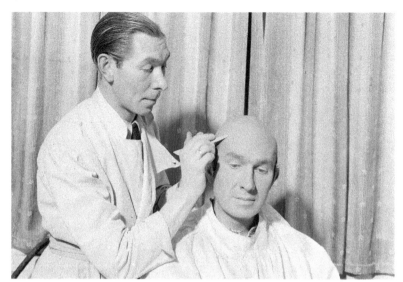

ix. Bernard Miles (right) in the makeup chair for his transformation into Newman Noggs for Alberto Cavalcanti's The Life and Adventures of Nicholas Nickleby *(1947).*

x. Bernard Miles (far right) joins James Stewart, Doris Day and Brenda de Banzie in Albert Hitchcock's The Man Who Knew Too Much *(1956).*

xi. The contractors (Marshall Andrew and Co. Ltd.) move onto the Puddle Dock site and work begins.

xii. The first view from the front of the house looking at the stage.

xiii. The seats covered with dust-sheets in position.

xiv. Laying the stage with the revolve in place.

xv. "its right and proper home" - the Mermaid Theatre, Puddle Dock.

Part Two

FROM BERNARD'S APPOINTMENTS diary, detailing some meetings with Novello, Daubeney and Glynne previously, it is clear that he had already had the conversion of the hall in mind (Novello, Glynne and Daubeney were, indeed, the theatre's first Trustees.) Bernard was a clever publicist and knew that the coup of having the world's leading soprano to sing in a converted barn would attract huge amounts of press coverage. He linked his idea to the Festival of Britain, announced by Herbert Morrison (leader of the House in the Commons) as a nationwide affair to celebrate the country's traditions and creative potential – "a national gesture of faith in the future, a Festival of Britain." Bernard liked the sound of that and, as the south bank of the Thames between Waterloo and Westminster Bridge began to see the creation of several key festival buildings, he determined to be a part of it. Dealing with the Eyre Estate which owned Duff House took time but eventually the Estate agreed to the development of the hall. In their early careers both Bernard and Josephine had appeared in many of the 'little theatres' in and around London; they knew that from unlikely origins several theatres had emerged – Hampstead's Everyman had been a drill hall, the Sheffield Playhouse also – and Bernard's ideas for the hall were crystallising. From the outset he had in mind an Elizabethan playhouse. Others had preceded him, most notably William Poel who used mainly amateur actors (the young Edith Evans included) for his Elizabethan Stage Society. Once described as "half genius, half crank, wholly fantastic", Poel abominated what he called "Lyceum Shakespeare", meaning the heavily cut, lavishly designed productions of Henry Irving at the Lyceum and Beerbohm Tree at His Majesty's and wanted to use an open platform stage, which could allow the kind of fleet, textually faithful productions which he was sure how plays by Shakespeare and his contemporaries were originally presented. Poel approved of what one of his heroes (one of Bernard's also) – Shaw – no Bardolator but a champion of the Elizabethan stage, had said of Poel's productions – "the more I see of them the more I am convinced that their method of presenting an Elizabethan play is not only the right method for that particular sort of play but that any play performed on a platform amidst the audience gets closer to home than when it is presented as a picture framed by a proscenium." Perhaps not surprisingly for a dramatist who saw his work as "a terrible art of sharpshooting at the audience", Shaw insisted that the platform stage was of "immense advantage to actors, making for a much more intimate relation to the audience" (it was no accident that Shaw became virtually the house-dramatist at Puddle Dock.)

From boyhood at UCS's Assembly Hall stage under Cecilia Hill to the stage thrown between two destroyers at Scapa Flow ("I remember saying to Josephine: "This is what the Elizabethan theatre must have been like!"), Bernard championed the open stage and as actor in revue and in solo performances he loved close contact with the audience.

When contemplating his own theatre he initially followed the work of Ronald Watkins and Maurice Percival at Harrow School where they presented an annual Shakespeare production, of which Bernard had seen some, in the Speech Room using a stage and tiring house "approximating to that of Shakespeare's Globe." Bernard showed some of his rough sketches for his own theatre to Watkins and Percival, reporting to Josephine that "they were thrilled with the plans and thrilled that we are ADVENTURING!" Clearly he had reservations about some of their more purist notions: "We mustn't use lights! Just flat daylight as in Shakespeare's day!!"

He worked away on his plans while trying to decide on the season's plays; having just read Jack Lindsay's radio version of *The Pilgrim's Progress* he considered that "it cries out for the swiftness and east of the Elizabethan stage." At that time he was considering three productions – a Shakespeare (*Macbeth*, which he had been denied at the Old Vic), Bunyan and/or Fielding (he had plans for a forgotten Fielding play, *Rape Upon Rape*) alongside *Dido and Aeneas*. He was right about the masses of publicity this obtained – "Flagstad to sing in old school hall" – much being made of her contracted salary of two bottles of stout a night.

Work on the design of the theatre continued with Bernard working alongside Michael Stringer, a bright spark who had been assistant art director on *Chance of a Lifetime*. Still young but with a good deal of experience (he went on to a distinguished screen career – *Genevieve* and *Fiddler on the Roof* included.) They worked well together – "he was full of ideas, all very practical" Bernard approved.

The St. John's Wood adventure was now, officially, The Mermaid, named after the famous tavern in Cheapside which in Elizabethan London was the regular watering hole of the literary men and dramatists, Shakespeare and

Ben Jonson included ("What things have we seen / Done at the Mermaid! Heard words that have been / Set nimble and so full of subtil flame!" wrote Francis Beaumont.) Now things were moving at a faster pace. The theatre was founded with an initial capital of £750 – Novello, Bernard and Daubeney each contributed £250 with Ernst Freud as honorary architect. But the actual stage was not finalised, as Bernard updated Josephine:

"Yesterday I had a long talk with Freud. He had made plans for an ordinary proscenium theatre and it took him some time to see the idea of the Elizabethan stage. But finally he was quite convinced. He has made what I think is a very good lay-out!"

He added the perennial worry of theatre designers:

"The chief thing is where to put the lavatories if the audience is not to use ours."

With Stringer's help, Bernard worked through as many as possible of the enormous amount of academic books on the subject and they discussed at length possible shape and structure. He knew he and his associates had not quite cracked the vital questions of the size and shape of the stage but he knew how crucial this was, especially as he was already thinking beyond the initial short (six-week) season. When writing to Kirsten it was decided to cut one production, leaving *Dido* and *The Tempest*:

"After all if the Mermaid is successful at all it will CONTINUE and not just be a brief flash in the pan."

Amidst the hectic planning Bernard fitted in another contribution to the Festival of Britain playing a cameo role in the Boulting film *The Magic Box* tracing the career of a pioneering figure in British cinema, William Friese-Green. Bernard played his cousin with two short scenes.

Then he was off to America for the first time, partly for *Chance of a Lifetime*'s New York premiere and also to catch Kirsten's farewell performance at the Metropolitan Opera. The decision of the Board of Trade Selection Committee (chaired by Lord Drogheda) had been unanimously in favour of the film being screened as a first feature on one of the circuits. A victory, except that none of the circuits wanted it. The practice was to draw lots to decide. Woodrow Wyatt, journalist and Labour MP, in *The Tribune* wrote that this was "a landmark" in the history of the British film industry – "one of the great circuits is staging a film not because it wants to but because it has been ordered to by the President of the Board of Trade."

As luck would have it, Rank 'won' the draw – its Odeon circuit would have to show the film. Wardour Street's moguls were hugely exercised by what they saw as political interference in their business. Rank admitted he had not seen the film, "but I am advised it is not a good one. There is nothing in the act to protect us if we lose a great deal of money by showing it." Unsurprisingly this raised hackles at the Board of Trade with its President, Harold Wilson, retorting, "Criticism of this kind seems hardly likely to be an inducement to the public to see the film." He also wrote a tart letter to Rank saying that he expected the film to be given the same publicity and treatment as if it were one of Rank's own.

This did not happen. John Davis, the feared Rank henchman, stopped negotiations with British Lion "as they were not provided for in the Act." The unsatisfactory outcome was that negotiations for the film's showing had to go through the Board of Trade with no distributor involved. As Wyatt wrote: "It became clear that Rank were determined to smash the film if they could."

The film premiered at the Leicester Square Cinema (no red carpet) with scant publicity. The notices were in the main positive although all tended to mention there was no love interest. It was described as "refreshing" and "different" but such adjectives hardly made for 'selling notices.' *The Times* wrote:

> "The film has a theme and an idea and the cinema is as frightened of both as was the late nineteenth century theatre before Mr. Shaw came along to shake some sense into it. The film's triumph lies in the integrity with which it draws its picture of factory life and it is flawlessly acted."

However business was patchy, as the Beaverbrook press seemed gleeful to point out, with admonitions that there should be no more interference from Harold Wilson. The Rank v Miles differences erupted once more when *The New Statesman* printed an open letter from Bernard to Rank, reminding him that his first film, *Turn of the Tide*, when Rank was just an independent producer, could not find a fair showing. For millionaire Rank the solution was simple – he bought a chain of cinemas and a distributing agency. Bernard had "ten tins of film and nowhere to show them." He conceded that on paper the film might not fit into the accepted categories of entertainment but that did not make it uncommercial. He was desperate for more involvement and commitment from Rank but they did nothing, putting it on unpublicised general release in July, never the best month for cinema attendance.

In New York it was well received ("highly enjoyable" said *The New York Post*) but, of course, the subject lacked the charm which had appealed to American audiences in *Tawny Pipit*. He had to take his cinema encounters on the chin, returning to London at an exciting stage in his great adventure.

His Mermaid work with Stringer had been fruitful. The stage and tiring house made it clear that this theatre was not to be a painstakingly antiquarian reconstruction, more "a free experiment in the Elizabethan style." An old friend of Bernard's, Max Gayton, once manager for the Baynton company, suggested he might get his boss, Val Parnell, powerful director of the Moss Empire chain of variety theatres including the jewel in their crown, The London Palladium, to come and see Bernard at the Players' with his "Clod" act with the cartwheel.

"On May 18, Max was as good as his word," wrote Bernard. "There was a good house and I got a good solid hand at the end." Bernard was offered half a dozen dates on the road "to warm him up" and then – the Palladium!"

While he was 'working the halls' in Brighton, a new collaborator burst into Bernard's life. In his dressing-room he was told a young man wanted to see him:

"A few minutes later Walter Hodges was sitting at my dressing-table, excusing himself for trespassing upon what he called my "valuable time" and protesting he intended to stay only a few minutes. He then opened his bursting portfolio and out poured on to the floor dozens of delightful drawings which I realised at once were the answer to the whole problem."

Walter lived a few miles along the coast. A former stage designer, he had also written essays on the Elizabethan stage ("my passionate obsession.") He was exactly the kind of enthusiast, game for "adventuring", to whom Bernard responded. Walter outlined his thinking:

"I am sure you are on to a terrific thing. This Elizabethan idea, if it is put across alive, that is not a piece of picturesque antiquarianism, will be an experience unlike anything any of us have ever seen in the theatre."

Luckily when Bernard told Hodges that another designer was on board there was no resentment and both Hodges and Stringer took to each other, unhesitatingly agreeing to redesign the stage together. Hodges said:

"We worked together in the most amicable harmony throughout. It must have been by some outrageous magic of Bernard's own that he could plant two artists together in such a way and made such a project prosper, as it did."

The trio scrapped the received idea of the Elizabethan theatre, its heavy pillars, thatched roof and half-timbered façade (what Hodges describes as "A poky old hybrid of a mousetrap and a Tudor tea-garden") and abandoned most of the academic theories on the subject. The final design of The Little Mermaid was much simpler; a rectangular 'tiring house' hardly more than a tabernacle of posts and curtains with, on the upper storey of gallery and two windows, all standing proud upon a platform stage. The stage would be two feet high and the structure decorated in what Hodges called "a style of Renaissance Mannerism." Bernard described it as "a proudly-painted mixture of pseudo-classic British folk and popular Baroque – a gorgeous playing-space."

By now Bernard's brain was fizzing. As well as working on the stage design he was writing often to Kirsten, outlining his ideas for *Dido*. While he was in America the stage and tiring house had been built in the workshop of Nettlefold Studios at Walton on Thames where Stringer was working. On returning from America Bernard found that everything was ready to be assembled and painted, all stacked in pieces. The work was now intense, including digging a tunnel for access to the downstage trapdoor from which in *Dido*, the Sorceress and her retinue would crawl, covered in mist and steam (using two electric kettles).

Sally, now a teenager, watched her home becoming a theatrical workshop –

Gradually all the rooms in the house became offices, property shops and wardrobes. "By the time the first production was under way I had ten dancers dressing in my bedroom."

It may sound rather amateurish but The Little Mermaid was run with meticulous and professional efficiency. The key issue of gathering subscriptions was well under way and doing well, as was the exhibition telling the story of the Elizabethan theatre being assembled by Walter Hodges. By early July the tiring house was reassembled to await painting and work began on the 180-seat auditorium for which Ernst Freud used a frame of tubular scaffolding, erected within two days. More tricky was the flooring of the raked seating for which it was estimated they would need 900 square feet of really solid timber and in 1951 many things, timber included, were in short supply or still rationed. Somehow people got to hear of supplies on a kind of grapevine. News came of old packing cases stashed in a scrapyard in Gospel Oak. Made of stout Oregon pine the cases were ideal; they were bought on the spot for a knockdown price and transported to Duff House in a local butcher's van. Then Bernard heard that seating might be available at a blitzed Baptist Chapel at the Elephant and Castle. The basement had once been used as a Sunday school and they were welcome to have them if they could find them. Hours of digging and rummaging revealed 36 pitch-pine benches, all usable after a thorough cleaning and painting. By August, rehearsals for *Dido* were under way – on stage if possible, in the various outbuildings, even in a nearby pub. Michael Stringer and the paint crew often had to work overnight. Walter Hodges said:

"I remember that summer of 1951 in that garden in Acacia Road as something quite splendid and wonderful with the voice of Flagstad in rehearsal floating across the evening lawn. And sunshine. It was always sunshine. Of course it really wasn't but so it may be remembered."

An enthralled spectator at rehearsals for *Dido and Aeneas* was a young boy, Terry Wale, who would go on to play Ariel in *The Tempest*. Everything was new to him – Flagstad's sublime voice (he had never heard opera at home in Hounslow), the camaraderie between performers, affecting him so much that he would attend rehearsals even if not called. He wrote touchingly of his time at Duff House in his later book '*Pretending to be Somebody Else*', vividly recalling Bernard of whom he admitted being afraid: "he scared the pants off me" not because of any unkindness ("he was just totally unpredictable.") The highlight for Terry was his entrance in *The Tempest* to deliver his speech to the conspirators ("You are three men of sin"), as devised by Bernard and Julius – Terry had to be up on the roof of the theatre, held by a parachute harness and then flown down to deliver Ariel's remonstration. After that he was totally stagestruck – a successful boy actor's career (Puck in Benjamin Britten's *A Midsummer Night's Dream* at Covent Garden included) and then a long professional acting life in repertory theatre, at Stratford-on-Avon and in the West End.

There were remarkably few panicky jitters on Sunday 9th September 1951 when *Dido* opened. The draughty old hall had been utterly transformed –

dazzling green and gold with the ceiling painted a deep blue with gold and silver stars set among clouds (another Hodges notion.) The orchestra, dressed in periwigs, velvet coats and lace cravats were seated in the stage gallery, conducted by Geraint Jones who had made a superb new orchestration of the entire opera. Partly due to the sheer unexpectedness and beauty of the venture, it was an unquestionable triumph. Critics had only praise for Bernard's production and the glorious singing from Flagstad, Maggie Teyte (Belinda) and Thomas Hemsley (Aeneas). Remaining tickets sold out quickly.

Directed by Julius Gellner, *The Tempest* opened ten days later and was similarly successful. Especially praised was the opening shipwreck scene which used sound (thunder, torrential rain), lighting and simple but striking effects (the trapdoor was used to represent the hold within the gallery as the poop.) As the mariners scattered ("We split! We split!") ropes fell down into the trap which closed while the lighting and sound faded into soft music and gentle waves. In 20 seconds, the audience had been transported to Prospero's island.

Designed by Stringer with Hodges's costumes, with Clifford Evans's commanding Prospero and Bernard's unsettling Caliban, *The Tempest* was also a sell-out for most performances (Josephine played "goddess of corn" Ceres, her only appearance in that first season.) The two productions played a total of 58 performances plus other recitals and concerts including Elisabeth Schuman in her last London recital. Altogether the first Mermaid season was a succès fou. In the 1951 Prospectus Bernard had quoted from *Macbeth*:

"I have begun to plant thee and
Will labour / To make thee full of growing."

This was a clear indication of his plan not to end the Mermaid adventure after the Festival of Britain season. It took some complex negotiations with Mr. Ragg of the Eyre Estate and his first approach was rejected. But Bernard was nothing if not persistent. He expected people to share his enthusiasms and was clearly puzzled when they did not. He badgered Mr. Rudd until finally, in late January 1952, Rudd agreed that the Trustees would grant another licence for a six-week season but it was abundantly clear that no future season would be permitted. Bernard was not going to let the Mermaid adventure collapse and, desperate to find a new home, was somewhat surprised when Rudd suggested another site on the Eyre Estate. Bernard and Josephine thought this – only a short distance from Acacia Road – was perfect and at once told Rudd ("When can we start clearing it?") Bernard needed to replenish the coffers (most of his money was poured into the Mermaid) so he played his solo act for a Palladium season and then on tour. Providentially a film came along – *Never Let Me Go,* a so-so affair set against a Cold War background, shot in Cornwall involving Clark Gable, Gene Tierney and Kenneth More in a people-smuggling plot. It was not a particularly good part but well-paid so Bernard settled down to a few weeks during a balmy Cornish summer, reading widely until director Delmer Davies asked him not to bring books on to the set. When he remonstrated that he had to do something Davies explained: "Yeah, but Gable and these he-man types get kinda uneasy when they see a book."

He returned to disappointment. The Eyre Estate had agreed to allow a ten-year period of use on the new site but, when the plans went before a meeting of St. Marylebone Council, it was "refused; the Council had designated the whole site for housing." So when the second Duff House Mermaid season went into rehearsal the future thereafter seemed decidedly uncertain.

That season opened with Flagstad in *Dido* again, even more successful than before, followed by Bernard and Josephine leading the *Macbeth* cast with Peter Sallis an hilarious Porter. The reviews were respectful – the production was played "in the speech commonly employed by educated Londoners of the 17th century," something of a Bernard hobby-horse but not a box-office blockbuster. The surprise success of the season, directed by Joan Swinstead, was Thomas Middleton's *A Trick to Catch the Old One* which, as one critic put it, "rose riotously from oblivion." Bernard was in ripe comic form as the country tapster who cons gullible old men into the trap in the form of Josephine's Courtesan. Bernard had chosen this piece to oppose "the chronic Shakespearean fixation" and this bustling, speedy production proved how rich the Elizabethan / Jacobean repertoire could be. He would not forget this when the Mermaid was established in its final home.

IN THE MEANTIME the following year finally seemed secure. A neighbour of the Mileses, a good friend called Major R.A.B. Smith had invited the Lord Mayor of London, Sir Leslie Boyce and his wife to the theatre and gave a small supper party afterwards. Sir Leslie had very much admired the theatre and the performance and when Bernard told him that the stage and tiring house were easy to dismantle and could be easily re-erected in any suitably-sized space, he suggested that Bernard bring the Mermaid into the City of London to celebrate Queen Elizabeth's coronation. It was Lady Boyce who suggested "Why not the Royal Exchange? You know you don't know what to do with it." Over the next few months the Boyces helped the move.

Right at the heart of the City of London, between the Bank of England and the Mansion House stands the Royal Exchange, built in 1568 as the Bourse, a two-level structure surrounding an open courtyard with covered walks around it and accommodation for merchants with shops above it. Destroyed in the Great Fire of 1666 it was rebuilt on the old foundations before burning down again in 1838. When rebuilt it had only offices, no shops, and reopened in 1844 with a rather po-faced statue of Queen Victoria dominating the now-roofed quadrangle.

The process of fitting the Mermaid into the Royal Exchange had more hazards than in Acacia Road. Encouraged by the Boyces, the Mileses were invited to present their plans to the arcane City institution of the Joint Grand Gresham Committee – "The City Fathers" – and Bernard wrote a polite account of this in a 1953 Brochure describing how they were treated most courteously. His private account was less reverent. It was clear that the Committee had not met for some time and regarded the meeting as an excuse for a slap-up lunch (the servitor who greeted the Mileses told them, "They are now on their ninth decanter of port.") When admitted, they found themselves in a room thick with cigar smoke and a less than cordial atmosphere. Bernard outlined the Mermaid's plan "to restore the living drama to its ancient cradle here in the square mile" which produced only "an angry stir along the table and some ominous muttering. Apparently I had touched a dangerous chord."

Leaving the meeting Bernard and Josephine were in low spirits, certain that he had failed. They were surprised then to receive a telephone call from the Deputy Town Clerk, John Murphy, who would be a loyal supporter, to say the Coronation Season had been approved. Very soon Bernard began fund-raising helped by an initial £5,000 from Sir Leslie Boyce and also began to assemble a group of 'patrons' who would add cachet to this new venture.

Now the major task of turning that awkward Royal Exchange space into a theatre began. Not the least of the problems was the massive (three-ton) statue of Victoria dominating the centre of the quadrangle. Moving it required long negotiations with a special committee (more port) of the Mercers' Company. The floor of the quadrangle turned out to be the original floor, made of Turkish honestone, the stone walked on by Elizabeth I when the

Exchange was proclaimed "Royal." There was no question of drilling into it to provide tunnelling for the trapdoor. The seating configuration would have to be different from the frontal arrangement at St. John's Wood, necessitated by the hall's narrow dimensions. At the Exchange the audience would be raked on three sides. Invention was required on numerous occasions; the acoustics at the Exchange were poor and the problem was finally solved by creating a huge false ceiling across the quadrangle, so big and heavy it had to be made in sections and hung by 6,000 feet of steel wire. Once again the ceiling of the same deep blue was studded with silver stars. A delicate issue was the famous Royal Exchange chiming bells which played a selection of British airs (plus '*Waltzing Matilda*' and '*The Maple Leaf Forever*') every three hours. Tactful negotiations resulted in approval of the request that they be silenced during performances.

The increased size of the space meant that this Mermaid would have nearly 1,000 seats divided into enclosures each named after a City street, livery company or personage (Leadenhall, Vintners, Lombard etc. – an idea carried into the final Mermaid in naming the dressing-rooms.) Everyone involved realised that filling that number would involve much more work than at the Little Mermaid. There were worries – the City was not a residential area and so somehow the enormous number of people who worked there and left at the end of their day would have to be persuaded that they should stay on for a play when most City restaurants, bars and pubs closed early. Conversely would audiences be persuaded to travel into the City for an evening? Also the competition in Coronation Year would be massive, with all sorts of special events and attractions. All the St. John's Wood subscribers were targeted – seat prices ranged from 2|6d. (12½p) to 12|6 (72½p) and a tiny box-office (a tarted-up contractor's hut) was erected at the west site of the Exchange, with encouraging early bookings.

The repertoire for this season consisted of a final revival of *Dido and Aeneas*, *As You Like It*, *Macbeth* and *Eastward Ho!* by Jonson, Chapman and Marston. Twice-nightly performances meant that City workers could catch the 6pm showing while audiences from further afield could attend the second performance. Bernard would direct the first two productions, Joan Swinstead the other pair.

Publicity was paramount. Bernard, no slouch in that department, decided that as an opening salvo the companies of all the plays should enter the City on May Day, all in the style of old strolling players ("I think that actors should bang the drum and wave the flags whenever possible and march through the streets.") That year, May Day was freezing and extremely wet, but an undaunted Mermaid company assembled in costume in Regent's Park. Bernard had arranged for four dray-carts drawn by Shire horses; some of the company were packed into the carts while others walked alongside with four of the strongest marchers leading the procession and carrying a little mermaid throned in a chair. A rubber fish tail was protection from the rain. It was five damp miles to reach the Exchange where the Lord Mayor along with his Sheriffs and the Common Cryer, all rather different from the welcome for past Strollers, the "rogues and vagabonds" fitted only to be booted out of the Square Mile. But because of this troupe's undampened high spirits the occasion, with the Cryer's orotund greeting ringing out, was a truly joyful affair although all the company were glad to get back to Regent's Park for dry clothes and a hot drink.

By happy contrast the weather for the opening night was benign. A packed house responded with enthusiasm to *As You Like It* with Josephine's Rosalind and the variety artist Reg Varney finding unexpected laughs as Touchstone. Bernard gave one of his doubles – a smouldering Duke Frederick and ripe rustic comedy as William. The press had one major moan – at the doubtless authentic but distractingly noisy rushes strewn over the stage, soon banished. *Macbeth* was so successful that its run was extended by a week while *Dido* was genuinely sublime, perhaps because Kirsten, aware that this would mark her farewell to opera, was in especially fine voice. The surprise of the season was the rarity of *Eastward Ho!*; audiences loved the rich language and the infectious energy of a cast of real individual characters (Bernard was a stand-out as Slitgut.)

Over 70,000 people paid to see the productions, higher than anticipated and making a uniquely delightful contribution to Coronation Year. Now the Mileses were more than ever convinced that a permanent Mermaid could be viable in the City. So convinced was Bernard that only halfway through the season he applied to the Gresham Committee for further use of the Exchange. But nothing persuaded the members to opt for the kind of City Arts Centre suggested by Bernard. It was a previous Lord Mayor, Sir George Wilkinson, who advised the Mileses to search the City for another site, possibly a blitzed building or church: "Sir George assured us that, although in the matter of financial aid he could not speak for the Corporation, he could guarantee a warm welcome." Finance was a top issue at the end of the season. Without subsidy it had played to over 70% capacity but that still left a deficit of £7,000:

"Certainly we would never be invited again if I did not clear the deficit – and three days after we closed I was offered two weeks at the Palladium as third top to Kay Starr followed by a fourteen-week tour. I could write to all outstanding creditors that if they could afford to be patient they could expect settlement in full within the next few months."

In the end Bernard slogged for over eight months around Britain's variety theatres, setting out with his now-celebrated wheel, billed as "The Uncrowned King of the Chiltern-Hills." Then, just as he was finishing, an offer came in for the role of the Manxman in the film of *Moby Dick* to be directed by John Huston (Bernard loved his film of *The Treasure of Sierra Madre*.) Before shooting he made a brief visit to Kirsten, still vexed by what she saw as shabby treatment from HMV and the Chairman Walter Legge but Bernard calmed her down and eventually had her contract moved to Decca. Then he flew to Dublin before going on to the Cork location in Youghal to join Gregory Peck (Ahab), Richard Basehart (Ishmael) and Leo Genn (Starbuck), an unforgettable experience. Bernard took greatly to Huston ("a magical man over 6ft. long, lean as whipcord and so relaxed that he bends in the middle.") It was never likely to be an easy shoot; when the unit moved to Elstree Studios, the work became even harder. The Pequod was made in two sections, the forward half on one soundstage and the other on a second. Each half was mounted on a steel cradle attached to hydraulic rams. Bernard was used to filming in water but *Moby Dick* was something else:

"For the storm sequence six tip-tanks each holding 1,000 gallons of water were set up on 30ft. towers. One after another the tanks were tipped and 6,000 gallons came down in solid sheets, tearing us from the rigging. This went on hour after hour for ten bitter November days."

With that in the can, filming moved to warmer waters. The cast still, however, were in for a tough time:

"At Las Palmas Huston really let himself go, day after day, tipping boatloads of men into the Atlantic 20 or 30 miles from land while he circled round in the camera boat, smiling."

Despite the rigours and the sense that it was not going to be a great movie, Bernard became friendly with both Huston and Peck (who told Bernard years later that he had hated playing Ahab although he did not admit it at the time.)

Although anxious to pursue Mermaid plans, when another film came along, Bernard could not refuse the chance to work with Alfred Hitchcock. This was a remake of his 1934 film *The Man Who Knew Too Much*, this time in colour with James Stewart and Doris Day then at the height of their stardom. Bernard and Brenda de Banzie were cast as the dubious Mr. and Mrs. Drayton. Filming began most agreeably in Marrakesh, then Bernard had a break while the complex Albert Hall sequence was shot before he was off for the first time to Hollywood. As always, he fretted over money; he had requested a modest hotel but was booked into a luxury establishment which involved long and expensive cab rides to the studio. But producer Hal Wallis's secretary found him a cosy small service apartment for only $105 a month where he was perfectly happy. He met up again with Gregory Peck who invited him to dine at his beautiful house ("My word, when they're in the money...!"), drove him to see a bullfight at Tijuana and also took him to the summer theatre co-run by Peck at La Jolla where he was impressed by *The Rainmaker* ("beautifully acted and produced.") He enjoyed working with Hitchcock ("He never said he thought actors were cattle to me or to anyone I heard") and admired the smooth-running efficiency of the studio. He came up with one of his best performances, relaxed without losing sight of the internal tensions of the character, master-spy Drayton. A subtle performance – convincingly understated when this hirer of assassins takes on the role of a nonconformist minister taking a service; it is full of little touches of detail filling out a complete portrayal of a complex character.

Whenever he had time off from London filming and on his return, he and Josephine continued to search for a Mermaid home. At the Architect's Department at the Guildhall they were shown maps demonstrating the devastation of the area in the Blitz (over 160 acres were destroyed) with possibilities of redevelopment and estimates of how long each restoration might take. They clambered through shattered churches, Livery Company halls and old warehouses. A late exploration took them down to the river and to the ruined warehouse (only the four outer walls of the ground floor remained) at 3A Upper Thames Street, next to a little inlet called, since Elizabethan days, Puddle Dock.

FROM THE FIRST look at the site they both agreed it could be ideal for their biggest adventure of all; he once said that looking down at it from the street above was his equivalent to Cortez standing on a peak in Darien. Few shared this view.

The site, especially in rainy weather, seemed unpromising – just a narrow strip of land with rubble everywhere and what the Luftwaffe had left after a night of devastation, destroying what had been City Mills Buildings, a seven-storey warehouse now merely a shell about 14` high and 4` thick of sooty London brickwork studded with windows at the river end and, at the other, four cast-iron columns pitted by German shrapnel. Often the site was used as a car park by local office workers. Weeds, mostly willowherb, were rampant. Puddle Dock itself, a narrow Thames inlet, once crowded with boats unloading cargo, had rarely been used for years, now mostly a rubbish dump or a berth for a battered old barge. All a sad decline from its glory days as a principal water-gate into the City, part of a busy residential area of London; according to Stow in Survey of London, in 1598 there were "many fairhouses, lodgings for nobles and others" and Shakespeare bought a house nearby in Puddle Dock Hill (now St. Andrews Hill.) The Blackfriars Theatre in which Shakespeare was a shareholder was close by, acting as the winter base for the Burbage / Shakespeare Company (later called The King's Men.) The City Fathers were decidedly hostile to more theatres on their patch. New theatres did appear but on the other side of the river where the City had no jurisdiction. Before long the players abandoned the area, leaving the City without theatres for 300 years, apart from a few short-lived ventures. When the Mermaid opened the theatre historian W. Macqueen Pope wrote: "The Mermaid stands outside the so-called magic circle of the West End, but it has as its neighbours mighty ghosts of the past. Where it stands was once theatre land – and may well be so again." Like Macqueen Pope, Bernard viewed that area around Puddle Dock as "theatrical holy ground."

From first viewing of the site to opening night it took over four years, involving the Mileses and a few devoted helpers in hard and dedicated work to see the building rise, giving Bernard time for only a few lucrative engagements, most of the reward going into the building fund. From the outset he had imagined a theatre "subsidised in a negative way by being free from rent," built by subscription and endowed by covenants and grants.

The necessary negotiations with the City were prolonged and far from easy. Bernard wrote to Robert Walker, the City Surveyor in the autumn of 1955 outlining plans to build "a temporary theatre to seat 650 people, designed mainly to serve the working population of the City." Budgeted at "not less than £20,000" building would commence "by Lady Day, 1956" and be completed fifteen months from that date. The City was asked to grant a lease to begin at Christmas 1955 with the rent proposed to be "a peppercorn" for the first year rising to £150 for the 6th to 10th years. At the end of the lease, the lessees would remove the structure and clear the site unless the City should wish to buy it. This submission closed with Bernard's heartfelt plea:

"Besides showing that the City can be a source of cultural and spiritual refreshment as well as a daily workshop, a river theatre on the North bank would excite world-wide interest and would also draw many thousands to the City for their evening's pleasure."

Mr. Walker replied, in Bernard's absence, to Derek Glynne, that the proposals would be put before the next relevant meeting –but the City's wheels grind slowly; the plan subsequently would have to be put before the City's governing body, the Court of Common Council. At times Bernard felt that the City workings were as labyrinthine – and at times as secretive – as those of the Vatican.

During this waiting time Bernard appeared in one of his most peculiar films. *Zarak* sounded alluring – a stirring tale of derring-do during the Raj – but during filming, virtually all on location in Morocco, it rained without a break. The casting was on the wayward side; Victor Mature as a Afghan outlaw, Frederick Valk an Afghan, the perennial Scot Finlay Currie a Mullah and Bernard, exotically clad in turban, a sheepskin coat and an eyepatch, as "the one-eyed Hassu." Box-office returns were low.

An untanned Bernard returned to snow and ice. But soon there was glad news – the City Fathers approved the Mermaid Puddle Dock plans at a Court of Common Council meeting in the Guildhall. The euphoria was slightly tempered by some minuted Members' objections, most strongly from Captain Alfred Instone who pronounced:

"to be successful a theatre must be situated among residents and a night life… Mr. Miles's first performance should be *Desert Island Discs*."

Captain Instone would be heard from again.

Television had not involved Bernard much previously but its popularity (audiences of 14-17 million in that era) persuaded him to star in *The Titlarks* as a variation of his "Clod" character, "poet and peasant and a bit of a poacher too." Press and public loved it ("one of the most amusing characters on the screen") but after only four episodes the writer James Lansdale Hanson, who had worked with Bernard assisting John Boulting, suddenly died. The series had enormously increased Bernard's standing and so it was a stroke of luck that Bill Naughton – later a key Mermaid author – was able to take over.

Television for Bernard was also a great educator. He came up with a series which he devised and presented in 1956, using the Bible as inspiration. Called *This Book is News*, he aimed to interpret "the most relevant of books in the language of the people, using passages from every possible variation of the Bible barring the Authorised version." Each programme used guest dialect, linked by Bernard who read his extracts in the Chilterns dialect. There were a few mutters that Holy words were spoken in dialect but the press loved it ("outstanding from every angle" said *The Star*.)

The drive to fill coffers while waiting for crucial building decisions took Bernard regularly to the film studios. At Pinewood (for J. Arthur Rank, no less) there was a tepid version of Marjorie Allingham's *Tiger in the Smoke* with Bernard transformed in dark glasses and an extraordinary white wig as an ex-Army man opposite Donald Sinden. Then came two for Frank Launder and Sidney Gilliatt – excellent as a conniving blackmailer in *Fortune is a Woman* starring Jack Hawkins. His favourite of this period was in *The Smallest Show on Earth* in which he gave a beautifully-shaded performance as the old commissionaire of the decrepit and unloved Bijou Cinema under new management (Margaret Rutherford, Virginia McKenna and Peter Sellers co-starred.) He stood out with a most touching and endearing performance, extremely moving in the scene after he has been told the Bijou must close. Finally he returned to Shepperton for *St. Joan*, heavily directed by Otto Preminger, playing a forbidding executioner.

AT LAST – in October, 1956 – the Mermaid was ready to be announced. With an Arctic blast blowing off the Thames, a marquee was erected on the bleak site – rum punch was wisely produced – and the Lord Mayor ("not too solemnly") cemented a brick from the old warehouse walls with what the press described as "a brick provided by Mr. Miles" reputedly from the Salzburg house in which Mozart was born (1956 marked his bicentenary.) The conjoined bricks were intended as something more interesting and arts-centred than a foundation stone. Bernard hastily changed the subject when one inquisitive young reporter questioned the origin of the Mozart stone – especially as the birthplace was still standing. Later he changed the story (a familiar habit) to say he had bought it for three schillings from an old lady guarding a bicycle park.

On view at the little ceremony were drawings and plans of the new building. But they bore scant similarity to what eventually was built at Puddle Dock. Bernard was impatient by nature – he'd have liked the whole enterprise completed yesterday – but in a crucial area such as the shape and size of the building (and auditorium) very wisely he took his time, rather as he had done back in Acacia Road. *The Times* described the building in the drawings seen that day as resembling a cross between a modern church and Mr. Peggotty's upturned boat of a house in *David Copperfield*. Sketches of the new theatre showed that it was to have a tiring house and a stage like those at Acacia Road and The Royal Exchange. Bernard promised a broad repertoire of what he called, rather high-falutinly, "selective eclecticism." Certainly Shakespeare but also the bountiful Elizabethan and Jacobean repertoire would be programmed, alongside new plays, revivals or musicals. That day he said he'd worked at the Old Vic and on the Halls and had come to the conclusion that "there was not much to choose between them." Basically, he said, he wanted to find "a common platform between so-called high-and-low-brow theatres by presenting 'a bird's eye view' of the world's drama in ten years." Equally important, he insisted (and would, to the end of his time at Puddle Dock) was the intention to keep ticket prices as low as possible. That chilly day there was, pleasingly, a good deal of warm enthusiasm from most City dignitaries present and, crucially, from the press.

Which is where a cheerful young man called Gerald Frow came in. Bernard was an adroit publicist but he knew he had to hand that area to an able assistant while he concentrated on building plans and fundraising. The Mileses had moved from Duff House, now living in Camden Town, as yet ungentrified, in Albert Street near Camden Town tube station and Gerald was summoned to meet Bernard one sunny morning in February. Aged 26 he had been married for a year and he and his wife Jacki were living in a cramped Kensington basement. He broke into journalism on the unromantic-sounding *Gas Journal*; he now worked at the daily newspaper *Lloyd's List and Shipping Gazette* and it was a colleague there, sharing Gerald's interest in the theatre, who told him that Bernard was searching for a publicity director as well as someone to guide him about fundraising among Lloyd's Members and City bigwigs generally. Gerald's journalism occupied him from 1pm – 8pm so if his Mermaid work could be done in the mornings then it would be possible.

When the two men met they had a long discussion about London theatre, still – despite the occasional surprise like *Waiting for Godot* or *Look Back in*

Anger (both 1956) – trapped in the commercial aspic of light comedy, musicals and intimate revue which they both deplored. Bernard offered him a three-month trial period (£3 a week, promptly accepted.) Then he handed over a file marked PUBLICITY which turned out to have little use except to provide a list of London theatre critics with telephone numbers. A week later he was sent a file marked PROPAGANDA which contained only some old publicity material on the Royal Exchange and many copies of pieces covering what Bernard liked to call "the brick-sticking." He added that the £3p.w. salary would commence on Monday 4th March. This was still more than three weeks away. As Gerald said, but without real rancour: "Typically he was getting my first three weeks for nothing!"

In fact, Bernard acquired a genuine bargain in Frow who quickly revealed an impressive knack for dreaming up publicity and who had a good deal to do with the Mermaid's initial success and with its convivial atmosphere. His initial suggestion was clever; he carried out a blitz on in-house magazines, arguing that it was a good idea to take the Mermaid story to date to the many employees of City firms who were being targeted for subscriptions. In those days there were many such publications and they proved a valuable source of companies and businesses ripe for Bernard's schmoozing. Quite some time – seven months – had passed since the brick-sticking ceremony. The site remained derelict. Fundraising moved sluggishly. The Mermaid Trust had £9,000 in the bank and 'promises' (covenants etc.) which could bring in around £6,000 more over the following six years. But Gerald – robust in argument – argued that something should be happening so the public knew that the project was still active. Plans were made for an 'Open Air Concert' to mark the launch of the Building Programme, to be held on site on Friday 19th July, 1957 beginning at 9pm, admission by invitation only (there were many notices advising that a collection would be taken.)

Theatres old and new then seemed prominent in the news. As the Mermaid was getting underway the St. James's was under threat after more than a century. Under Sir George Alexander it had presented prestige work by Oscar Wilde and Pinero, with the star couple of Laurence Olivier and Vivien Leigh co-starring in Shaw and Shakespeare. But now there was controversy over its possible demolition and Bernard worried that the St. James's publicity might overshadow the Mermaid campaign but, in fact, it worked to its advantage, the St. James's cramped seating and dreadful sight-lines hardly helping its cause. With the Savile, an unlovely barn (later a cinema) and the huge Stoll and Gaiety also doomed, the Mermaid could be seen as a ray of hope in a threatened theatrical landscape. Vivien Leigh garnered massive publicity by protesting vocally in the House of Lords and organising marches (which Bernard attended.) On the day of the Mermaid concert, there was a public march to protest against the St. James's closure but rain made it sadly a small affair. By evening skies had cleared although the rain had left the site looking like another Thames tributary. Usually at his best faced with crisis, Bernard prevented a quagmire by tracking down a sawmill which rapidly delivered 50 sacks of sawdust to spread and soak up the water. The evening turned out to be extremely clement. *City Press* wrote:

> "Mr. Miles erected a bare stage of scaffold poles and planks and with the stars for a roof succeeded in creating an atmosphere of complete magic."

With those participating including Larry Adler playing *Dido*'s lament plus 'interpolations' from Edith Evans, Kenneth More, John Mills and Max Bygraves, all informally presented by Bernard, by midnight the effects of theatre lighting on a derelict site and the crumbling walls began to assume an enchanted beauty. Near the end, coming on after her *Titus Andronicus* performance, Vivien Leigh read a letter of support from Winston Churchill and pleaded with the packed house to support the St. James's. "It was," said the *Birmingham Post*, "all very stirring and had something in its unrehearsed spontaneity which only the theatre could give."

Nothing could save the St. James's and then Bernard had a sharp reminder from the City Surveyor pointing out that no progress seemed to have been made at Puddle Dock, reminding him that the terms of the agreement for the building had dates for the opening and the end of the work. Promptly Bernard replied, assuring him that "Building proper commences this coming Thursday." That produced another letter from the surveyor politely stressing that the City, as freeholders, had not seen plans of the proposed building. Again Bernard replied at once: "The work in progress consists of preparing walls and clearing the site. These plans will be in your hands within the next ten days." That was followed up by a piece in the *Evening Standard*, a long editorial lauding the Mermaid's aims and policies – the Mermaid generally had a warm relation with arts editors if not always with critics, largely due to Gerald's genial hospitality. The work mentioned by Bernard about "preparing walls and cleaning the site" consisted of a site foreman and two labourers with a wheelbarrow and a ladder, not exactly high-tech. The architect – Elidir Davies again – recalled:

> "The contractors, who had worked with me at the Royal Exchange, had to build as the money came in – a most unusual contract for the building industry. We often had to change the pace, but we never had to stop the work."

Bernard's decision to take his time before committing to a final design was wise. The exterior changed – no more upended boat – and he blithely chose to forget the notion of a 'temporary building', reasoning that should the theatre succeed the City would adapt plans for the site; he knew there were plans for a new road along that section of the Thames north bank but it would be possible to build the road past it rather than through it. Crucially, the interior underwent considerable change. Early drawings and models showed Walter Hodges following previous designs with a stage and a tiring house but Bernard persuaded them that a different approach was needed for the Puddle Dock site. His thinking now was to have a simpler design, a spacious open stage stretching the entire width of the auditorium (its walls – stage and auditorium – were to remain the Old Mills bricks) for which Elidir Davies designed a revolutionary barrel-vault roof of reinforced concrete. The whole design was unique – a low, simple platform with no proscenium, with unbroken continuity of stage and auditorium walls. He had fretted for some time with his colleagues about the longitudinal section of the theatre, what height the stage should be – he had been less than happy with the 4` height at the Exchange (the blocks of side seats suffered especially). Finally, it was decided that the stage (incorporating a trap and a revolve) would be only 9" high with seating (now 498) set on a raked concrete ramp (he called it "the democratic slope"), each row one foot above the other and none more than 65` from the stage. Directors would find sightlines virtually perfect and the acoustics superb (both Mermaid musical compilation-revues *Cowardy Custard* and *Cole*, did not need to be miked.)

Gradually on-site work continued. Gerald Frow, now full-time, at last had an office (a tiny hut) among the huts and sheds which gave Puddle Dock the appearance of a shanty town. He gave himself the title "Press Representative and Head of Publicity" (salary now £10p.w.) and he made a good, if occasionally fiery, team with Bernard, as Bernard said: "We responded, I think, to each other's sense of humour. We were both adventurous, both irreverent. We fitted in with each other."

Fundraising now became even more paramount. Previously the business of raising money had been conducted mainly from Derek Glynne's offices. Now it moved to Puddle Dock, to start a serious drive to build from the £20,000 already contributed or promised. Subscribers included the Bank of England, all the main clearing banks as well as Lloyds, the Stock Exchange, Insurance and City Livery Companies, Charitable Trusts and many more.

Bernard liked to give the impression that raising money involved a kind of carefree amateurishness bu, in fact, he took it extremely seriously, never forgetting (as he had often to remind the City) that while he was being given money for his own special project, it was aimed to entertain those who subscribed. He told the *Daily Mail*:

> "It's no good hating money. There's plenty of it about and you've got to establish a claim to make some of it available to you. Besides, going round the City collecting is a marvellous education."

The fundraising campaign was carefully planned. Craftily he had chosen as fellow Trustees three wise men who could guide him through the maze of the City's interlocking interests – of course Sir Cullum Welch, former Lord Mayor and always a Mermaid friend, Major R.A.B. Smith, former neighbour from St. John's Wood, then the wild card of Hugh St. Denys Nettleton King-Farlow, retired lawyer with nearly 30 years' Shell Group experience. He also put together an 'Advisory Council' of City worthies, subsequently enlarged to include a generous number of theatre people.

The Times of 16th September 1957 carried a prominently-placed letter in its correspondence column, signed by 16 prominent names from commercial and industry worlds as well as from politics and the arts – Lord Chandos, the M.P. Bessie Braddock, T.S. Eliot, Laurence Olivier, Edith Evans and Harry Secombe included. This was designed to stress the Mermaid's ambition to cover a wide range of tastes, strongly urging more support for the theatre, "a further £25,000."

That same day saw the launch of the most ingenious of all the fundraising efforts – the 'Buy a Brick' Campaign, Gerald's brainwave ("You know, Gerald, you were wasted at Lloyds. Be grateful I rescued you," said Bernard.) It gave the City's 'small investors' the opportunity of helping to build the City's own theatre by buying 'bricks' for half-a-crown (12½p) a go. They were token bricks, slips of coloured paper, eventually all to be buried beneath the Mermaid stage, a tiny bit of immortality. The launch took place on the steps of the Royal Exchange (it rained) and Cullum Welch, surrounded by a group of actors, bought the first brick, throwing his half-crown into an iron-band-chest, the first of thousands.

The scheme widened. 'Bricks' were to be sold in the City between noon and 2pm on weekdays for a fortnight. The City granted permission for appeal tables to be set up at the Exchange, on the forecourt of St. Paul's and other City sites. Then the brewers Charrington and Whitbread allowed collection in all their City premises. Bernard decided that he and Gerald should have a trial run. Pubs in the Square Mile mostly closed early but the pair marched boldly into the White Lion in nearby Upper Thames Street, a lovely old-style pub with a coal fire and etched glass. Not by nature 'a pub man' he became so much in his element, as did Gerald, that they never got to the other pubs scheduled for visits that night.

Realising that they would need help, Bernard came up with the idea of attractive girls – "shock brigades" – and dragooned students from the Guildhall and 'resting' actors to join the collectors. Many of Bernard's famous friends were cajoled into helping – John Mills, Donald Wolfit and Laurence Olivier took their turns. Every day Bernard did his bit, collecting box round his neck – he had the slot in the top widened so it could take notes as well as half-crowns. The reactions were nearly always friendly ("I think they liked us because we were so insane!"); this Buy-a-Brick Campaign received a great deal of publicity.

More time-consuming and rather more boring but necessary work was the direct mailing. For many months Bernard and Josephine were joined by a small group – Gerald, Denys King-Farlow and the retired acrobats who would run the Mermaid coffee-bar, José and Caroline Moreno – who sat stuffing envelopes with appeals (typed and always personally addressed and signed.) He made a heartfelt plea in those sent to big businesses:

"Industries and business houses are giving more and more thought to the welfare of their employees in the belief that happy and healthy workers are good workers. How better this could be done for the residents and workers of the historic Square Mile than by providing them with good entertainment at a reasonable price, on their very own doorstep?"

Bernard's success in extracting money from hard-boiled magnates became legendary. His colleague from the Little Mermaid, Maggie Teyte, said to him:

"You must possess the tongue of a humming-bird to reach the hearts of those City tycoons!!!"

He was on especially fine form in the face-to-face meetings, mainly because he assiduously did his homework. Just before his first term at Oxford he went to tea with a girl he had known at school but among her friends he was tongue-tied and shy, so he made it a lifelong habit to find out what he could about people before meeting them, often flattering them by his seeming interest in their hobbies and pastimes. He would use Josephine too; after their sales pitch they would leave only for Josephine to run back on her own to reclaim the spectacles or scarf she had deliberately left behind and thank the tycoon again, her wide eyes looking at him in the appeal: "You will help us, won't you?" A later Chairman of Whitbread remarked: "He was really the most fantastic salesman. He rang up and arrived on your doorstep and you found yourself parting with money like nobody's business."

One other proxy to the fundraising was 'Gifts in Kind', beginning with Critall's Windows and then Adamses who supplied all the Mermaid's toilet fittings. All this hard graft paid off. On 21st October 1957 the contractors finally were able to get on to the site and building was under way. By early November scaffolding had been erected in order to have the roof shuttering put up to hold everything in place for the roof concrete to be poured.

The builders worked well. And quickly. But the bank account was being drained quickly too. The unusual contract with Marshall Andrew broke building work into 'parcels' which were then costed. Each month the Mermaid handed over a cheque. Progress depended on the size of the cheque. While Josephine and the team carried on with mailing Bernard had to raise more cash. His return to the film studios was for *Tom Thumb*, filmed at MGM studios, which mixed comedy (Peter Sellers and Terry-Thomas) with fairy-tale and dance. Bernard played an amiable woodcutter (close cousin to Joe Gargery), delighted to be photographed by the great George Périnol, a regular collaborator with René Clair, whom Bernard greatly admired. He knew it was not his finest hour on screen but – vitally – it paid well.

Filming had to be juggled with some crucial Mermaid issues. Two weeks into filming there was an early morning meeting on site; Bernard and Denys King-Farlow were there to meet his friend and Mermaid supporter Harold

Drayton who was driving up from his country home and stopping at the Mermaid before going on to his Consolidated Trust offices. He wanted no tea or coffee, took in the building progress, asked a whole string of financial questions then was off in his chauffeured car.

At this time, just after Christmas, the mood at Puddle Dock was glum. Just a few days into 1958 Bernard asked Gerald and his secretary Betty Forbes to come to a meeting in his office. They had never seen Bernard, usually so unquenchably buoyant, in such low spirits. He told them, falteringly, that funds were drying up and that building work might have to stop. Gerald sensed that this was the lowest point for Bernard to date. Building was able to continue for a couple of days and then Bernard learned that a donation of £5,000 (the largest single donation the Mermaid received) would soon be forthcoming from the Edmund Howard Charity (Howard was senior partner in a major company of architects and surveyors.) Drayton had contacted him following his Mermaid visit. Additionally Drayton brought in the Dunlop Rubber Company and Associated-Rediffusion Television. The original Mermaid at Puddle Dock had many City friends but Harold Drayton, who kept most of his charity work quiet, was easily one of the best.

By the middle of January, the roof shuttering was in place, ready for the pouring of the cement. Bernard was booked for a Variety appearance so the job went to Betty with Gerald sending the many press photographers up too, high up on the roof with a stiff breeze from the river. Bernard in Cheltenham back on 'the Halls' was on crutches, having fallen backstage, damaging his ankle. He began with an improvised section, the Uncrowned King's encounter with "old 'Arry Partridge":

"I says to 'im 'ow you feeling, 'arry? "Well," 'e says, "I'm better than I was," 'e says "but I ain't so well as 'wot I was afore I was as bad as wot I am now… I've never 'ad a bath in me life. Not that I know of any 'ow. I don't want one, neither. That's why I 'ope I never 'ave to go into hospital. I bin private all my life and I wants to stay private. I don't want a lot of young girls takin' down my particulars."

Variety and the Halls supposedly were on their last legs but this show at least was immensely popular, going on for a long run at the Saville Theatre headlined by Frankie Vaughan with the singing King Brothers, Petula Clark and ballerina Nadia Nerina alongside Bernard in support. He also squeezed in a second series of *This Book is News* for the BBC, produced by George Angeloglou who wrote in the *BBC Staff Magazine* that it was "memorable television, though a little before its time." He put together a superb team of readers including Peggy Mount, Flora Robson, Peter Sellers and Edith Evans who point-blank refused to read any of the suggested translations ("I was brought up on the Bible of King James and when I die I shall be buried with it.") This series, Angeloglou thought, was "innovative, adventurous and courageous" in the way it attempted to interpret the most relevant books in the language of the people: Its success, he claimed, was "a tribute to the enterprise of Bernard Miles."

By the time he could be more involved again at Puddle Dock the roof was finished. Progress was on schedule. But, as Gerald knew, the main problem with lengthy building projects and fundraising was how to maintain interest without wearying the public. He and Bernard aimed to stage a major publicity event every six months or so, one of the most successful of which was the "Roof-Warming Party" in March, 1958. It was a freezing day but six coke-fuelled braziers helped as did a cauldron of mulled wine plus barrels of beer sent over from Whitbread's. Marshall Andrew's men hoisted a white 50' flagpole – the flag would come later.

At noon six hundred quests gradually arrived amid the piles of bricks and bags of cement; as the *Glasgow Herald* said, this was like "something between the break for elevenses on a building site and a fashionable theatrical première." Bernard and Gerald had had another of their brainwaves, arranging twenty of the Tiller Girls chorus at the Stage Door of Drury Lane for a press photocall (the girls wore fishnet tights and blue sweaters with gold sashes proclaiming MERMAID, donated by Marks and Spencer) before the girls kicked off a relay run in twos carrying "the torch of the theatre" from the Lane via Aldwych, Temple Place and the Embankment to the Mermaid – from London's oldest theatre to its newest. The *Daily Express* cheered it as "the cheekiest stunt in years." Denys King-Farlow, with whistle and stopwatch, saw the girls off; they fell slightly behind schedule so Bernard, with a Tannoy system, kept up an improvised commentary on the imagined progress of "these magnificent specimens of English womanhood." To loud cheers the last pair panted into Upper Thames Street and handed the torch to Norman Wisdom, wearing his 'little-man' suit and cap who joked his way into the on-site party to light the logs under the wine cauldron. Then a vast Red Ensign was run up the mast by ballerina Beryl Gray and Norman Wisdom climbed up a ladder to join the builders on the roof for the traditional topping-out ceremony before Donald

Wolfit pronounced the roof "well-and-truly no longer open." At which point the guests could tuck into the trays of plump pork sausages sent over from Smithfield. It was a triumphant occasion (no rain), summed up in *The Star*:

"Quite the jolliest, yet most significant event of the week is that the Mermaid put her hat on."

In one of the on-site huts, Bernard and Josephine held regular lunchtime meetings mixing City bigwigs, actors, writers – half a dozen or so on each occasion – craftily bringing together people who might help the Mermaid. He said:

"We've found it invaluable to get people down on to the site. It's the only way we can really give them a sense of the adventure of a building rising. Down here with the noise and the general litter of builders' materials, the excitement is catching."

This sense of an adventure was surely what so many of the visitors responded to. For City entrepreneurs, used to lavish lunches, the Hut's menu of frankfurters, stone-ground bread, English cheeses and apples, washed down with Austrian vin rosé, was novel and enjoyable. Denys King-Farlow now was saying that "The Law of the Bandwagon", in the wake of such thorough and intelligent fundraising, was taking effect. As fundraising went on all over the City the captains of finance and industry would be shown the list of subscribers to date while Bernard's follow-up letters would gently remind those still to contribute that they had time.

For the early summer of 1958 he had to leave Puddle Dock affairs to his colleagues while he flew to New York to record a TV version of *Wuthering Heights* for producer David Susskind's *Show of the Week*. Bernard found the tight schedule tricky but he ended up enjoying it and making Mermaid subscribers out of the star, Richard Burton, and Susskind. But the Mermaid was always on his mind: then on his return he agreed when Gerald told him that the Moscow Art Theatre, still in a time of Cold War, was visiting London. He and Gerald caught *The Cherry Orchard* at Sadler's Wells after which the entire Russian Company was invited to the Mermaid soon afterwards. Not wanting to stiffen the atmosphere with interpreters, Bernard invited all the Russian-speakers he knew with everyone given a badge denoting that he or she spoke Russian or English (Gerald was lucky – he was able to have a long conversation with the great Gribov, playing Firs). The event was a great success (and much covered by the press.) Trestle-tables set under the new roof and an English menu of roast beef and strawberries and cream made for an informal atmosphere with a great deal of laughter. The Mermaid was made an honorary member of the Moscow Art Theatre; its legendary seagull emblem would be fashioned out of a template (Bernard used an old tin can) and eventually embedded in wet cement. Typically Bernard would seize on any possibility of raising money. Drilling one day revealed an old bottle, undamaged, with "J. Schweppe and Co., Genuine Superior Aerated Waters." In an old reference book he discovered when exactly the company became Schweppes Ltd. He then promptly wrote – as the bottle – to the Chairman:

> "Surely the fact that I have been found on the site of the proposed Mermaid Theatre at Puddle Dock indicates that the firm of Schweppes is predestined to play some small part in bringing this unique venture to fruition."

He signed it "J. Schweppes" and sent it off, neatly boxed, to the Chairman of Schweppes. The company did not have an example of the bottle found at Puddle Dock and Frederick Hooper, the company Chairman, was altogether delighted:

> "Your note and enclosure irresistible. Herewith my cheque for 100 guineas."

Gerald had the notion of producing an occasional newsletter, co-produced with the weekly and very supportive *City Press*, to be sent to all subscribers and on sale for 6d. on site. It paid its way with advertising and kept subscribers in touch with progress. As well as corporate supporters there were over 400 individual subscribers including Noël Coward, Doris Day, Cecilia Hill, John Huston and Tom Hopkinson. Still Bernard was always dreaming up new schemes – 100 guineas to become a Foundation Member allowed those contributing to have their names added to the several red panels in the foyer gallery, while all this time the sale of bricks continued. In the end, over £12,500 worth of bricks was sold.

Outside work for Bernard to swell the coffers had to be squeezed in. Bernard had a good supporting role as Harris, a quietly-spoken, gentle man, a "Gilder and Sign Glass Writer" for producer Michael Relph and director Basil Dearden in *Sapphire* with racial undercurrents strong for the time. Low-key but gripping, this had fine performances from Yvonne Mitchell and Nigel Patrick too. Even more happily for the finances, Bernard was able to fit in a series of commercials for the Egg Marketing Board playing a *Titlark*-like character counselling "Go to work on an egg." Some were written by Bill Naughton, a good friend. He could make 20 in one week for a handsome fee and residuals. Also, whenever it could be fitted in, he was "on the night shift" as he put it, touring on the variety circuit.

The next *Mermaid News* reported "enormous progress over the past few months as work goes full speed ahead" and that Michael Stringer and Walter Hodges would soon start work on the interior. The headline for that issue bannered: "YOUR FIVER – AND WE ARE HOME!" Total cost of building and fitting out the theatre was estimated at £61,000. More than £50,000 had been raised. So, as Bernard wrote, a further £10,000 had to be raised in the next few months if the Mermaid was to open debt-free; a fiver from each subscriber would do it.

He was not the only one after money. He had received the first of many letters, from many places, from a peripatetic Del Giudice. Rather on his uppers, the first letter came from Dalkey near Dublin, full of Del's characteristic optimism – "a new financial man" (of whom nothing further was mentioned) was going to join him in a new company. With fulsome promises of repayment Del asked for "a contribution" from Bernard. Over the years Bernard always replied, usually enclosing a tenner and adding "no repayment necessary." He found out that he was not the only one being 'touched' by Del but he could not forget his ebullient friend's support on his films.

The Mermaid's opening night was approaching. The final issue of *Mermaid News* (February) mentioned "we are aiming for an opening about May 24th" and gave a run-down of final work. The gallery, which ran the full length of the building, linking the two staircases to create a promenade over the foyer area, was in place, as was the stage revolve. The foyer itself was adapted late in the day. Elidir Davies had designed the entrance from Upper Thames Street to be an open paved area which led to a glass wall with doors giving access to the (60` x 35`) main foyer. Suddenly Bernard began to worry if the paved courtyard was really necessary. Davies was not fond of it himself but he had been told it was the City's requirement to prevent taxis and vehicles blocking Upper Thames Street, the idea being that vehicles could turn into the courtyard, drop passengers and return to the road. Using little Dinky toy cars, Bernard and Davies realised this would involve several sharp right turns in a very narrow space. A recipe for trouble. When Bernard called the City Corporation he was told the courtyard idea had nothing to do with them and must be an architect's whim. So the courtyard was covered over, greatly extending the depth of the foyer and allowing, in addition to the long bar under the gallery at the back of the foyer, space for a coffee bar to the right and another smaller bar to the left. This would become the famous 'Connie's Bar' for years; Connie was a Mermaid character, a stout, cheerful woman sporting a cropped silver wig (which could shift alarmingly, even coming down over her eyes, if she hit the gin bottle excessively.) Journalists for *The Times* and *The Observer* just across the road loved the bar for Connie just as much as the fact that City licensing laws permitted its opening half an hour before other licensed premises.

One final – important – change to the design occurred when Bernard was just in time to stop the plasterers from covering the brickwork of the auditorium and foyer. He was right – buildings can have their character informed by their walls and material and within the walls of the old City Mills many generations had worked. He felt that to cover them would be a kind of desecration.

AND NOW HE and all involved at Puddle Dock had the feeling that the adventure was now very close to realisation. The huts were removed; the extraordinarily tolerant firm of Marshall Andrew had with great generosity made a gift of a block on the second floor looking over the river providing a space for Bernard's office, "the direct gift of contractors and subcontractors to Bernard Miles," said Elidir Davies. There were also a few smaller offices at either end, one of which was to be Gerald's office. As he said "those in the huts surfaced from the mud, dust, rubble and din of life in the huts, like pearl divers coming up for air." Bernard loved hailing the river traffic with a megaphone; Ned Sherrin told the story of being in Bernard's office with some dignitaries one summer afternoon when a barge was gliding along in midstream when Bernard grabbed his megaphone to hail it, quoting John Masefield:

"Ahoy, there, mariner!
Where be you sailing,
With your cargo of ivory,
And apes, and peacocks,
Sandalwood, cedarwood and sweet white wine?"

There was no megaphone on board but someone in the boat had stout lungs, because faintly but audibly came the reply:

"Fuck off, you silly old bugger."

At weekends now, Bernard and Josephine often went to their "country place", a small mill cottage near Dunmow in Essex which had cost only a few hundred pounds (the first property he had owned.) It was like life back in the early days of their marriage – oil lamps, water from a well down a hill. With help from Elidir Davies this became a cosy, simple retreat. Sally, with whom Bernard's relationship often could be stormy, was now working in the Mermaid press office and living in her small Camden Town house, having embarked on a passionate relationship with Gerald. While the Miles's John, a gifted photographer, would photograph some of the Mermaid's progress before finding his ideal niche as a racing driver and then motoring journalist. Their youngest child, Biddy, had become a talented sculptor, married to the artist John Noakes, living in the country.

xvi. Lord Mayor of London, Sir Cullum Welch launches 'Buy a Brick' campaign with Bernard Miles (1957)

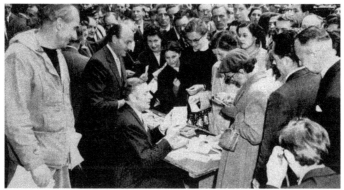

xvii. Sir Laurence Olivier selling 'bricks' in front of the Royal Exchange as part of the fundraising efforts (1957).

xviii. Norman Wisdom joins Tiller Girls as part of the publicity torch relay.

xix. Caroline Hawkins, the little mermaid, is carried into the opening ceremony of the new theatre by the Lord Mayor of London.

xx. Ronald Searle's cartoon first appeared in Punch *in 1959. The original hung in the theatre foyer.*

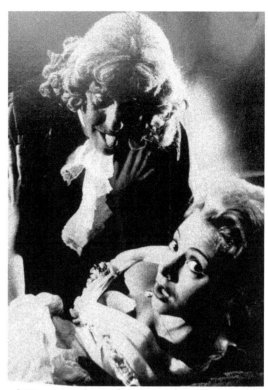

xxi. Stephanie Voss and Harry Locke in the original production of Lock Up Your Daughters *(1959).*

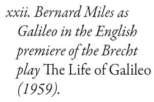

xxii. Bernard Miles as Galileo in the English premiere of the Brecht play The Life of Galileo *(1959).*

xxiii. John Neville as Alfie (1963).

xxiv. Bernard Miles and "a few close friends" in On The Wagon *(1966).*

xxv. John D. Collins and Spike Milligan in
The Bed-Sitting Room *(1966).*

xxvi. Michael d'Abo in Gulliver's Travels *(1969).*

xxvii. A demomstration of how the ear works from The Molocule
Club's *O.K. for Sound (1967).*

*xxviii. Noël Coward pictured with members of the cast at the pre-
miere of* Cowardy Custard *(July 1972).*

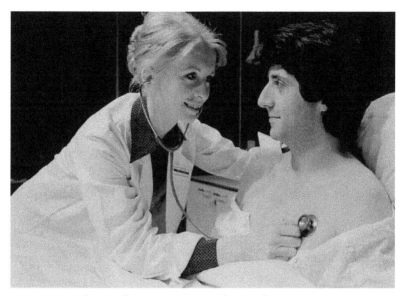

xxix. Jane Asher and Tom Conti in Who's Life is it Anyway? *(1978).*

xxx. Trevor Eve and Elizabeth Quinn in Children of a Lesser God *(1981).*

xxxi. Bernard Miles as Long John Silver with his trusty companion Jack Spratt in Treasure Island *(1959).*

Part Three

AT THE END of March the Mermaid box-office opened with the first night fixed for 28th May. Press and public interest was intense. Bernard contributed some "stray thoughts of an ageing Character Actor" to the trail-blazing theatre magazine *Encore*, describing the Mermaid as "my life's work and a blueprint of things to come." He mused on the problems of attracting and holding a regular audience, explaining that too often he found theatre-going dispiriting, not least the commercial West End theatre, woefully inhospitable – "no feeling that what is being done is for us alone. Where is the welcoming voice when you arrive, who is the host at the party, who makes you feel your presence is needed and who sees you off the premises and hopes you will come again?"

He aimed to have the building used for as many hours in the day as possible – in signal contrast to a West End where doors to the auditorium were opened not long before the performance, interval drinks gulped down usually in cramped bars and the audience shepherded out on to the pavements at the end as soon as possible.

The call for change would be resoundingly echoed by a new arrival on the Mermaid team. As 'resident art director' Bernard brought in a remarkable character, a 26 year-old, denim-clad Irishman, Sean Kenny. His involvement at Puddle Dock was fairly short; after his Mermaid success he was snapped up for West End and Broadway productions such as Lionel Bart's *Oliver!*, his designs for which were truly influential and which took him to international success. Bernard and he bonded partly because of their shared passion for the work of designer Edward Gordon Craig, but the designer in Bernard realised at once that this was a major talent. Kenny despised the West End with its prevailing painterly style. He aimed for an entirely new approach, somewhat akin to that of another young and influential designer, John Bury, who had produced some superb work for Joan Littlewood at Stratford East and would soon bring his style, using steel, concrete, wood and a more abstract approach to the work of the R.S.C. Once Bury in his dungarees was hailed outside the Stage Door of the Stratford-on-Avon theatre by fellow-designer Lesley Hurry, immaculately dressed as always with "Go home, you fucking cement-mixer." He would have said the same to Kenny, who likewise would not have cared a jot.

Sean's mantra was simple:

"Let us free the theatre from the cumbersome shackles of outmoded tradition."

Generously, Walter Hodges respected the newcomer:

"I didn't like him at all, largely because he appeared almost contemptuous of me – well, let's say cool, no – let's say rude."

But he acknowledged:

"Sean Kenny was one of Bernard's great 'discoveries' (not great – greatest), a meteoric career which in fact created and was created by the Puddle Dock Mermaid style."

In essence, although the two men were at polar extremes in temperament, Hodges was not so far off Kenny's main aim when he said:

"How wonderful it is to see a new playhouse of fresh form rise up amid the confusion of our enfeebled theatre – the Mermaid is our empty room, let's use it – all of us – playwrights, directors, designers, actors, spectators – everyone."

With rehearsals for *Lock Up Your Daughters* in full swing by May, Bernard began what he called "sea trials" testing the restaurant and the bars with family and friends. The company of *Lock Up* and Sir John Braithwaite performed the ceremony of burying under the stage a metal box full of the names of every subscriber, foundation member and buyer of bricks. On 22nd May dress rehearsals began, including two on the 27th (the twice-nightly routine 6:10 and 8:40pm.)

Then at last, on a balmy May evening Bernard and Josephine had to climb into their glad rags to welcome the Lord Mayor and party before the opening ceremony, a meticulously planned and timed event. Gerald, coping with the organisation of all the elements of the opening, kept in mind Bernard's threat of dreadful vengeance if the performance did not begin on the dot of 6:10.

Walter Hodges perhaps summed it up most neatly:

"The whole 'Mermaid' style was Bernard's style. The Mermaid's personality was his personality."

Lock Up quickly sold out for weeks ahead. Bernard had set his face against long runs but he could be a pragmatist when necessary and the financial logistics – some building debts remained – persuaded him to keep his smash-hit running for the rest of a lovely summer. He had always said that he wanted the Mermaid to be, above-all, accessible, open for as many hours in the day as possible. In his *Encore* article his declared ambition was to see the theatre become "a power-house of activity." For now he had to forget the plan to have early-morning prayers and businessmen's breakfasts but with the bars, restaurant and coffee-bar open most of the day and twice-nightly performances, the Mermaid was active for twelve hours each day. The coffee-bar was immediately wildly popular with reasonably-priced soups and sandwiches, not to mention the occasional display of juggling (with plates) from the Morenos. The sandwiches all had names. Actress Frances Jeater, when taken as a child to *Treasure Island*, asked what was in 'The Bernard Miles' to be told by an unusually laconic waitress: 'Ham!' Across the foyer, Connie's Bar regularly would be crowded with thirsty journalists from Printing House Square across the road. And, in the restaurant, drifting elegantly through the tables, the manageress Wanda Krazynska, reputedly a Mitteleuropan aristocrat, ushed customers as if leading them to some exotic Slavic feast.

So busy during the pre-opening period, Bernard had no time to visit Kirsten but later in the summer he spent some time with her at Amalienborg, trying to tempt her into something he had written for her, what he called "an opera-musical" centred round a retired opera star visited by a former tenor colleague. She enjoyed tinkering with the script with Bernard but remained implacably opposed to any stage return at 65.

It was luck that *Lock Up* was running happily. Gerald had been diagnosed with TB and was ordered to rest for at least six months. Sally took over the Press Office although with *Lock Up* extended again that department was less busy. She visited Gerald in hospital every day – tongues began to wag – and Bernard visited often too. He was busy initiating a long-nurtured scheme – a series, initially for ten weeks, of lunchtime films and record recitals which he dubbed "Bob-a-Nobbers" (no advance bookings and a 'bob' – one shilling – a seat.) They were enormously successful with City workers; the record recitals attracted presenters such as Benny Green, Antony Hopkins and Bernard too.

Busy as the Mermaid was, it had not been forgotten that sooner or later the redevelopment all over the City would reach Puddle Dock. In October the City Corporation announced the first phase of a planned underpass running under the railway bridges at Blackfriars between the Embankment at Victoria Station and Queen Victoria Street. Sharp eyes would have noticed in *The*

Times a mention that the Common Council was about to be asked formally to give the green light for the creation of a "residential neighbourhood in the Barbican area", still a post-war wasteland. Only a handful of insiders might have guessed that a Barbican Theatre was then a possibility; the 1956 Report on the site's redevelopment had suggested that any Arts Centre would not be a profitable proposition in an area then of low-population density. That, of course would change – Bernard had suspicions early on, as Josephine intuited. She once wrote to Derek Glynne: "He always feels there are many waiting for the chance to throw mud at him – and perhaps he's right." There had been a few Mrs. Grundys and even some Mr. Grundys (including a couple on the City's powerful Court of Common Council) who found some Puddle Dock productions, including *Lock Up*, offensive.

Even they could not possibly have objected to the second production. Finally closing *Lock Up* – Bernard was beginning to worry that long runs could make staff grow complacent and a favourite saying was heard regularly – "Prosperity and a fully flowing cup are bad teachers" – he opted for another long-planned venture, a new version of R.L. Stevenson's "immortal classic of the sea" and piratical adventure in *Treasure Island*. He knew it would make an ideal choice for the Christmas holiday period and had long coveted the role of Long John Silver, a strong choice for his first Mermaid appearance although he later admitted that he hadn't an inkling it would become a Christmas perennial for years. Bernard was the most frequent Long John but others to take on the parrot, Jack Spratt, later revealed to be Jill Spratt (bought from a pet-shop in North London and long-lived), and crutch included Donald Wolfit, Barry Humphries, Peter Bayliss, Christopher Benjamin and Tom Baker.

Treasure Island involved many of the *Lock Up* team – Peter Coe directed and worked on this new version with Bernard and Josephine along with Sean Kenny whose set was astonishing; generations of younger audiences marvelling at the on-stage assembly of the 'Hispaniola' using the units of the Spyglass Inn and the Benbow house, the crew all tightly choreographed to the rhythm of the sea–shanties supervised by A.L. Loyd. Similarly memorable were the thrillingly athletic fights staged by Paddy Crean which included the jaw-dropping cutlass fight in the rigging. Bernard's Silver was one of his finest performances. It had been – in a very different version – a regular role of his mentor Baliol Holloway but Bernard was proud of the Mermaid version and of his performance:

"I think nobody has ever done certain aspects of Long John Silver anything like as well as I have. I don't mean the text. I mean the cat-like ferocity and the demonic speed like a cat pouncing on his victims as I learnt to do with my crutch."

His Silver, turning on a sixpence from affability to frightening venom, was indeed an original, ripening with each re-creation.

During *Treasure Island*'s run, Bernard worked with Julius Gellner on his long-planned version of *Henry V in Battledress* which Julius directed. Rehearsals were uncomfortable; it was an icy winter and the set for *Treasure Island* and its many matinees prohibited onstage work. Instead the cast froze in a room near the Mermaid. Julius always seemed older than he was, a somewhat forbidding figure wrapped in a heavy coat, a muffler and a hat, all brown, who could be somewhat taciturn, except during breaks when he could give long lectures on the art of the theatre. But it was all the same an intriguing production – the King wore flannels, coolly handing his cricket bat to a French courtier, there were World War I tanks instead of horses, '*Roses of Picardy*' on a harmonica and Princess Katherine under a hair-dryer. Out-of-period Shakespeare was nothing new but, for some reason, this was controversial with critical reaction polarised. Purists were aghast – Philip Hope Wallace was outraged: "one of the worst productions of the play I have seen in the last 35 years", but then he did admit that his idea of theatrical heaven was Bayreuth with the stage picture glowing in the dark. On the other hand Harold Hobson, Agate's *Sunday Times* successor admired it greatly:

"The whole production flows with the open delight of the liveliness, the dash and speed of a revue."

It was another box-office success. Then Gerald Frow, returning from his convalescence, was told that the writer commissioned to adapt *Great Expectations* for the theatre had failed to deliver so he would have to do it. Quickly. Perhaps the deadline spurred him on but over one long weekend he did a first-rate job. As did Sean Kenny, a clever but unshowy design essentially of two low platforms with a bridge behind leaving an open, uncluttered acting area between. Sally directed this with considerable flair with a strong cast including Paul Curran as Magwitch, Josephine a Miss Havisham seemingly carved of marble and Gary Watson as Pip. In a couple of smaller roles was Ron Pember, a clever cockney actor who had already appeared in *Henry V*; he would become a Mermaid mainstay. This made for a fourth success in a row; J.C. Trewin, a Dickens expert, claimed that the version "put more of the Dickensian narrative upon the stage than we are ever likely to see again in a single night." It must have been strange for Bernard, with his Joe Gargery for David Lean on film behind him, to watch Dan Meaden in the role. Bernard was busily occupied on his next project – one of the Mermaid's triumphs and a prodigious achievement – the British première of Bertolt Brecht's *Galileo*.

This masterpiece had a convoluted stage history, written during Brecht's exile from Germany – he left with his wife Helene Weigel in 1933 following the Reichstag fire and spent the next fifteen years on the move, France, Finland and Los Angeles included. He worked on *Galileo*, first produced in Switzerland in 1943 and then, after revisions, in Los Angeles where it was directed by Joseph Losey with Charles Laughton starring. After this production was seen in New York, Brecht continued to cut and revise the text and the production when he and Weigel returned to Berlin after the war, when the play triumphed at the Berliner Ensemble in Berlin's eastern sector.

Bernard first read the play in 1958 and was bowled over by the muscle and sinew of the writing. He produced, directed and played the title role at the Mermaid. Brecht was not unknown in the UK and indeed the Berliner Ensemble had played a notable season in London just after Brecht's death, although *Galileo* was not in that season. Bernard had visited Berlin in 1959 and had seen the Ensemble's production directed by Erich Engel which he acknowledged strongly influenced his own. He and Helene Weigel got on very well and she approved of his plans (then still to be fixed) to produce the play at the Mermaid. There was a BBC Third Programme production, also in 1959, and both the critic and radio director Martin Esslin and Julius Gellner gave Bernard considerable help as he prepared his own production. He also brought on board a Fellow of the Royal Astronomical Society, Colin Ronan, as an advisor on the scientific content – this would plant a seed, certainly in Josephine's mind, for what would become the Molecule Club.

Prior to rehearsals Bernard returned to Berlin, taking Gerald and Sally with him. Weigel greeted them warmly, approved of the sketch of Michael Stringer's design and even arranged for key props to be collected while the Ensemble played Paris to be used at the Mermaid.

Galileo has a large cast and is lengthy; it would have to play to solid business to recoup its costs (it could play only once nightly plus two midweek matinees.) Bernard wanted no showy performances, just what he called truthful, "piping-hot" acting. His own was certainly one such performance – he had a grizzled wig and beard, and was totally believable as a dreamer within a tough, pragmatic exterior, with the occasional touch of slyness. Not unlike Bernard himself. In a long, demanding role this for many was his very best performance and the production a revelation. The London critics were bowled over with Bernard Levin in the *Daily Mail* writing:

"This play is visibly one of Europe's masterpieces and this production by the brave madmen of Puddle Dock is one of the greatest theatrical occasions we have seen since the war."

While Harold Hobson in *The Sunday Times* described it as:

"The finest dramatic experience that any production of a Brecht play in this country has given us… From this judgement I do not exclude the presentations of the Berliner Ensemble."

Bernard's cup surely ran over when Helene Weigel travelled to see the production and pronounced his *Galileo* superior even to that of the Ensemble's Ernst Busch.

The production played to excellent business although the midweek afternoon performances saw some empty seats. But it covered its costs and Bernard was already contemplating a future revival.

Since opening, the Mermaid had somehow maintained unbroken success both at the box-office and in the press. Only distinctly qualified success, however, greeted a "new musical play", *Mr. Burke, M.P.*, a satire inspired by reports of monkeys in space for which Gerald, perhaps over-ambitiously, came up with book, music and lyrics, another large-cast venture, directed by Sally. Its comedy, at times reminiscent of Stratford East's work, was hardly subtle, centred round two convicts, recently released from prison who are persuaded to bring a chimp to Parliament and get him elected. Intended as a spoof on advertising it was greeted variously as anti-Semitic, Fascist or Anarchist and its score was found wanting. Ron Pember and Brian Rawlinson were good value as the two ex-cons.

That Christmas, when *Treasure Island* played a Christmas season in the recently-opened cavernous O'Keefe Center in Toronto (Sean Kenny somehow managed to adapt the set without leaving acres of space empty) and while Bernard gave his Long John, much admired, the Mermaid saw an adaptation, by Julius Gellner, of Erich Kastner's perennial favourite for younger readers, *Emil and the Detectives*. It was a lively production tracing young Emil's efforts with his new chums in Berlin, to recapture money he was meant to take to his grandmother but which was stolen. Scenically it was rather lacklustre with not much of the atmosphere of 1930s Berlin, but it did steady if not spectacular business.

Design was more of a problem when Bernard returned from Canada to rehearse Ibsen's penultimate and problematic play, *John Gabriel Borkman*. This was nobody's finest hour. The set, supposedly one room above another in which the disgraced tycoon paces unseen before descending, was an uneasy compromise between naturalism and stylisation. Many actors have come to grief to various degrees with Borkman, Paul Scofield a notable exception (Ralph Richardson rather worried his director, Peter Hall, when he said not long before opening "I've got John, I think I've got Borkman but I know I haven't got Gabriel yet.") Bernard's was really no good. He gave no impression of a big man felled by avarice but defiant – this financier might have robbed a child's piggy-bank but embezzlement on a grand scale he just could not suggest. The reviews were scathing and public interest scant.

But one of the striking aspects of the Mermaid was the ability to bounce back, even with little subsidy and often with projects seeming unlikely successes. After the unwise excursion into late Ibsen, Bernard programmed a project nurtured for a long time and about which most at Puddle Dock were deeply sceptical – the first production for over three centuries of *The Wakefield Mystery Plays*, the great medieval cycle telling the Christian story from the Creation to the Day of Judgement. Written between 1350 and 1450, the cycle contained 32 plays of which 18 were included at the Mermaid brilliantly edited by Martial Rose, a teacher at Bretton Hall, a noted college for teachers of music and drama. Originally presented literally on the road, on carts by different guilds, each with its own play, the Mermaid version was a revelation with the gravity and comedy fused together by glorious medieval music sung by the Ambrosian Singers. A large cast included the young James Bolam, spellbinding as Christ. Another bonus was Bernard's design, his first set for many years. He wrote in a programme note:

> "In this collection of *Mystery Plays*, written around 200 years before Shakespeare was even born, we see powerful dramatic minds at work, masters of situation as well as English versification. There is truth and insight in abundance. The impudence of Lucifer as he sits in the Father's throne,

the daring of Cain, prototype of Melville's Ahab, the age-old squabbles of Noah and his wife; the face-to-face battle between Christ and Satan in the Harrowing of Hell and Satan's pathetic request to go with the saved souls back to Heaven – the total effect is one of gathering magnificence, the picture of a coherent and departed civilisation in which life was a unity – swear words, sexual references, prayer and devotion unashamedly mixed."

Bernard did in-depth research, spending time in cathedrals and churches which housed much medieval craftmanship, finding special interest in the glowing stained-glass windows in the great cathedrals. He was also able to study the illuminated bibles in Harley Drayton's library; Gerald said he seldom saw Bernard happier than when he was working on his set models surrounded by balsa wood, glue, paints and brushes. The design was a crucial element in a project carefully nurtured and delivered most absorbingly. Bernard was delighted when the Queen paid a royal visit despite the fact that, as he gleefully told the press, the plays "abounded in vigorous four-letter Anglo-Saxon words." Her Majesty seemed not remotely shocked when she met the cast. Subsequently she visited the Mermaid several times.

The theatre was back on an even keel financially as it entered its third year but subsidy would always remain a nagging worry at Puddle Dock. The Arts Council grant for 1959-60 was £5,000, dropping to £1,250 for 1960-61 (*Lock Up*'s extended run and income explained that.) Not until 1965 did it 'struggle up' to £8,000. And only in that year did the theatre receive anything from the City ("Six years after we opened the Corporation held a fiery meeting and voted us £2,500 a year.") Compare this with a 1965 Arts Council Committee report on subsidy to London theatres which stated that the Mermaid required "at least £50,000 a year of which, if possible, the Arts Council's share should be in the region of £40,000 a year." Bernard described his task as "shoestring work – all very well but the shoestrings must be strong enough to keep them on your feet."

In the meantime he came up with another unexpected success with *The Andersonville Trial* by Saul Levitt, first produced in 1959 in New York. This was based on a little-known case, the 1865 trial of a Confederate Captain, Henry Wirz, who was accused of the deliberate extermination of Union troops imprisoned in the southern camp in Georgia at Andersonville (more than 45,000 had been incarcerated there and almost 30,000 had died.) The trial was held in Washington D.C., in the United States Court with Bernard directing a gripping production and (using the name Giles Fletcher) designing an austere setting using the width of the Mermaid stage with the auditorium assuming that moral force which certain theatres can have. With that potent continuity between stage and auditorium walls the audience became complicit in the action, drawn into the gripping arguments on both sides. An impressively committed cast was headed by Maurice Denham in terrific form. "Levitt's spare, illuminating text dramatizing one of the earliest war crimes trials deserved such a fine production and it is not likely to have achieved it by a commercial West End production," wrote the *Daily Mail*. The box-office was busy throughout the whole six-week run.

During *The Andersonville Trial* the Mermaid acquired the impressive brass bell from "HMS Mermaid"; Bernard disliked electric bells and since opening the Front-of-House manager, Sami Swaminathan, had rung an old school handbell but the Mermaid bell had a much more resonant ring. This acquisition was widely covered in the press while, more controversially, was Bernard's gesture when he offered a job to Frank Haxell who had been Secretary of the Electrical Trades Union but was fired following allegations of ballot-rigging in Union elections. In the *Daily Express* Haxell revealed that he was on the dole and unable to find a job. Without telling a soul Bernard sent him a telegram assuring him that the Mermaid was "a strongly democratic, all-party interdenominational, multi-racial and lingual organisation deploring victimisation and restrictive practices of all kinds." He offered Haxell a standby electrician's job for the following production, guaranteeing him five weeks' work, which he accepted. This sparked much press controversy and (possibly partly intentionally) upset some City traditionalists, fanned by Bernard's insistence that "I'm happy to have given the City the honour of being once again first."

He rather hoped that Sean O'Casey's *The Bishop's Bonfire* would cause controversy, even if not quite the same as the riots at the Abbey in Dublin back in the 1920s which had greeted *The Plough and the Stars*, Bernard and O'Casey were kindred spirits; there was a physical similarity – two lean, beaky men, both natural anti-authoritarians. Bernard loved the full-blooded fusion of robust comedy and pathos in O'Casey, as well as his drive to move theatrical goalposts. *The Bishop's Bonfire* had been premiered in Dublin in 1955, the first new O'Casey to be seen there for nearly 30 years, greeted with grudging reviews there but much praised in British and American newspapers. A programme note for the Mermaid production glossed the play's denunciation of contemporary Ireland's puritanical stranglehold on life with an ignorant priesthood teaching an ignorant peasantry. Set in the village of Ballyoonagh before the arrival of a prodigal son, Bishop Bill Mullarkey and the planned burning of books containing temptation, the play incorporated song and dance which Bernard responded to. He admired the play greatly – he loved O'Casey's description of it as "A Sad Play with the tune of a Polka" and was proud to present the play's London première. Its success at once led Bernard to contemplate future O'Casey productions.

Also pleasing was the success of a play from the Elizabethan and Jacobean repertoire, the first production in London for over three decades of John Ford's dark masterpiece of incestuous passion, *'Tis Pity She's a Whore*. Bernard always felt that Shakespeare had been allowed to crowd out productions of other major dramatists and carried a torch for several of them, including Ford. It, too, marries scenes of lust, revenge and cruelty with a vein of gallows humour, something which he found invigorating in the theatre. This production had mainly excellent notices including an often hard to please Bernard Levin:

> "Scene after scene strikes home by reason not of the lust and cruelty in it but by its dramatic power... its strength and force show Ford for the mighty man he was and help to bring him out still further from Shakespeare's overwhelming shadow."

Like many dramatists, Bernard Shaw had slipped from popularity in the years immediately following his death but Bernard, who still rated *Saint Joan* extremely highly was determined to bring him back into favour. Largely on the advice of the Shavian scholar Hesketh Pearson he produced a clever pairing of the relatively accessible *Androcles and the Lion* with the rarity of the Wild West-set *The Shewing-Up of Blanco Posnet* which delighted audiences. Harold Hobson asked, "Does this herald a Shavian revival?" It did. Shaw would become virtually the house author at Puddle Dock. His 1913 fable saw Androcles, a gentle Christian slave, saved along with his friends by mercy of a lion from whose paw he had drawn a thorn. The second play of the double-bill was described with characteristic mischief by the author as "a religious tract in dramatic form" which sounds unappealing but, set in cowboy country it revolved round the local drunk, Blanco Posnet and the local tart, Feemy over the theft of a horse. Jill Bennett and a wonderfully pickled Ronald Fraser headed a fine company and when the box-office boomed Bernard was soon leafing through the Shavian canon.

A great admirer of R.C. Sherriff's enduring First World War play, *Journey's End*, Bernard was keen to produce his *The Long Sunset*. Set in 410 AD just as the Roman legions are about to depart and the Roman Empire's power begins to wane, it had been seen at Birmingham Rep. and produced on radio but Bernard thought that the London public would respond to this new play and be as fascinated as he was by the portrayal of one civilisation dying and another yet to be born. A Roman family headed by Julian, a farmer, has to face Saxon invaders but is helped by both Gawain and Arthur, Sherriff's attempt to demythologise legendary Arthurians. The main Romans are killed towards the end of the play but the ending carries the nationalistic sense that Arthur's resistance will in the end succeed with the dawn of monarchy as independent rule.

It was a fascinating subject and Sherriff, passionate about history and archaeology alike, certainly knew his history but despite some powerful scenes the play is hamstrung by its flat-footed dialogue, rather as was Rattigan's *Adventure Story*, his history play on Alexander the Great. The play needed consistently more daring than Sherriff's politesse could provide.

Treasure Island returned for Christmas before an unfairly jinxed production, launched with the best of intentions. *The Bed Bug* by the tragic figure of Vladimir Mayakovsky, "a paradoxical pantomime" written in 1928 and first seen in Moscow directed by the great Vsevolod Meyerhold, remains one of the most biting of social satires on Russian Statism. It had never had a professional London showing – it had a large cast and demanded music (Meyerhold had Shostakovich.) It needed bravura staging as it traced the 'hero's' journey from his wedding day, when he becomes frozen in a basement, to fifty years later when he is thawed into an utterly transformed world, a kind of communist utopia. As an example of the vices of a previous age and a warning to the future, he becomes an exhibit in a zoo. The bedbug was frozen along with Scrofulovsky and becomes his companion. A multi-layered, fast-moving piece, with only four weeks' rehearsal, inevitably this was a somewhat breathless production. Joss Ackland, just coming to prominence after three years of leading Old Vic roles, played Scrofulovsky. He had seen a production of the play while on tour in Moscow and so was aware that the Mermaid version was somewhat underpowered – although Bernard had had to take on a supporting role at short notice and so had little time to polish the production which, again, he credited to "Giles Fletcher" (his programme credit claimed he had been a deep-sea diver and that his grandfather had been hanged for sheep-stealing – some critics who fell for this were by no means pleased when Fletcher was exposed.) *The Beg Bug* received 'mixed' reviews (i.e. good and rotten). *The Evening News*'s Felix Barker enthused:

> "Never have I seen the open stage of the Mermaid used or a large cast more effectively than for this startling, spectacular production."

Nevertheless much still rested on the Sunday notices, especially that of Harold Hobson in the influential *Sunday Times*. The ever-unpredictable Hobson did not review it but simply wrote at the end of his column that since the play had no curtain call the Mermaid would not see a review printed, one that would have been the theatre's "pride and joy." Since the play ends with Scrofulovsky locked in a cage with the audience being told to leave the auditorium quickly, a curtain call would have been redundant. Bernard appealed to Hobson (the play was struggling at the box-office) but he refused to listen. His review appeared in *The Boston Herald*; it pronounced the production as "One of the most remarkable theatrical experiences I have ever had."

Too late. The production was too costly to keep running although a stop gap of *Arms and the Man*, quickly mounted, proved again Shaw's appeal. It played to solid business. During the *Bed Bug* run, Bernard had asked Joss Ackland "Why is this play not working?" to which Ackland bluntly told him "Confused direction and bad casting." Ackland subsequently wrote:

> "For about ten minutes Bernard did not speak to me. His sly and cheeky face creased into a sullen scowl. Then after a long, tense silence he mumbled: 'Bad casting, eh? Why don't you come and do it?'"

And, for nearly three years, Ackland became the Mermaid's associate director. It was demanding work; six days a week from nine in the morning to whenever at night. He acted, directed, helped choose plays and cast them (soon there would be a splendid casting director, who had worked at the Royal Court, Corinne Rodriguez.) He left one of the best thumbnail pictures of Bernard:

> "He could be infuriating, iconoclastic and stubborn, a mixture of naïve child, a scheming prankster, brilliant and foolish, kindly and cruel. But it was these very contradictions that, against all odds and heavy opposition, had enabled him to build the Mermaid in the heart of the City and produce a throbbing, exciting theatre in a cultural wasteland… Thanks to Bernard and Josephine the Mermaid always had that greatest of theatrical qualities

– danger. Each production had to cross a high wire and live dangerously… Without danger the theatre is dead."

A crucial problem at Puddle Duck was the length of the runs, always something of a gamble. *Arms and the Man* was a stopgap that played to capacity and could easily have run for longer but of course the next production was in an advanced state of preparation. An Easter Holiday production by the scientist Fred Hoyle, *Rockets in Ursa Major* did not match the appeal of *Treasure Island* but the young audiences loved this tale of space travel. Set in the next century, exploratory space probes had become lost without trace, including DSP15 with a crew frozen in suspended animation but which reappears on radar screen in England. No crew is on board but a message etched on the metal interior warns "If this ship returns to Earth then mankind is in deadly peril." Indeed it is. Aliens – one group hostile, the other friendly – arrive on Earth. Hoyle, pioneer of astrophysics and a sceptic of the Big Bang theory, had a profile beyond academia; his play was another element which reinforced Josephine's idea of teaching science to young audiences through theatre.

Shortly before rehearsing a revival of *Lock Up* Bernard had a dream about Kirsten from whom he had not heard for a while:

"One night I dreamed I was sitting in my office hanging over the river when one of the commissionaires came round and said that Kirsten Flagstad was in the foyer looking for me. I rushed out of the room and made one of those horrible processions through false openings and blind corridors which happen only in dreams and at last came into the foyer in time to see her get into a taxi and drive away. She was dressed in the white fur coat in which I had first seen her in 1936. I rushed through the glass doors on to the pavement shouting 'Kirsten! Kirsten!' but she was gone."

The timing was tight but he was determined to get to Norway (Biddy says that Josephine persuaded him that he must go.) When he arrived it was clear that he had reached the hospital just in time. He had brought her English roses but although her eyes shone with welcome she was not strong enough to take them. Her leukaemia had taken such a firm grip that she could no longer hold a cup of water to her own mouth.

They spoke of old times – of the early days of their relationship in Holland and of "that magical tour" of Norway in 1948.

"I knew she was remembering everything. All this while I had been holding her hand and bent down to kiss her. As our heads came together for the last time I whispered softly in her ear the words I had not spoken for so long and she breathed a soft "ja", just a low sigh. I walked backwards to the door and our eyes were locked and she was smiling with her lips slightly parted."

He saw her one last time before his return flight the next day. She was unconscious now, "her skin stretched tight over those marvellous cheekbones in whose cavities had rung and rung thousands of thrilling notes."

Bernard had watched his mother and father die and was convinced that Kirsten was close to the end but she fought on for ten more days. It seemed fitting that apart from her daughter Else and son-in-law Arthur, Bernard was the last person to see her alive in hospital. A few weeks after her death Bernard received a little package from her daughter. It was a brooch, always worn on one of Kirsten's Isolde costumes, which Bernard kept always. He showed it to me once – it was kept in his office, always speaking of her most tenderly. He clearly had loved her very much; he said he realised later that the affair had made his marriage to Josephine stronger.

With Bernard as Squeezum and Hy Hazell back as Mrs. Squeezum, *Lock Up* opened at Her Majesty's Theatre in the West End where it ran for over a year. Typically Bernard programmed another high-risk enterprise back at Puddle Dock – three O'Casey plays in a revelatory season under the overall supervision of Peter Duguid. Two of the plays – *Purple Dust* and *Red Roses for Me* were virtually unknown in the UK although *The Plough and the Stars* was more familiar. The season aimed to touch on the three principal phases of O'Casey's work – the early anti-heroic tragedies, the visionary plays and the later comedies – and was a beautifully-mounted tribute to the 82 year-old dramatist. Outstanding casts enhanced the venture – great Irish actors Marie Kean and Donal Donnelly included, alongside such actors as Leonard Rossiter, Anette Crosbie and Peter Bowles. *Purple Dust*, set in the spacious, gloomy room once the drawing-room of a ruined Elizabethan mansion contrasts three workmen questioning the wisdom of the upper-crust owners and their plans for the house. It emerged as a ripe rediscovery. *Red Roses for Me*, one of O'Casey's crowning achievements, is more expressionistic in technique (several notices of this production drew comparisons with Toller and Kaiser), a powerful piece set against the background of the Dublin lockout in which O'Casey had participated. His astonishing ability to convey the contradictions in human behaviour was most potently expressed in the masterpiece of *The Plough and the Stars*, over which the Easter Rising looms, juxtaposing fiery nationalism and the resulting suffering mainly by the women in the play. Joss Ackland directed this with compassion and flair with memorable performances from Katherine Blake as the tragic Nora, Donal Donnelly as the Young Covey and Marie Kean in magisterial form as Mrs. Gogan. Once again the risk came off; the box-office was busy throughout the season, as it was for the subsequent pair of rarities from the English classical repertoire, Bernard's favourite *Eastward Ho!* and *The Witch of Edmonton*, each programmed for four weeks.

Eastward Ho!, which was a happy, buoyant production, is credited to Chapman, Marston and Jonson (all of whom spent a brief time in the clink for satirical references to the Scots.) *The Evening News* said that "This roistering, flamboyant romp of goings-on in 17th century London fits the Mermaid like a gaudy tail." *The Witch of Edmonton* had another trio of writers – Thomas Dekker, William Rowley and John Ford, written in 1621 but not professionally staged in London since 1936. A dark play shot through with some robust comedy, this met with mixed reviews but most echoed the *Daily Telegraph*:

"This is just the kind of production that the Mermaid exists for."

1963 was something of an annus mirabilis for the Mermaid; at one point no less than five Puddle Dock productions were running simultaneously in the West End. There was an assumption that money must be rolling into the Mermaid coffers but that, of course, was not the case. The theatre could not risk the costs of moving a production itself – these could be heavy – and all the theatre received from West End runs was a small royalty (usually between 1% - 2½%) bringing in £100 - £200 a week.

After *Rockets in Ursa Major*'s Christmas run, the year began with an unqualified delight – *The Bed Sitting Room* by Spike Milligan and John Antrobus. Initially a short play first seen at the Marlowe Theatre, Canterbury it was extended and revised for the Mermaid. Set in a post-apocalyptic London nine months after World War III, "the Nuclear Misunderstanding" (which lasted precisely 2 mins, 28 secs., "including the signing of the peace treaty") strange mutations begin to appear caused by nuclear fallout – Lord Fortnum of Alamein finds himself turning into a bedsit whilst another bigwig becomes a parrot. Still wildly funny, this version had an extra edge, with more undertones of existential despair than the *Goon Show* to which Milligan was an essential contributor. The audience never knew quite what to expect, not least when Barry Humphries (soon to unleash Edna Everage upon the world) stood in for Graham Stark as Lord Fortnum's doctor for a time. There were clever visual gags, as when "Mate" (Milligan) entered wearing an assortment of ragged military uniforms from across the centuries. Attached to his boots were long strips of canvas which were attached to pairs of boots. As he marched across the stage the empty boots marched in time behind him. On board were several familiar Milligan collaborators including Johnny Vyvan, John Bluthal and, as Lord Fortnum, the sepulchral-voiced Valentine Dyall. Many theatregoers – some of whom made several visits to the Mermaid and then to the Duke of York's on transfer – remain still torn trying to decide whether *The Bed Sitting Room* or *An Evening of British Rubbish* which starred the surreal trio of The Alberts (who sometimes collaborated with Milligan) remains their funniest evening in the theatre.

A very different kind of comedy – some said "neo-Chekhovian" – saw the first play by Bill Naughton at the Mermaid. Naughton's lovely autobiography, *On The Pig's Back*, does not cover his later years and theatrical ventures but makes clear his compassionate, non-judgemental view of human nature. He became good friends with Bernard, a fellow Savile Club member. Although born in Ireland, Naughton's plays are mostly set in the north of England and while he had written for radio and television (*All in Good Time* was originally a television play) this was the first of his plays to be seen in London. It made an enormous impression on the metropolitan press:

"Salute Bill Naughton, former Bolton lorry-driver, who last night became a leading and probably unbeatable candidate for the title of the best new playwright of 1963." - Herbert Kretzmer, *Daily Express*

Although seemingly small in scale – one set, smallish cast size – its reach is universal in its premise of a young couple, living with the bride's parents but unable to consummate their marriage (family jokes, paper-thin walls etc.) Joss Ackland was slated to direct this and had offered the central roles of Ezra and Lucy Fitton to Eric Portman, a brilliant but troubled Yorkshire-born actor and a major star, and Marjorie Rhodes. Not long before rehearsals Ackland was given an instance of Bernard's devious and occasional ruthless side. He and his wife were invited along with the Naughtons to enjoy a traditional Sunday lunch chez Miles after which the conversation turned to *All In Good Time* when Bernard announced that it would have to open a week earlier than scheduled, the first mention of this Ackland had had:

"Not possible," I said. "Eric Portman won't be free". Bernard's eyes gleamed. "Well, we'll have to get someone else." "But he'll be wonderful – we couldn't get anyone better." "No one is irreplaceable," said Bernard, "I could always do it." I took a deep breath, "But I don't think you're right for the role," I said.

"Well then," said Bernard, "one of us will have to go, won't we?"

The play opened a week earlier than scheduled. Josephine directed. Bernard actually was impressive as Ezra Fitton but could not quite mine the inner sadness, even despair, which Portman would have explored. It was a major commercial success and transferred to the West End for a long run. On Broadway with Donald Wolfit it sank like a stone.

There was already another Naughton play aimed for the Mermaid but wisely it was decided to programme another production before it opened. The musical *Virtue in Danger*, based on Vanbrugh's Restoration comedy *The Relapse* trailed too many echoes of *Lock Up Your Daughters* for comfort. With book and lyrics by Paul Dehn and music by James Bernard, this was only too reminiscent of the British musical of the 1950 – rather too relentlessly arch and with a routine score. It did have some first-rate performances – John Moffatt's blissfully self-adoring Lord Foppington and Patricia Routledge as Berinthia ("a prospecting widow.") It looked ravishing in Alix Stone's beautiful designs but while packing the Mermaid for its limited run, it was a rapid flop in the West End.

More sex – of a more modern nature – informed *Alfie*, the new Naughton play which opened in June, and marked something of a departure from *All In Good Time*. London-set, its randy wide-boy title-character was a sharp-witted amoral charmer, an egotist whose frank philosophy sometimes redeems his predatory sexuality:

"I mean the average man knows in his own heart wot a rotten sod he is – 'e don't want to keep being reminded of it with somebody good around him. Know wot I mean? A bloke will always turn down a good woman to marry a rotten one."

This spiv (the word was coined by Naughton) and his busy sex-life made it a diamond-hard comedy, often extremely funny but with a cold, clear-eyed look at 1960s metropolitan mores and manners. It was directed by Donald McWhinnie, an unusually laid-back director who seemed to do very little actual directing, working by a kind of osmosis but with an excellent ear and eye, possibly because of his earlier radio work and on early Pinter. Sadly his career was destroyed by alcohol. For many, John Neville's anti-hero was a surprise; associated more with classical work, it was Joss Ackland who pushed for him, realising he was more of a character-actor than people assumed. He was superb, never for an instant softening the character and heart-rending in the scene with the abortionist. The women were equally strong – Gemma Jones, the young Glenda Jackson and the formidable Margaret Courtenay as the "lust-box" older woman, Ruby, who gives Alfie a comeuppance of a kind. *Alfie* transferred to the West End, to Broadway (a rapid failure, even with Terence Stamp) and to the screen twice.

Galileo was never a candidate for a West End transfer – too large in scale – but it deserved another Mermaid run and was revived with Joss Ackland this time in the title role. Staying with Brecht, Bernard programmed the first British production of *Schweyk in the Second World War*, Brecht's version of *The Good Soldier Schweyk* directed with panache by Frank Dunlop. He, like Joss, believed when casting to start at the top – he suggested Charles Chaplin as Schweyk, Peter Sellers as Hitler, Spike as Goebbels and Harry Secombe as Goering. No chance of them but they still found a fine ensemble for Dunlop, including Harold Innocent (Goering), Dudley Jones (Hitler), Bill Fraser and Bernard as the intrepid Schweyk. The original Hans Eisler music was used and Dunlop found exactly the right tension between anarchic comedy and the dark shadow of the Reich.

There were changes at Puddle Dock during this time. Sally and Gerald, now married, had launched their venture, the Margate Stage Company which took all their energy, not a little of their money and some of their zest when audiences were slow to come. Biddy was happily married to a fellow-sculptor John Noakes while John too was married and found his niche as a racing driver himself becoming a highly-respected motoring correspondent. Unsurprisingly he tried hard to avoid being driven by Bernard who had – somehow – managed to pass his driving test. Bernard had next to no road sense and tended to ignore corners (and, on occasion, traffic lights) but he enjoyed collecting people to take to the theatre – he drove to Hillingdon Station to drive Cecilia Hill to the Mermaid. Financially he had a good deal with Mackeson for his series of commercials ("Looks good, tastes good and by golly, it does you good!") directed by Lindsay Anderson who enjoyed making them ("Our Mackeson days were full of fun.")

Bernard did not direct *The Possessed* adapted from Dostoevsky's tense novel by one of his favourite authors, Albert Camus, but he was much diverted by backstage goings-on. Camus thought that Dostoevsky, not Marx, was the great prophet for the next century in his depiction of the consequences of ideological fanaticism. His dramatization of the novel, dealing with a group of nihilists in a small Russian town 50 years before the revolution, was written in 1959, the last major work which Camus completed before his early death in 1960. For him *The Possessed* was "one of the four or five works that I rank above all others." Julius Gellner was set to direct, but was ill before rehearsals so Joss had to cast it for him. Whether intentionally or not he gave Julius a collection of genuine eccentrics, often known in the theatre as 'difficult.' Kenneth Griffith and Ernest Milton definitely were two such but the volatile Ina de la Haye outclassed even those maestros. Joss was playing the suicidal Kirilov and was well aware that the play required vivid, passionate and sometimes violent performances. On a few occasions such as when the eccentric Ernest Milton chased Ina de la Haye with an axe backstage, maddened by her upstaging tricks, the backstage atmosphere resembled the second act of Frayn's *Noises Off*. According to Joss, Ms. de la Haye behaved in such a monstrous manner that everyone else was open-mouthed, even the notoriously temperamental Kenneth Griffith being lost for words. She was the only member of the cast to have a dressing room to herself. Hearing of the shenanigans, Bernard composed a letter from a fictitious fan telling her how superb she was while the rest of the cast clearly did not understand Dostoevsky. The company all knew about the letter and waited. Sure enough, Ms. de la Haye knocked on every dressing-room door and read the letter to each straight-faced cast member.

As Ackland spotted, Bernard thrived on danger but he took a major risk when, in conjunction with the equally risk-taking impresario Oscar Lewenstein he presented New York's avant-garde group *The Living Theatre* run by Julian Beck and Judith Malina. *The Brig* trailed America in its wake and, of course, Bernard never was averse to publicity. A bleak, documentary-style portrayal of the gruelling routine of life in a US Marine Corps. detention camp *The Brig* indeed was widely publicised but hardly in a way calculated to have crowds besieging the box-office. Most critics admired the tight choreography of the escalating violence but their tone – Levin describing it as an unforgettable experience but both horrifying and inexorable and the *Daily Mail* calling it "a sickening parade of violence and fear" – did not help its cause. Bernard remained unrepentant, but was forced to close the play early.

It was not quite crisis-time but belts had to be tightened until the fail-safe *Treasure Island* at Christmas. A fill-in play, *Don't Let Summer Come* by Terence Feely, described as "a cross between a Freudian case-book and a farce" had a decent run, helped by the publicity over more "filth at Puddle Dock." Frank Gordon, Clerk to the Mermaid Governors, assumed from a billboard trumpeting this that the hygiene of the Mermaid's kitchen was under attack. It was, rather, a complaint – becoming familiar – from some members of the Court of Common Council, principally Douglas Young who from the outset had opposed any subsidy for the theatre. Now he argued, in the light of publicity over an anonymous letter to the theatre that Liz Fraser and Caroline Mortimer who had done a "striptease" (it was in fact a token strip – both actors wore bikinis over black body suits) subsidy would be killed unless the play was taken off. Cynics assumed this was a typical Bernard stunt to boost business but it emerged that similar letters had been sent to other theatres previously and an arrest was made. Mr. Young regularly fulminated against "filth" at Puddle Dock; he and a handful of supporters regularly argued for "wholesome plays."

At a Common Council meeting at that time only a small number voted against the grant to the Mermaid (a princely £2,500.) In retrospect, more worrying than the accusations of "filth" was the report two weeks later after the funding meeting that approval was given by the Court of Common Council for a theatre to be built in the Barbican (at a projected cost of £1,307,500) while a report presented to the Corporation suggested that the Arts Complex in the Barbican (theatre and concert hall) would require an annual subsidy of between £1,000,000 to £1,500,000 per year. Bernard had good friends in the City in the early days but now, as redevelopment of blackened ruins into the gleaming glass of temples to Mammon marked the City, he became more watchful. The City had made tentative moves to oust the Mermaid when the lease had only a short time left to run. Bernard acted quickly: "I sought help from the most prestigious sources", one being Lord Astor whose *Observer* offices in Printing House Square were across the road from the theatre, the other the portly legal eminence gris Lord Goodman. Lord Astor called the

Town Clerk while Goodman rang Kenneth Cork, a Mermaid Governor and City panjandrum, both saying the same:

"With the greatest respect, that if the Corporation tries to extinguish this brave little venture at Puddle Dock whilst trumpeting plans for a 30 million artistic development in the Barbican, it will be hit by the biggest load of political bricks in its long history."

That silenced the City for a time. But with the Barbican project to the north and the National Theatre rising across the river to the south, soon the Mermaid would seem like an adventurous tug sandwiched between two mighty ocean-going liners. Arts funding was proving vexatious for many smaller theatres. Gerald and Sally had struggled with their Margate adventure to build an audience with only tiny subsidy and had to call it a day and return to the Mermaid. Sally directed the *Treasure Island* revival while Gerald had to find some publicity angles for the rarity of Gogol's *The Marriage Brokers*, the first production for 1965. The play had been a notorious flop in its first St. Petersburg production but at the Mermaid it was a major success. The simple plot of the wooing of a Russian rosebud by a middle-aged suitor, its warm comedy was deftly played by such comedic masters as John Moffatt and Robert Edison. As the *Daily Express* wrote:

"An evening of unalloyed pleasure that should keep the Mermaid one of the warmest places in town for the rest of this chill winter."

The risk of another repertoire season proved mostly successful; the revival of *The Shoemaker's Holiday*, a Shavian rarity (*Fanny's First Play*) and a revival of *The Wakefield Mystery Plays* all did well, just carrying the season home despite Bernard's unwise choice of the Oedipus plays (*The King* and *At Colonus*) in which, miscast, he elected to play the title role. Kenneth Cavender's new versions were fine but the plays could not survive Bernard's rough and ready portrayals, sadly lacking any sense of tragic grandeur.

Almost as harshly treated critically was his new show when he and Gerald re-worked Dryden's *Amphitryon* into a misguided musical as *Two Hundred Brass Halfpennies* with Gerald's lyrics and music by Kenny Graham. This played to thin houses while Pinero's *Dandy Dick* did better. At the centre of this repertory season was a new play specially-commissioned by the City of London to celebrate the 750th Anniversary of the Magna Carta. This was fraught with peril; the City had made elaborate preparations for a visit by the Queen for a St. Paul's service and then the play at the Mermaid. Bernard had been approached early in 1964 by the City to suggest the kind of thing suitable for this great event. Bernard porposed a play – the City had £13,000 to spend and it was proposed that half should, in time-honoured City fashion, be spent on a good blow-out and the other half on the actual event. Bernard proposed Robert Bolt as an ideal dramatist but he was too busy on the film of *Dr. Zhivago* to accept. Bernard's next choice was John Arden, closely associated with the Royal Court, including the writing of *Sergeant Musgrave's Dance*. Out of the blue Bernard was called by the committee's Clerk who said that:

"unless I could within the next 48 hours produce a dozen testimonials to Arden's suitability they would not wish to proceed with the commission. The testimonials should be from people of substance and repute in the fields of literature and the drama."

By happy chance Bernard was due to attend a theatrical reception at Buckingham Palace the next afternoon. The place was packed, but while the Coldstream Guards band played selections from '*Lilac Time*', Bernard with a notepad and pencil mixed with the throng and was able to slip away with nine recommendations, securing the final three from Peggy Ashcroft, Kenneth Tynan and Milton Shulman by taxi that evening, all laid out on the Town Clerk's desk by 9.30 the following morning. All seemed set fair but another contretemps arose over the title, *Left Handed Liberty*:

"This really got the Committee's hackles up and I was called to a special session to explain: 'We don't want any of that Pink stuff here,' growled one angry senior Member."

Somehow Bernard convinced the Committee that present-day connotations were far from Arden's mind. But more trouble arose when members were sent the script, aghast at one scene with the Barons waiting in the City and one of them given the line:

"Fetch me three strong whores from Billingsgate."

This put the cat properly among the pigeons. Three alderman called urgently on Sir James Miller, the Lord Mayor, protesting that such a slur was an insult to Billingsgate but, more importantly, that such a line should not be delivered before the Queen and Prince Philip. "But Jimmy Miller soothed their brows and the line stayed in. The Queen did not turn a hair."

In the end *Left Handed Liberty* was worthy but somewhat unexciting. It needed more fireworks although Patrick Wymark as King John did his considerable best.

Bill Naughton, loyal to the Mermaid, brought his new play, *Spring and Port Wine*, to the theatre where it ran over Christmas while *Treasure Island* played matinees. A family row when the patriarch (Alfred Marks) refuses to allow his younger daughter (Jan Carey) to skip her tea-time herring is the fulcrum for a subtle play on the institution of family and the undercurrents which fuel its indestructability. John Alderton and Melvyn Hayes, both just on the cusp of television fame, were strong in support. It had a memorable first night as Fergus Cashin reported in *The Sketch*:

> "Some of us had waited patiently for ten years, others perhaps more, but last night it happened. Suddenly the whole wonderful damned sterile business of the live theatre burst into tears and cheers as they stood and yelled and bayed out that long-forgotten chant of "Author! Author!"

The genuine and profound compassion which fuelled Naughton's play was something which marked many plays at Puddle Dock. It was there in abundance in *Spring and Port Wine* (which went on to run for over 1,000 performances in the West End) and it also stamped Bernard's solo performance, described by him as "an attempt to explain myself without explaining myself completely away." *On the Wagon* was, he said, "a variation on the common chord of art and agriculture"; it could be said that the search for that common chord was central to his life. For the show the stage was virtually bare – a screen for some evocative slides, an accompanist (Alan Clare) and an old Essex farm wagon. There was a good deal of re-shaping and cunning placement of material for what in performance came over as a kind of informal conversation. He quoted from his grandfather – the one he had never known but evoked to such convincing effect – and talked of men who used to tame unruly horses by talking through the night to them, of actors and opera stars. There were snippets of his material from The Players including *The Uncrowned King* and *The Cockney Bandsman*. Peter Lewis conveyed the tone of a unique evening:

"He brought back the warmth of forgotten summers… The effect is to produce the most relaxed atmosphere I have known in a theatre. The gap between the man and his audience disappears. It is like spending an evening with a friend in a pub."

Certainly there are not many actors who could get an entire audience, including hard-boiled drama critics, gently singing '*Jesus bids us shine.*'

On the Wagon initially played nightly at 9pm. Later it played Tuesdays, Thursdays and Saturdays at 8:40. Its popularity was such that it returned in March to play twice each Monday, running well into the summer. So for most of December 1965 and January 1966 the theatre was presenting three performances a day. Eighteen performances a week plus, still, the Lunchtime Films and regular exhibitions including one of John Piper lithographs and one of sculptures and drawings by Roy and Biddy Noakes.

Despite this ceaseless activity and hard work, the Mermaid's relationship with the City was revealing more cracks and fissures. The Court of Common Council met in May, 1966 to discuss various grants, including a Music Committee grant of £24,000 suggested for the Mermaid to put towards reducing its accumulated deficit. Bernard explained that the theatre had opened "with a building debt of £54,000 which we had foolishly tried to pay out of revenue and that this had hung around the theatre's neck ever since." This occasion produced no shortage of opposition. Alderman Edward de Courcy Howard thundered:

"The Mermaid is in my opinion bust. To pour money into an insolvent cause is much the same as pouring water into a leaking barrel. Empty seats and uneconomic tickets are all gall to the Music Committee."

Once again the shopworn-old charges were repeated. Douglas Young had not changed his mind, although it transpired he had seen very little of the Mermaid's work:

"There is no prestige in the prestige the Mermaid has for vulgarity… it appeared that more money by muckraking than from wholesome plays."

He wanted a stipulation "that the theatre be used for Christian purposes."

The grant application was refused. The following week's issue of the *City Press* newspaper – which had ace reporters – carried a piece by Bernard rebutting much of the Court of Common Council's view. It also coincidentally carried a brief report on the City's Arts Banquet at which the Lord Mayor claimed for the Corporation "a full and expanding share in the civilising mission of promoting the arts." The main representation of the theatre present was Peter Hall, then Director of the Royal Shakespeare Company, boundlessly ambitious and eager to have a permanent London home. It was already whispered that the RSC would be a likely tenant for the Barbican when finished. Nobody from the Mermaid received an invitation.

With an eloquent two fingers to the City Puritans, Bernard turned to the Mermaid's most regular dramatist, Shaw, with the provocatively-titled *The Philanderer*. This dry-run, rarely produced, for *Man and Superman* came as a big surprise to modern audiences with its picture of a man, Leonard Charteris, who flirts with women but dodges commitment, juggling between a cool, pragmatic widow and his other love object of "a new woman." This pugnaciously ludic play proved again Shaw's strength at the box-office. Even more of an unlikely hit was *The Beaver Coat*, Gerhart Hauptmann's 1893 comedy, benefitting from a powerhouse performance from the redoubtable Peggy Mount as Mrs. Wolff, with a kind of Falstaffian native cunning trouncing pompous officialdom audiences loved.

Then, by stark contrast, two Molière plays in a double-bill – *The Miser* and *The Imaginary Invalid*, adopted by Max Loding, was one of those ideas which should have been strangled at birth. Apparently Loding's aim was to remove the "Baroque cocoon" surrounding Molière, but the cutting required to fit both plays into one evening left only the skeletons of plots.

French farce fared infinitely better with the runaway success of a neglected piece, (Divorçons) *Let's Get a Divorce!* by Victorien Sardou and Emile de Najac, niftily translated by Angela and Robert Goldsby. Set in late 1890s France, it dealt with the comedic possibilities of the new divorce laws then going through the French parliament. *The Daily Sketch* pithily described it as "a gorgeous, wiggy, bustley – cleverly staged – piece of busty nonsense of a love cuckold and a cockalorum husband." At its centre was the orchidaceous, wittily costumed Fenella Fielding who scored a personal success, giving London audiences, who knew her from her intimate revue camp persona, a glimpse of a range better known to regional audiences (a blazing Hedda Gabler in particular). This went on to the West End where it ran for nearly a year.

That was a surprise hit. A disappointing failure was Bill Naughton's Mermaid return with *He Was Gone When They Got There*. It sounded promising

– a simple countryman managed to outwit all attempts to bring him into bureaucratic line – but a light-hearted satire on convention ended up as a decidedly plodding piece. It had to close early, the gap being plugged by an enjoyable reading from *Pictures in the Hallway*, filleted from Sean O'Casey's autobiography. But yet again it was Shaw who steadied the ship, with two rarities – his Napoleonic play *The Man of Destiny* and the first public performance of a very funny play, *O'Flaherty V.C.* about a young war-hero briefly visiting his Irish home which turns out to be less than a holiday from the war, with his Fenian mother appalled to find he is fighting with the British against Germany and his girlfriend less than pleased that the V.C. does not come with cash. Ian McKellen made a big impression as the beleaguered solider now longing to escape back to the trenches.

The coffers still needed some replenishing, which was happily achieved by a revival of *The Bed Sitting Room*, slightly revised but again with the ebullient anarchy of Spike Milligan and the gang. This transferred to the West End and then toured. While Sally directed *Treasure Island* with a baleful Donald Wolfit as Silver, playing matinees under the lunacy of the evening show.

Bernard continued to avoid playing safe and 1967's productions had a bravely ambitious range, also honouring O'Casey and Shaw. A cleverly-structured trio of short Shavian pieces, included the outrageous *Passion, Poison and Petrification*, described by Shaw as "a new, startling, original, Pathetic, Blood-Curdling and Entrancing Tragedy in One Act and Ten Mechanical Effects by the Chelsea Shakespeare, George Bernard Shaw", of which one critic wrote that if Shaw's shade was not chuckling away at his three half-forgotten pieces – "then I'm a leprechaun." These squibs buried away in the Shavian cupboard were proving rich material.

Through the Mermaid's occasional popular Poetry Evenings (on Sundays usually) Bernard had come to know and admire the work of American poet Robert Lowell and had read of Jonathan Miller's production of a trilogy of Lowell one-acters under the title *The Old Glory* off-Broadway. The longest – and best – of the trio, *Benito Cereno* was directed by Miller at the Mermaid. The novella by Herman Melville on which Lowell based this unsettling piece made a strange, haunting play (for years John Huston dreamed of filming it) and Lowell's version maintained Melville's hallucinatory atmosphere, helped by a pitch-perfect, slightly stylised production. Set in the early 1800s, an American ship's captain, Delano, sees a Spanish slave ship in disrepair and with its Captain, Benito Cereno strangely distracted. A complex work of interwoven dualities – Old / New Worlds, Africa / Europe, Black / White, Freedom / Slavery – inexorably leads to the revelation of hideous violence and rebellion as Cereno's ship reveals further violence and mendacity. This ambitious dramatic poem met with totally mixed notices; London's literary world and intelligentsia made up most of the audience. Bernard came to admire Miller's polymathic personality highly and Miller loved the freedom of the Mermaid stage and the atmosphere of the theatre; both hoped that before long another venture might reunite them.

O'Casey returned with a double-bill – the robust comedy of *A Pound on Demand* and the better-known *Shadow of a Gunman*. They were well-contrasted; the first play is a comedy of two drunks desperate for another pound to spend in the pub. *The Shadow of a Gunman* (1923) the first of the dramatist's 'Dublin Plays' is a powerful tragi-comedy set in a decaying tenement during the Irish War of Independence. The poet Donal Davoren is mistaken for an IRA gunman on the run, his admirers include a naïve girl Minnie Powell who is arrested and shot by the Black and Tans. Like all the O'Casey ventures at the Mermaid, this was a very popular evening.

In hindsight, however, perhaps a more important and more lasting in influence of Mermaid productions was the establishment and the first production of The Molecule Club. This was Josephine's brainchild. She had noticed the widespread interest from younger audiences in the background talks on such productions as *Galileo* or *Rockets in Ursa Major*. She suggested an organisation to continue such talks but also to dramatize basic facts of science using sketches, dance and song for audiences focused on schoolchildren between 8 and 12. The idea gathered pace and soon publications like *The New Scientist* were noticing:

> "The Molecule Club has shown that the theatre can be used to make a serious textbook subject come to life. Such a delightful and practical exercise in the fusion of The Two Cultures may well contribute to the ultimate vigour of British science and technology than all the high-level councils, committees and commissions yet contrived."

The first Molecule show, *Lights Up!* was written by Nicholas Stuart Gray, known for his children's plays and pantomimes with catchy songs by Robert Webb, with performances at 10am and 1:45pm. It was a major success, at once leading to the planning of future productions and tours. Watching a Molecule show with a full house of enthralled children made it clear why the Mileses were so proud of Josephine's creation.

The Greeks rarely brought the gift of success to the Mermaid. Jack Lindsay, a prolific author and fellow Savile Club member planned with Bernard an ambitious version, mooted for production at various times of *The Pilgrim's Progress* (never produced although often on the "to do" list.) He also translated four Euripides plays under the umbrella title of *The Trojan Wars*, all transposed to the era of the Austro-Hungarian Empire. His versions were judged over-colloquial but the cast carried the production to a modest success.

As so often, Bernard rang the changes for the following production, a new play by a familiar television dramatist, Keith Dewhurst. *Rafferty's Chant* was written first as a radio play then revised and extended. It was an energetic and often wildly funny play with a corrupt scrap-dealer the leading character. It received mostly enthusiastic notes:

> "You can shoot enough critical holes through *Rafferty's Chant* to make a colander. Equally it is one of the most promising plays I have seen this year."

Set in a dilapidated area of Manchester where an unemployed conman tries to flog hopelessly battered cars, this acid comedy showed a less appealing side of the Swinging Sixties.

The revival of the plays of D.H. Lawrence – rediscoveries essentially – was mainly due to Peter Gill's loving productions at The Royal Court in 1968 but the Mermaid had led the way the previous year with *The Fight for Barbara*, very different from the mining-background plays at the Court but still a fascinating find. It surprised many with the vitality of Lawrence's treatment of love and marriage. Written in 1912, a crucial year for Barbara (based on Frieda von Richthofen) and Lawrence's decision to leave a costive, industrialised England. An outline makes it sound like a Strindberg play – the omnipresent battle of the sexes, Barbara's feeling that Jimmy (the Lawrence figure) is set on dominating her to take her will away – but Barbara speaks for women in tune with the 'new woman' of the era. Set in an Italian villa, this had passionately full-blooded performances from a vibrant Adrienne Corri and Stephen Moore as Jimmy. Directing, Robin Midgley balanced their relationship beautifully with the arrival of Barbara's conventional parents.

This somewhat pick'n'mix of productions at this time took in a well-intentioned revival of *Nathan the Wise*, Lessing's fervent plea for religious and racial understanding in the Jerusalem of the Third Crusade. Maurice Denham, an old colleague of Josephine's rep. days gave a mighty performance in the title role and audiences did come, although visibly bracing themselves for the ordeal. A happier rediscovery arrived with another surprise – *The High Bid* by Henry James. The great novelist's involvement with the theatre – he wrote occasional dramatic criticism and was a strong advocate for Ibsen – brought only unhappiness when his own plays failed commercially. *The High Bid*, originally written as a vehicle for Ellen Terry, was reworked into a short story when Terry never got round to it, and then turned into a play. It came as a revelation to most critics and to audiences. Not for the first time James combined a somewhat melodramatic central situation with sophisticated comedy – a vulgarian rich businessman offers to buy the country house inherited by less rich Captain Yule provided Yule marries his daughter while a visiting American, Mrs. Gracedew falls in love with the house and urges Yule to accept the offer. The plot twists and turns intriguingly and *The High Bid* rose like a soufflé on the first night with Edward Woodward and Fenella Fielding like two expert fencers handling James's elegant dialogue. One critic wrote "Bernard Miles has discovered an Edwardian comic playwright to rank with Wilde – Henry James." Some others found it creaky but the public flocked to it. It could have run much longer, especially in light of another of Bernard's misguided self-castings when in the next production he chose to play a patriarch from New York's Little Italy. In *Climb the Greased Pole* by Vincent Longhi his performance was not remotely in key with Libby Morris's truthful acting as his wife and his accent was all over the place but rarely in New York. He seemed to see similarities between Bill Naughton and Longhi – tyrannical fathers and quietly resourceful wives – but the writing has none of Naughton's compassion. Bernard needed a rest – all the battles to get the theatre built, nearly ten years of programming and running the organisation had taken its toll.

Recently, tipped off by friends, the Mileses bought a tiny, primitive and remote house on the Balearic island of Formentera, sited at the higher and least inhabited end of what was then a rarely visited place (although rich hippy adolescents were beginning to arrive, forming queues at the American Express office once a week to collect the parental cheques.) The Miles home was basic – two rooms and a tiny kitchen and bathroom. There was no telephone (no mobiles yet) and only one bus a day to and one from the central village down on the plain. There was no real garden, just swathes of thyme and rosemary bushes and a fig tree. The Mileses did little to it apart from installing a better and more efficient bathroom. It became a haven, a perfect spot for total relaxation.

Back at Puddle Dock, Josephine's brother George Hinchcliffe, now retired from the oil business in the Middle East, had joined 'the crew'; laconic, usually dressed in well-worn tweeds and a pork-pie hat, pipe permanently clenched in his mouth, he worked away on the books and figures in one of the remaining sheds. He persuaded Bernard, rarely averse to money-making schemes, to abandon the 'penthouse' office and rehouse the office staff in the old office building next door always known as 4X. The 'penthouse' remarkably quickly became a second restaurant, greatly increasing the number of covers the catering operation could accommodate. And costs were always increasing – top-price tickets were now £1 (still cheaper than the West End.) But Puddle Dock was about to enjoy one of its most successful periods, beginning with another unexpected find – Peter Luke's *Hadrian VII*. Bernard knew the novel by Frederick William Rolfe, self-styled "Baron Corvo" and had noticed it was scheduled to open soon at Birmingham Rep., in association with commercial producers Bill Freedman and Charles Kasher, who had persuaded an initially reluctant Alec McCowen to play Rolfe ("It didn't sound promising to me – a man imagines he's the Pope and then discovers it was all a dream") but after a period out of work, he took it on. It was directed by Peter Dews, the phlegmatic but savvy Birmingham supremo who, after some performances at Birmingham (to small houses), had some crucial rewriting done and shrewdly junked all the elements of a costly realistic design. Bernard sent his general manager at the time, Ken Smalley, to cover it. He liked it although remained somewhat dubious about its London chances, but Bernard had "a hunch" about it, having re-read the book and took it on. It opened on 18th April 1968 to virtually no advance bookings in the kitty and became a runaway sell-out. Audiences responded to the wish-fulfilment of Rolfe's dreams, recreated in some stunning theatrical sequences such as when the theatre's two back doors opened and two lines of Catholic clergy in all their striking finery, complete with thuribles and incense, came through the audience and down the aisles for Rolfe's elevation to the Papacy, a superb coup de théâtre.

And McCowen was masterly – acerbic, ironic, casually amusing in turn but fuelled by a subterranean rage against a world slow to recognise his genius. Weary from the strain of 5-week runs, Bernard decided that since Freedman and Kaster were happy to keep *Hadrian* at the Mermaid, which suited it so well, he would keep it running – eventually for over 300 performances, subsequently moving to the Haymarket and then to Broadway.

There were several arrivals and departures at this time. Although Gerald and Sally were now divorced (both soon later remarried) they were back at Puddle Dock. As was Sean Kenny, back as suddenly as he had departed, now internationally famous from spectacular designs for musicals (*Oliver!*, *Maggie May*, *Blitz*) with Lionel Bart. In denim jacket, neckerchief and ever-present cigarette, he looked exactly the same and was keen to find a project to bring him back to his favourite stage. Bernard did his best to lure him into *The Scharnhorst* docudrama but the idea did not attract Sean. In the meantime Bernard and Vivian Cox beavered away, trying out various notions for using magnetised ships moved over metal maps to represent the naval battles.

After a short Formentera break, the Mileses returned to find *Hadrian* still playing to sell-out business, allowing Bernard to fit in a good deal of radio work including a series for Radio 4's *Ten to Eight* slot, the New Testament stories told in the dialect of the Chiltern Hills. Later published as a book, these were immensely popular. He also fitted in an appealing film, *Run Wild, Run Free* adapted from the book '*The White Colt*', with his friend John Mills and the Oliver Twist from the filmed version, Mark Lester. These engagements made it impossible for him to attend Gerald's third wedding. Josephine was deeply involved with two Molecule Club plays scheduled to tour after the Mermaid. Then he could concentrate on Sean's ideas for *Gulliver's Travels*. Inevitably there were heated arguments. Sean was set on using all four sections of the book while Bernard, curiously cautious in this instance, felt that young sensibilities might recoil from the later books with the immortal Struldbrugs and the bestial Yahoos. They argued, often noisily, right up until the opening. Its development – of all four books – was as rapid as that of *Lock Up*. Within only a few weeks the show was outlined and costed (budget £10,000.) Sean and Gerald had a script ready by late September, the show was cast during October with rehearsals scheduled for 8th November.

Before *Hadrian* had opened, Bernard had scheduled a month's run of a programme *Open on Sundays* – a kind of Jewish scrapbook of the music and comedy of a tight-knit small Jewish community. The co-creators, Ron Pember and Michael Landy covered both Old and New Testaments, with Moses acting as a straight man, Chaplin partnering Hitler in a custard-pie routine and the Marx Brothers (Karl and Groucho) doing a rapid-fire cross-talk act. Critics were unsure how to pigeon-hole it but it was very popular with audiences.

Gulliver's Travels had a dizzying rehearsal period with Bernard still muttering about the two later books and Sean and Gerald trying to avoid him as much as possible. It was cast quickly – Mike d'Abo from the Manfred Mann Group as Gulliver – alongside comedic experts (like Willie Rushton, John Bluthal and the *sui generis* double-act of anarchic mayhem, the Alberts.) David Toguri, also involved with the London production of *Hair*, choreographed, Andrew Loog Oldham, former Rolling Stones manager, supervised the pre-recorded musical montage, all that work totally in tune with Sean's remarkable vision of Swift's masterpiece. His technical innovations were often breathtaking; back projection which had been seen rarely to date in the British theatre (Tony Walton's use of it in two Michael Codron revues and a West End musical, *On the Level*, with projections by Robert Ornbo) but *Gulliver* took the technique to a whole new level. In *The Observer* Ronald Bryden hailed Sean's work:

> "so radical a landmark in theatrical technology that its suggestion of limitless possibilities for theatre as to place it on the cusp of a revolution as fundamental as Appia's introduction of electric lighting."

Michael Billington was similarly enthusiastic, noting that the basic set was comparatively simple, a group of curved, lightweight and easily moveable screens which could become a three-dimensional backcloth for some arresting projections or rearranged so that two screens placed parallel to each other could become the sails of a ship. Despite his differences over the script Bernard described *Gulliver* as "surely one of the most inspired productions ever seen in European theatre." The opening was especially memorable – Gulliver walking from upstage into a spotlight to speak, simply, the first sentences of the book before a massive crash as the storm strikes the ship and the vessel's timbers fall apart. Then all goes silent before the lights come up and the audience sees the soles of a pair of vast buckled shoes, each 12` tall, projected on to a pair of screens, one on each side of the stage. Obviously the shoes' owner is lying on his back while his legs and upper body disappear upstage in the shadows. Actors are securing his enormous body with ropes, walking over the rostra forming his legs and tying him down tightly. Then at the back of the stage an enormous head and shoulders are seen as he sits up on the screen to roar at the Lilliputians to take care with their ropes. The illusion of a man at least 70` tall is complete and the audience shrieks with delight.

Billington was right to stress that the most ingenious feature of *Gulliver* was the way it kept shifting the visual perspective. In Brobdingnag we see Gulliver as resembling a tiny doll (radio-controlled, six-inch high) through the eyes of the awed inhabitants then suddenly we get Gulliver's-eye view of the same world with wasps the size of balloons buzzing over his head.

Intriguingly B.A. Young in the *Financial Times*, much as he admired the first half, thought the second if the more philosophical the more interesting, finding the island of Laputa to be like *Dr. Who* territory while the chilling Struldbrugs, with their unenviable immortality, take on an extra significance in an age of transplants and medical advances.

In the rush of technical and dress rehearsals nobody had given any thought to a curtain-call and so after the final black-out the lights came up on some uncertainty. Richard O'Brien (later of *The Rocky Horror Show*) had removed his horse's head as one of the Houyhnhnms and yelled "Come on, kids! Help me shake the yahoos out of the trees" which made a joyful ending to the production – it was retained.

Gulliver and *Hadrian* made up a glorious finale to the Mermaid's first decade (McCowen left to lead the Broadway company while Douglas Rain took over in London.) *Gulliver* had been scheduled for a six-week run playing twice daily but the run was extended to thirteen weeks, while *Lights Up!* a new Molecule show played a season of mornings before setting off on tour. Bernard had always hoped to maximise the opening hours; with 24 performances a week against most theatres' eight, he did not have to worry. Yet he did; walking round the foyer one evening it occurred to him that the foyer space could be an ideal informal performance space. Discussing the idea with Sean Kenny, they made some effective plans by removing an obstructing central panel and putting in a simple lighting rig behind the main beam and a moveable screen placed in front of the long central bar. Called SIGHTLINE, the space was ideal for occasional Sunday nights of new plays.

Both *Hadrian* and *Gulliver* closed on 31st March. To coincide with a *Lock Up* revival, opening production of the 10th Anniversary season, there was an unusual exhibition ('Sweet Chastity') of chastity belts, remarkably popular. Russell Hunter was a ripely lubricous Squeezum and the musical seemed as appealing as ever. In a review (*Mermaid 10*) of the theatre's first decade, Gerald included a survey of all the theatres built in the UK since 1959, ranging from small spaces to the behemoths (to be completed) of the Barbican and the National Theatre. A small proportion included proscenium – arch theatres but most were very clearly to varying degrees indebted to the Mermaid – seats on a raised tier, mostly open stages, all incorporating Puddle Dock's innovations of coffee and drinks bars, restaurants and provision for film shows. Ronald Hastings of *The Daily Telegraph* summed up the essence of The Mermaid:

> "We have accepted the Mermaid as a friendly club, the one theatre in London where no one takes himself too seriously. Informal enthusiasm and a sense of humour make up for much. It has not become a haunt of sybarites, not does it treat the players and the public as living on separate planets."

All around the City major changes were in process, Puddle Dock included. Old wharves and warehouses were vanishing and a major stretch of river wall between the theatre and the river was now in place. What did not change was the City's attitude. Despite all the protestations of goodwill surrounding the opening and early years, during the first decade the Mermaid's grant-aid from all sources amounted to precisely 4.6% of its global earnings. As Bernard put it with understated eloquence: "This must be a record unequalled by any other theatre of kindred size and policy." Always an optimist by nature, even during the celebrations and congratulations marking the 10th Birthday he could not help feeling there was little chance of persuading the Arts Council or the City to add much to their current £5,000: "constant strain and anxiety over financial problems would continue." A piece in *The Stage* on the first decade was a crumb of comfort:

> "A measure of the importance of the Mermaid and the affection in which it is held, might be gained from a thought on the reaction there would be if anyone dared to put a destructive finger on it. A critic, a lot of critics, may at times go for a production but I am sure these same critics, with thousands of the public to back them, would rush to the aid of the Mermaid should there be any question of withdrawal of financial aid or any sort of diminishing of its activities. It is a rare institution."

Bernard's energy was formidable – just as well as the second decade at Puddle Dock often threw up problems. At times it must be said he could be charged with taking his eye off the ball, not least given the amount of time he devoted to the *Scharnhorst Project*. The script was a closely-guarded secret but I did read it once. Vivian Cox told the complex story of a major sea-battle well enough but there were no vivid characters and nobody ever solved the problem of handling the battles visually. Sean still refused to be involved. Nevertheless Bernard gathered his troops and took the entire technical staff for a day's 'recce' to record ships' sounds in Plymouth while, in the evenings in his office, he would often pore over the script with charts and model destroyers.

The following week it was announced that he would be knighted in the forthcoming Birthday honours. The staff all received a memo declaring that anyone addressing him by his title would be instantly dismissed. New members of staff, unused to his eccentricities, would have a lot to learn. At that time they included an aspirant actor, hired to work in the box-office. Simon Callow had briefly worked in the box-office of the National Theatre and when a friend then working as number two in the Mermaid box-office returned to the National, he recommended Simon, who had given up University in Northern Ireland and, unsure of his future and impecunious, had been working as a cleaner in London. In the Mermaid Box Office he was working under Joan Robinson, signally different from the hatchet-faced old biddies who ruled over most West End box-offices. Joan was always impeccably coiffed and dressed (she had an impressive collection of bright summer dresses and always had fresh flowers from her Sanderstead garden in the box-office.) Bernard liked to spend some time in the box-office, having long chats with potential customers on the telephone, squeezing into Joan's tiny domain and on occasion managing to pat her bottom ("Stop it, Bernard!") For his first period at the Mermaid, Simon worked mainly with a delightful, but as it transpired, tragic young man Arthur ("Arfs".)

Joan smiled indulgently at their antics. When both *Edward II* and *Richard II* were programmed for a brief run in Prospect Theatre's productions, with a young and rising Ian McKellen in both leads nobody expected much activity at the box-office. When Simon and Arthur arrived on Monday morning they had not known of an extraordinarily enthusiastic piece by Harold Hobson in *The Sunday Times*, hailing McKellen as a great actor and they found a queue already long and the telephone ringing incessantly:

"We gave up putting the money in the till quite early on so that when Joan Robinson arrived at noon we were knee-deep in banknotes. Instead of being acclaimed as box-office heroes we were soundly berated for having let all the house-seats go and told to pick up all the money and not go anywhere near the window. Eventually poor Joan was reduced to buying back tickets from customers so she'd have something to give the ticket agencies on whose business she relied on during leaner times."

Prospect had only a few weeks available for its London run and Bernard drove a hard bargain with Iain Mackintosh, the Company's co-founder, insisting in the teeth of fierce opposition on a playing schedule of nine performances a week instead of the customary eight. Often Mackintosh (and Simon in the box-office) would catch Bernard outside, like an old-style barker, before each extra matinee, trying to persuade any waverers that Terence Wilton, McKellen's understudy was just as fine and that they would have a wonderful afternoon.

Simon greatly enjoyed his Mermaid times (although poor Arthur was found dead – partly burnt to death – in what seemed like a gay killing.) He responded particularly to the unpredictability – "inspired lunacy," he said – and Bernard's volatility, although he was sure Bernard never really knew who he was (he did, of course, which was perfectly clear when, after finally training as an actor, Simon appeared on stage at the theatre.) Simon, too, responded – in both acting and directing – to danger on stage, just like Bernard, whom he called "The Lord of Misrule."

In the February of 1969 the City's planning committee rejected an application to extend the Mermaid by building a new workshop, a new restaurant and a smaller theatre for the Molecule Club. Undaunted, in June Bernard submitted an even more ambitious scheme. He warned the staff that soon the City press would carry an announcement signed by R. Seifert and Partners on behalf of the Mermaid Theatre Trust to the effect that planning permission had been granted for the erection of a building at Puddle Dock and on the site adjoining Blackfriars Station for an office development containing a new Mermaid Theatre. He asked staff to give little away to the press although if challenged they could reveal that the Trust had applied for and been granted an Office Development Permit (ODP) by the Board of Trade for the building at Puddle Dock which would have a theatre, floor space for a car park and just over 67,000 sq.ft. of office space. He added that no detailed designs for the new theatre were yet available but that he and Sean Kenny would ultimately be responsible for this.

The scheme had been initiated by the property developer Instone Bloomfield and the crucial key – or golden goose – was the ODP. In 1965 a recently-elected Harold Wilson Labour government had stopped further office development in the City after a boom of several years. Under this Control of

Office and Industrial Development Act no more blocks could be built in the City without an ODP from the Board of Trade. ODPs were hard to come by but much sought after – Bernard had clearly charmed Antony Crosland at the Board of Trade. Bloomfield proposed that if the Mermaid Theatre Trust, a registered charity providing a public amenity, could acquire one for the Puddle Dock site they would then build a new theatre containing lettable office-space within the site area. A ground rent would be paid to the City of London (owners of the site) and the office space would then be let on a commercial basis. Bernard enthused:

> "It was envisaged that that properly financed, such a development could provide the Mermaid with a new home, plus a vital degree of permanent endowment."

Gerald's diary records the arrival of the precious ODP, which was with the inherent intention of subsidising a new Mermaid. He added that Bloomfield did not want it known that he was behind the development, which worried Bernard even more than did Colonel Seifert who had said "when the ODP comes bob's your uncle." He was frightened that he could be being used.

In light of subsequent developments Bernard might have handled the whole redevelopment issue differently and more speedily. He was well aware that in the City there had been some gnashing of teeth when it was discovered that Bernard held a coveted ODP, nor was Seifert universally popular. Many in the City saw the Puddle Dock site as theirs. The equation seemed simple – the Mermaid had an ODP but no money. What was required was a business partner without an ODP but with money. However it was to take seven years before a workable package could be put together. Bernard realised that he was going to need supporters around him. Several of his original Governors, most of whom had been most supportive, had died or left London. And he finally intuited, correctly, that the City was a different animal now and much less understanding of the very different world of theatre. His old friend Harold Drayton, had died in 1965; Sir Val Duncan, Chairman of the mighty Rio Tinto Zinc Company, replaced him as Chair of the Mermaid Board. He and Bernard got on well, with meetings held often at Duncan's Chelsea house or in his St. James's Square offices.

THE MERMAID'S SECOND decade began with less of a flourish than the first, with the only too predictable *Lock Up Your Daughters* running out of steam, catching the organisation on the hop. Alongside *Lock Up*, playing on a clever adaptation of Sean's set was a typically anarchic piece by Ken Campbell, another off-the-wall talent who greatly delighted Bernard. *Anything You Say Will Be Twisted* should have been a success. Originally produced in Bolton it was a brash, raunchy piece set in 18th century London, covering the exploits of the highwayman Jack Sheppard until his execution at Tyburn. But, for whatever reason, it somehow failed to draw audiences.

Although *The High Bid* had been a big success, another foray into Henry James proved to be a major disaster. *The Other House* was based on a novella, adapted by Bernard and a friend, the director Basil Ashmore, with Fenella Fielding scheduled to return to Puddle Dock. An unusual Jamesian piece – its plot involved a murder – critics at the time found it heavily influenced by Ibsen and indeed the main plot, one of a struggle for possession as three women vie to secure the affection of one man, has similarities with later Ibsen. A difficult piece to adapt, *The Other House* became a heated cauldron of rows, problems and general hysteria. Fenella left the production (Vilma Hollingberry replaced her), Bernard (directing) also stamped out for a while – poor Gerald had to have six versions of the poster designed as cast-names rapidly changed. Reviews of this were so dire that Bernard had to close it early. He was in a foul mood then – his instinct probably told him he had a major flop on his hands – and amongst all the *sturm und drang* he behaved with one of his occasional ill-judged and ill-tempered acts when he sacked Ken Smalley, one of the best general managers in the business. This was possibly connected with Fenella's defection (Ken was her partner) but this was unusually small-minded behaviour for Bernard. It also lost him another crucial member of staff in Lynn Haill, Ken's loyal assistant who before long was ensconced at the National Theatre, in charge of their programmes. It was usually such a happy atmosphere at the Mermaid but this was very far from a contented time.

The rest of the 10th Anniversary year was basically a series of stop-gaps, few initiated by Bernard. Prospect Theatre Company brought their double of *Richard II* and *Edward II*, both strong productions featuring a magnetic Ian McKellen as both monarchs, catapulting him to major stardom. Financially the picture was rosier with *The Bandwagon* co-produced with the West End's leading producer Michael Codron, by Terence Frisby (whose *There's a Girl in My*

Soup was still running in the West End.) Similar success was predicted for this new comedy. Set inside and outside the Botterill family's New Cross top floor household, sensationally all the female Botterill's family members give birth at the same time (the play had acquired some notoriety when Frisby refused to cut the line "My friend Sylv told me it was safe standing up" when the BBC planned it previously.) With Peggy Mount in awesome matriarchal form, the production by Robert Chetwyn was fast and funny but it did not transfer. And this production, too, had some unpleasant aspects, not least Frisby's fury when the play did not move to the West End. Bernard still seemed quarrelsome; he became involved in an argument about theatre design, focusing on the new Crucible Theatre in Sheffield under Colin George, much influenced by director Tyrone Guthrie and designer Tanya Moiseiwitsch, champions of the thrust stage in America and Canada. The Crucible would have a main 1,000-seat auditorium on a raked tier surrounding three sites of a promontory stage in an arc of 180o, about which there was some dissension. Bernard had not forgotten the Royal Exchange and considered the Sheffield plans a mistake. As did Laurence Olivier who cited his unhappiness with the Chichester stage, a hexagon with an arc of 120 degrees which he found a strain for actors and audiences. Bernard weighed in and went public in *The Observer* saying that Sheffield had got things badly wrong, citing Olivier's letter in support. He rather enjoyed stirring up controversy, but neither Olivier nor Sheffield was happy (Bernard had not consulted either.) Olivier fired off a stern letter calling Bernard "Naughty boy. Naughty boy":

"If I wished this letter to be published I would have done it myself – Do learn to manage the opening of your pretty mouth with a little more discretion, dear boy."

This seemed a time for spats and rows. Bernard's latest – with Sean Kenny – was more damaging. Sean had notionally designed *The Bandwagon*; it was not his kind of play, nor was Robert Chetwyn a director he respected and so most of the execution and supervision of the set was overseen by his assistant, Bob Bahl. A great to-do erupted during the weekend prior to the technical and dress rehearsals. Sean was nowhere to be found and Bahl was delayed on a new production at Billingham's Forum Theatre. Bernard stamped his feet. Very loudly. Dragging Gerald with him, Bernard set out for Sean's Chelsea apartment where a short but tempestuous scene followed, the upshot of which was Sean's refusal to get to the Mermaid but to fly home to Dublin for a screenplay meeting with Lionel Bart. Back at the Mermaid Bob Bahl appeared and the technical and dress rehearsals for *The Bandwagon* proceeded perfectly smoothly. Bernard, however, was in vengeful mood.

The next day he ordered the cancellation of the scheduled Christmas revival of *Gulliver's Travels* which had had posters outside the theatre since September. Gerald had to take down and replace all the existing publicity with any mention of Sean's name. The news reached Dublin during the week at which point Sean, boiling with real Irish rage, returned to London but getting nothing from Bernard except a lecture on his behaviour and a vague promise that if *Gulliver* could find another producer then "some arrangement might be possible."

Soon Sean had found a producer – Oscar Lewenstein who raised the possibility of the Round House or, less appealing, the unlovely barn of the old Savile on upper Shaftesbury Avenue. For the negotiations it was considered wise to keep Sean and Bernard apart as much as possible and so Sean's redoubtable agent Patricia MacNaughton negotiated for him. Not an easy task (Patricia recalled "a great deal of shouting and thumping of desks") – Bernard would change times of meetings arbitrarily and kept offering different financial deals. Also Jack Sprat the malodorous parrot, resident in Bernard's office between *Treasure Island*s, took against Patricia and gave her a nasty bite on the hand. The feeling grew that Bernard did not really want the show to be seen elsewhere and indeed negotiations fizzled out without resolution. *Treasure Island* replaced *Gulliver*.

The sour atmosphere at Puddle Dock continued – both Ken and Sean were extremely popular figures there. Bernard, obdurate to a degree, would not countenance changing his mind. The second decade had got off to a somewhat toxic start. Change in the City was in the air all around; smart boutiques replacing chains like John Collier or Burtons, gleaming glass towers instead of dirty old brick which had begrimed Dickensian offices. Bernard seemed rather lost then – his City's transformation somewhat unsettled him.

Hurt – as he saw it – by some of his staff, Bernard turned more to loyalists such as Ron Pember. In 1968 Ron had suggested the idea of an evening – *Open on Sunday* – suggested by a sketch of a Jewish boy by his friend Michael Landry, a play / revue set within a small community during different historical periods from Ancient Egypt to modern Bethnal Green. Bernard was hooked by Ron's idea for the opening – an empty stage with the loading-doors at the back open allowing the audience to see all the river traffic while, under music, slowly the cast would appear, pushing their carts down a ramp on to the stage, then proceeding to present anecdotes, folk songs, Hassidic tales, jumping through space and time before the company disappear. Ron heard no more about it until he picked up a leaflet in the Mermaid foyer announcing the opening alarmingly soon. It was a very popular show as was another of Ron's suggestions – *Enter Solly Gold* by the much underestimated Bernard Kops. This Jewish *Tartuffe* had marvellous performances from Joe Melia and David Kossoff and was a genuine audience pleaser.

A director much admired by Bernard was Jonathan Miller. In 1967 Miller was just embarking on his post-*Beyond the Fringe* career and in 1964 in New York had scored a success with an off-Broadway venture of three plays under the overall title *The Old Glory* by the American poet, a troubled genius, Robert Lowell. Now *Benito Cereno*, adapted from Herman Melville's eerie novella was chosen to bring Miller to Puddle Dock. Set on a battered slave-ship, a Yankee captain and crew board it, not realising there has been an on-board mutiny. Like many Miller productions this divided opinion in America – some more conventionally-minded critics like Walter Kerr loathed it while others such as the poet Randall Jarrell and *The New Republic*'s Robert Brustein hailed it as thrilling, seeing in Lowell's work a kind of allegory of US foreign policy and race relations. Miller, also a doctor, was able to cope with Lowell's psychiatric problems (he was Bipolar.) At the Mermaid he had two favourite actors – Peter Eyre as Cereno and Rudolph Walker the chief mutineer. Again the notices were divided but most audiences were mesmerised by both narrative and production with Miller using slightly stylised movement which gave the evening a disquieting sense of unease. Bernard was somewhat in awe of the polymathic Miller but the two men got on very well and Bernard stressed how much he would like to see Miller back at the Mermaid.

And in 1970 both Miller and Pember came back to be part of an ambitious season – six classical plays covering Shaw, Shakespeare and James Joyce. *The Apple Cart* had a magnetic King Magnus from John Neville with one of the best British black actresses, Carmen Munroe a bewitching Orinthia. Disappointingly the following production, both parts of *King Henry IV* which marked Bernard's return to the stage never quite took wing. Ron Pember chose to set it in a somewhat dull monochrome barn-like setting, reminiscent of Hogarth's '*Strolling Players in a Barn*' but with no real explanation of why it was set in the 18th century and also it was never entirely clear whether the actors were giving a performance or just rehearsing. The main prop, a large farm-cart, was no help to sightlines. The Mermaid's casting director, Corinne Rodriquez, had assembled a fine cast, several of whom would go into the following *The Tempest* and *Saint Joan* – Hwyel Bennett, a still, watchful presence as Hal with David Neal and Colette O'Neill vigorous Hotspurs. The big disappointment was Bernard's Falstaff. He looked right – well padded and sly – but there was little energy and no real bond between him and Hal. Benedict Nightingale spoke for most critics in describing the performance as sentimentalised. Even in the 'honour' speech he was slow and underwhelming.

Henry IV had a commanding performance as Henry from Graham Crowden, who remained at the Mermaid to play Prospero in *The Tempest*, directed by Jonathan Miller who also joined the Mermaid Board of Governors for a time. *The Tempest*, based to some degree on Frank Kermode's notion of the play as an allegory of colonialism, was one of Miller's finest productions, drawing on a wealth of sources anthropological and psychoanalytic, with Prospero's white colonialism set against the finely-tuned work from black actors (Norman Beaton an aloof Ariel, Rudolph Walker as Caliban with the Masque sung by three magnificently gowned black female singers to pastiche Monteverdi from Carl Davis.)

It was on *The Tempest* that I came in. Jonathan had directed a joint Oxbridge company in *Twelfth Night* (I played the worst part in Shakespeare – Fabian) for an American campus tour and asked me to assist him at the Mermaid. I had finished a research degree and was not yet sure of my path, but I knew the next six weeks would not be boring. Nor were they, and six weeks became six years. I started on £7 a week (just about possible to survive on in London then), although I sometimes had to make another pound or two by pulling pints in Connie's Bar, and Joan in the box-office who tended to 'mother' the impecunious young was usually good for a modest 'sub' on Thursday before Friday pay-day. Jonathan had a disconcertingly low boredom threshold and on occasion would jump up to say he had an urgent appointment at the National or the BBC (quite untrue) and say that I would stand in for the rest of the day. The actors must have been somewhat thrown; here they were, expecting to be directed by the great man, instead of which they were left under the charge of a spotty student. Somehow I got through those scenes – I began to realise how much I enjoyed directing – and the production, a very happy one, went on to receive excellent notices and packed houses. Then, not long before the end of the run, Bernard asked to see me and, much to my surprise, asked if I'd like to stay on "for a bit" – I could assist directors, read scripts, even sweep the stage.

I never knew why he offered this although I think he liked my Scottishness and also he could tell my heart wasn't really in the idea of an academic life which was another possibility. I really liked him – I didn't take long to realise how contradictory he could be, but I responded also to his absolutely burning commitment, a moral zeal, to the theatre.

My first collaboration with him was as assistant on *Saint Joan*, possibly his favourite Shaw, with Angela Pleasence who had been such an effective child of nature as Miranda in *The Tempest*. This should have turned out well; Bernard had the excellent idea of casting as the Inquisitor his old revue companion, George Benson, who played him with a deep sense of moral gravity, using all possible arguments to save Joan from the fire. John Tordoff was a singularly original Dauphin but it was a drab design with some coarse supporting performances and Bernard did little to elicit the kind of performance of which Angela Pleasence was capable – perhaps the Sybil Thorndyke performance was still too much embedded in his mind. In any event I spent a good deal of time in classic assistant mode, going after Angela to the dressing-room to woo her back to rehearsal. In the end it was a patchy production although, like most Shaw, it kept the box-office busy.

An even bigger success – more surprisingly perhaps – was a rare showing of James Joyce's only play, *Exiles* in a characteristically meticulous production by Harold Pinter. This British premiere fared well critically – some hailed a lost masterpiece, pinpointing the missing link between Ibsen and modern drama; unquestionably its exploration of sexual jealousy influenced Pinter in plays such as *Old Times* and *Betrayal*. What came over forcefully at the Mermaid was the play's bold modernity (it was written in 1918) in revelatory scenes such as that between Richard Brown, returned to Dublin after years in Europe with his wife and young son, and his old friend Robert when their candour reveals two men in love with the same woman. Joyce described the play as "consisting of three cat-and-mouse acts" and Pinter explored the relationships with riveting finesse.

This meant the following production for the Christmas period would be a break from *Treasure Island*, with a new play – *Dick Turpin* – by Ron Pember and Sally's second husband Tony Loynes. To run alongside Bernard persuaded me to direct the only full-length play by "Saki" (H.H. Munro) although I found the play less than a dazzling prospect. His short stories remain inimitable but Saki's country-house comedy of *The Watched Pot* (the title positively invites the headline "This Never Boils") is an odd hybrid – the first half has some sleek, barbed comedy but then it simply fades away, with no proper ending, not even a whimper let alone a bang. It was handsomely set (Bernard Culshaw's first Mermaid designs) with stylish actors (Lally Bowers and Moira Redmond in particular) who knew how to handle the literate dialogue but, rather as I anticipated, the reviews were muted. But I hadn't disgraced myself it would seem – Bernard asked me to direct *O.K. for Sound* for the Molecule and then in the spring one of my favourite Shaw plays, not seen in London for many years – *John Bull's Other Island*. I was relieved he had not asked me to take on a play he enthused about but which most of us at the theatre thought little of – a comedy by a prentice dramatist, Huntly Harding called *The Licentious Fly* (Fly is the name of the local randy rustic – possibly Bernard was reminded of his "Clods" on the halls) – wooing a similarly lusty local woman. Corinne Rodriguez had no little trouble casting this one – scripts were returned with extremely swift rejections. Finally Christopher Benjamin and Antonia Pemberton were heroic in the leading roles and despite generally downbeat notices this played to fairly good houses.

Josephine, much involved with the Molecule Club, directed a new autobiographical play by Bernard's old friend Walter Greenwood which was a sad disappointment, a play given no real chance by the press. *Hanky Park* (the area of Greenwood's Manchester childhood) in which he traced his own upbringing was no masterpiece but it was an honest, touching (not sentimental) and funny exploration of a particular world – the pre-war years before 1914-18 – and it was patronised by most metropolitan critics. Bernard Culshaw designed a cobbled and gaslit working-class district with many northern actors (Anne Reid, John Comer, Jean Boht) giving authentic, gritty performances. Those who came seemed to admire it greatly – there were many letters to the theatre about it – but it had a very large cast and it had to close early.

The theatre staff were loyal to most productions, including *Hanky Park* but there also seemed to be a feeling that Bernard was letting things drift. He was still elusive about the ODP and how to proceed with the precious paper. A sense of unease was prevalent – in the summer Harold Wilson was ejected from Downing Street and the Tories, under Edward Heath with a majority of 30, took over. For reasons best known to himself Bernard without warning sacked Gerald Frow claiming he could not afford him – risible in light of Mermaid salaries – and it took some time before a first-rate publicity replacement (Sue Rolfe and then Barry Walsh) could be found.

Early in 1971 the Mermaid's cherished ODP was absorbed into planning permission granted by the City Corporation, but, by May, Bernard was having doubts:

"I am of the opinion that certain measures of a very drastic nature must be taken before we proceed further with that brilliant and audacious scheme."

He pointed out that financially the Mermaid's situation was precarious just when new plans were being contemplated. Everywhere money seemed a huge problem – the City's Barbican Committee now admitted that their own theatre would require a minimum of £750,000 in endowment. He counselled "a major appraisal of the present situation." At this stage Bernard was much helped by another Jonathan Miller protégé. He never had much luck with general managers; he had, more or less on a whim, fired Ken Smalley and now he took on Jonathan James Moore, another Jonathan Miller suggestion, an ex-*Cambridge Footlights* star who had co-founded the Oxford and Cambridge Shakespeare Company. Sartorially dishevelled, ginger beard and hair all over the shop, Jonathan was a cheerful personality who rather shared my view of Bernard – most of the time inspiring, at others best avoided. He handled Bernard very well and gradually life at the Mermaid regained its beguiling atmosphere.

Still Bernard felt less supported by the City fatcats now more prominent on the Court of Governors. His staunch ally and St. John's Wood neighbour Major Smith had departed as had Spike Milligan who had been "suggested" to resign by one of the recent co-opted City 'experts' brought in to spearhead the redevelopment. Spike was offended by the cavalier treatment (he had done a great deal for the Mermaid – playing Ben Gunn in *Treasure Island* and *The Bedsitting Room* included – with no special fees), being told "we don't need actors for this theatre to succeed, we need business men" (somewhat ironic in light of later developments.)

Most of Bernard's time at this period was taken up with meetings (the Lands Committee, the Rates Committee), finally, after lengthy debate, agreeing that the City should become 'godfather' to the new development. This meant that the City should take over the ODP and then find an institution to provide the finance to build the theatre / office complex at Puddle Dock. No discussion seemed to have been held about a viable ground rent for the theatre. Sir Desmond Heap (comptroller and City solicitor) and Frank Gordon (secretary to the Governors) were very helpful in driving things forward. Sir Desmond was apprehensive because the dreaded Alderman Howard, no friend of the Mermaid, was to be the next Lord Mayor. In the event it would take five more years to resolve the matter. Bernard kept producing hard facts about subsidies, making a comparison chart of revenue grants as a percentage of box-office receipts for the year 1968/9, looking at 30 theatres nationwide and detailing subsides from the Arts Council and local authorities. It showed how much each theatre needed in grant-in-aid to earn every £100. The highest were Lincoln Rep. and the Northcott, Exeter (£250 and £230 respectively) while the RSC, still at the Aldwych required £35 per £100. Lowest of all was the Mermaid which received £15 for every £100 taken at the box-office. Bernard told Jonathan and me that he had prepared these figures at the request of *The Guardian* for an article in its Arts pages. He had asked the Arts Council to check the figures but, in his words, "they warned me off" and his piece was never published.

Shaw came to the rescue again. *John Bull's Other Island* had not been seen in London since 1911, it had four sets and a large cast and IRA unrest was still a menace in the capital. It needed extra-strong casting from English and Irish actors alike and I was lucky – Christopher Benjamin was an hilariously, seemingly blundering Mister Toad among the Celtic Twilight, Edward Petherbridge, incisive and sharply-bearded was like a younger Shaw, an exile in London, alongside some of the best contemporary Irish actors (P.G. Stephens, Dermot Kelly.) The play surprised many – regarded as a supreme prose-writer, Shaw here has some long, rhapsodic speeches on the seductive allure of Ireland, its mists, its sunsets, its devastating and dangerous charm. It played to packed houses; Eddie Kulukundis, a larger-than-life Greek from a shipping family, now a West End impresario, wanted to transfer the production but no suitable theatre was available.

Jonathan Miller and Robert Lowell returned for another rarity which totally divided critics but still did strong business. Lowell's version of Aeschylus's *Prometheus Bound* which Miller had previously directed in America at Yale with Kenneth Haigh displaying virtuoso vocal variety. A necessarily somewhat static evening, this – with Angela Thorne's driven Io – had a laser-beam concentration of focus and became a surprise success.

Michael Redgrave had never acted at the Mermaid although he and Bernard had remained friends since the *Thunder Rock* days. William Trevor, a highly-regarded novelist and short-story writer, had adapted his novel '*The Old Boys*' for the stage. As with many adaptations there were a few narrative flaws but in the main Trevor's story of old and bitter schoolboy rivalries again erupting over the election of a new president of the Old Boys Association remained taut and involving, the action divided between the home of Mr. Jaraby (Redgrave), keen to win the election, and the Rimini Hotel, a late-life resting place for many former pupils including Mr. Nox, Jaraby's old rival. The various ways in which the elderly can be exploited (not least by Miss Burdock, proprietrix or the Rimini) make a strong thread throughout, building to a surprising and life-affirming climax. Rehearsals began promisingly; Redgrave had not been on stage for five years, following a less than happy time at the Old Vic during the National Theatre's first season there, but initially he seemed on top of the text and fully energised. Sylvia Coleridge who had worked with Redgrave previously, thought he was beginning to build a very fine performance. But gradually there was a disturbing change when the lines were all over the place and his body-language tight and constricted. There were murmurs of "a drink problem" but certainly at rehearsal there was no evidence of that. To me it seemed like a barely cloaked internal dread. The other actors – like most, sympathetic to a fellow-performer in trouble, were as helpful as possible, going through his lines in the evening.

But when we moved into the Mermaid from the rehearsal room the barely-controlled unease returned. I had to see Bernard to tell him that I was far from sure we would be able to open. Bernard and Josephine came to watch a run-through – apart from being very slow, Michael was perfectly sound on the text until the closing scene, never a problem before.

Bernard tended to be good in a crisis. He said he had an idea and in about an hour returned bearing a machine with a small microphone and an earpiece which looked like a hearing-aid (perfectly in character for Jaraby to wear). One big problem – *The Old Boys* was a very busy show for the stage manager, with many cast calls for entrances, lighting cues and sound cues. It was impossible for her to prompt (possibly regularly) as well, speaking softly into the microphone for Michael to pick up dialogue through his earpiece. Bernard had heard about this device from a friend working in films. We had a test run that afternoon but it had fallen to me to do the prompting. The only place for a prompter at the Mermaid was in one of two slits in the side walls near the bottom of the rows of seats, one of which the stage manager used, while the other would house me and the machine for eight performances a week. I had the advantage of being able to tell from his eyes when Michael might 'dry.' A run-through that afternoon was partly successful despite his earpiece collapsing when he fiddled with it – Michael could hear me, nobody in the theatre could, but he was initially slow in reacting to his cues. That evening he was clearly very nervous initially, but gradually he gained confidence and by the end was firing on most if not all cylinders in his big speeches of defiance in the Rimini Hotel and improved further during the few previews. The notices were mixed for the play but mostly excellent for Michael. He clung to the safety-net of the prompting-system for most of the run (in a hot summer my perch hidden in the Mermaid brick was something of an ordeal.) After the Mermaid *The Old Boys* toured for twelve weeks – I put my foot down, telling Michael he hadn't dried for three weeks and that I had to get back to work at Puddle Dock. He never dried once during those weeks on tour. It was popular at the box-office on tour, as it had been at the Mermaid.

A worrying pattern was beginning to feature at times at Puddle Dock – a big and often money-spinning success would be succeeded by one or two productions which could drain the box-office disturbingly quickly. *The Old Boys* succeeded financially but everyone at the theatre worried about Bernard's next production – *Othello*, in which he would play his third Iago. As tactfully as possible it was pointed out that his age (he was 62) might be a problem, to which considerable umbrage was taken. Some Othellos ensure their Iagos will be sound without taking the spotlight; on this occasion it was the other way round. For his Othello, despite Corinne Rodriguez's reservations, Bernard cast Bruce Purchase, an amiable, burly actor who had been in *The Tempest*. He was not ideal physically, a big man but, to be frank, somewhat flabby and with a voice large but without much resonance. Without discussing the question of a director with anyone Bernard decided to have *Othello* co-directed by Julius Gellner (who had directed him in the play at the Old Vic) and a charming but madcap young Australian, Peter Oyston who had worked at Century Theatre. It was an uneasy mix and it became a fraught production. Julius was not well while Oyston was understandably somewhat unsure of how the chain of command should work and, of course, Bernard would keep chipping in with his own ideas. I saw a late run-through which was deeply worrying. Purchase was just about adequate but with little sense of a great warrior while Bernard was uncertain and (heinous crime in his book) often inaudible. Advance bookings were hardly encouraging, at which point Bernard's keen sense of publicity kicked in. He decided that for the deathbed scene towards the close when Othello kills Desdemona the actress should be naked, justifying this with some dubious textual readings and, more justifiably, insisting that a sexual woman like Desdemona might well want to persuade the enraged Othello to make love and become calm. But he had not mentioned this to the cast and the Desdemona refused to go naked. A hastily recast Sarah Stephenson took over. Bookings certainly picked up dramatically following a great deal of publicity in the press and on TV and radio. Even those critics who did not see the nudity element as unjustified could not approve of the production, however – both Bruce Purchase and Bernard came out of it poorly. Bernard's performance, indeed, was distressing; the tape he used to lift up his jowls kept coming loose and messing up his wig, altogether a sad spectacle.

Back with the old faithful, Shaw yet again came up trumps with the rarely-seen *Geneva*. This "Fancied Page of History" was written in 1938 on the eve of another war set at a summit conference aiming to defuse the increasingly belligerent behaviour of three European dictators – Herr Battler, Signor Bombardone and General Flanco. Rarely revived, this satire came up fresh in a sparkling, fleet production with Christopher Benjamin's pleasingly, pompously self-satisfied Bombardone.

For a second year running *Treasure Island* did not feature at Christmas and instead Bernard revived *Dick Turpin*, the fast-moving adventure by Ron Pember and Anthony Loynes. This did not match the success of the previous Christmas's showing but it was a foul winter and all London theatres were badly affected.

Then Bernard's long-nurtured project of Camus's *Les Justes* (newly translated as *The Price of Justice* by Robert Baldick) was put into production. Bernard was a big Camus admirer and really wanted this to succeed, giving it a taut production with Leigh Lawson deeply impressive as a riven would-be assassin in a revolutionary cell, based on the true story of the assassination of Grand Duke Sergei Romanov in 1905. Camus's scrutiny of the complex moral issues associated with terrorism still gripped but audiences, with London still freezing, were thin.

Another golden period was just beginning although neither of the next two productions was Mermaid-initiated. The first London revival of Pinter's *The Caretaker* packed the theatre for an extended run. It had a Rolls-Royce cast in a spectacularly cluttered set from Eileen Diss – John Hurt, Jeremy Kemp, Leonard Rossiter, all in peak form. This had some treasurable comic highlights, not least Rossiter as Davies, the truculent tramp setting the house on gales of laughter with his description of a visit to Sidcup in search of identity papers.

Bernard had a problem towards the end of *The Caretaker*'s run when a project collapsed at a late stage. I had heard of a production of R.C. Sherriff's World War I classic, *Journey's End*, touring after playing Manchester's Royal Exchange so I made the journey to the unlovely Harlow Playhouse to catch it. It was a splendid production, directed by Eric Thompson and with all-round truthful performances including those by Peter Egan, James Maxwell and Colin Procktor. Despite a tight schedule to get it into the Mermaid and with little time for pre-publicity, it eventually played to standing-room only before transferring to the West End.

A new kind of musical revue – first in London, initially at the Mermaid, and then in New York, began with *Cowardy Custard* in 1972. Noël Coward and Bernard had not seen much of each other with Coward mostly in Jamaica or Switzerland. But they admired each other – Coward was always drawn to people with the kind of enthusiasm Bernard had for the theatre while Bernard, miles apart politically from Coward, never ceased to wonder at Coward's range and variety. He had thought previously about including a Coward play for production, considering both *Peace in Our Time* or *Cavalcade* but neither was felt sure enough given their cast sizes. Then one morning in Bernard's office, Gerald – soon to leave London to become press representative for the Belgrade Theatre, Coventry – mentioned that Coward was in London. I had recently said that Coward's songs had been neglected – most of his sketches from revues had dated – and that an evening based on his music with a biographical element, might work well. When Josephine heard that Coward was in London she insisted "Ring him." Bernard demurred – he was at times surprisingly shy, an instance of his 'outsider' feeling, and felt unprepared. Still Josephine persisted: "Just ring him! Invite him down. Give him dinner." It emerged that Coward was to visit the Mermaid that very evening to see *Hadrian VII*; Bernard offered him dinner but he already had a dinner engagement although he would love to have a drink with Bernard and key members of the Coward "family" (Graham Payn, Cole Lesley.) The drinks extended into a late supper, ending – according to Gerald – "in the early hours of next morning" when Coward and Bernard were to be seen skipping down the iron staircase from the restaurant, arm-in-arm singing '*Dance Little Lady*' to the sleeping City.

Bernard's original idea for the show presented problems – he suggested a kind of morality-piece with Coward to be judged by a celestial judge and his angels and then devils to debate his candidacy for heaven, with songs produced as evidence. Gerald and I – I had been roped in as co-deviser – could not summon up enthusiasm for this notion – Bernard suggested a similar notion often, rather like W.S. Gilbert and the Lozenge device. Somehow over the next few weeks we managed to persuade him to reconsider and finally the idea of a kind of biography in song and dance, with some brief extracts from his plays and prose writings, was settled on. Originally Bernard scheduled it for the following year but that was already packed with revivals and other celebrations of Coward's Birthday week (dubbed by Coward "Holy Week") and so it was scheduled for 1972 as part of the City of London Festival. Its committee audibly sniffed at the idea – more rarefied music was the Festival's speciality but Bernard argued most forcefully that "Coward's roots, for all his cosmopolitan image, lie firmly in London." He was also irked that the Committee's grant to the Festival stood at £50,000 ("This for two weeks work per year – set alongside the yearly pittance to the Mermaid.")

When we got down to serious work – usually in a frigid shed near the theatre, I saw little of Gerald who, of course, had a full-time job in Coventry (no faxes or e-mails then) so I asked Wendy Toye who had so splendidly staged the Phoenix Theatre one-night celebrity birthday show, to help shape the production as well as direct and choreograph. Originally the show was to be called *Master Pieces* (but did the general public know of Coward's sobriquet of "Master"?) Everyone chipped in with suggestions; Bernard proposed *Cream of Coward* but a cable whizzed back from Jamaica "That," he said, "would be asking for trouble" and suggesting *Cowardy Custard*, which became the title.

Designer Tim Goodchild came up with a clever permanent set of varying levels, revolving periaktoids and with the onstage band stage right. The final script, which changed little in rehearsal, used more than 60 songs, many in an ingenious opening medley, zestfully sung (no microphones) by a superb cast – Patricia Routledge nearly every night stopping the show with '*I've Been to a Marvellous Party*', Una Stubbs reinventing '*Mad About the Boy*' while John Moffatt handled Coward's autobiographical poem '*The Boy Actor*' with moving affection. Those who saw a preview will still remember Jonathan Cecil bringing the house down with '*Uncle Harry*' but that sadly had to be cut when the second act proved overlong. The evening was a huge success – Coward in his chocolate-brown dinner jacket received not one, not two but three standing ovations. He made no curtain-speech but told Wendy Toye and me: "Don't change a thing."

Cowardy Custard was one of the Mermaid's biggest financial successes – it played to capacity for nearly a year and only closed when the Arts Council began to make noises. Bernard kept it running by going back to twice-nightly programming, alternating six performances of *Cowardy Custard* with six of Shaw's *Misalliance*, which I had a good time directing. This too had a hand-picked cast who played this comedy with the authentic Shavian zest – the peerless Bill Fraser as the underwear tycoon Tarleton, Caroline Blakiston as the Polish aviatrix and an award-winning performance from John Tordoff as the inept anarchist emerging from a Turkish bath in a Surrey mansion to declare: "Rome fell! Babylon fell! Hindhead's turn will come!"

Despite this run of successes this was a strange time at Puddle Dock. The landscape of the City was being transformed and when the 4X building next to the theatre, which had housed many staff lately, had to be vacated for demolition, most staff were housed in a communal office on Ludgate Hill. The country, too, seemed to be in O'Casey's "state of chassis" – a three-day week, power cuts, London at times under a pall of freezing fog. At this time Bernard seemed strangely subdued, curiously withdrawn. We all knew that he was anxious about the future and what to do with his apparently precious ODP but he rarely said much about this goose, supposedly soon to lay its golden eggs. He was also visibly deeply affected by Sean Kenny's death. Sean and Lionel Bart came into Bernard's office one afternoon – I was asked to join – to listen to some songs for a projected new musical of *The Hunchback of Notre Dame*. It seemed that all the past rancour between Sean and Bernard had melted away and it was a jolly afternoon while Lionel played a catchy number, '*Be a Performer*'. Suddenly Sean rose from his chair and moved to the door, and we assumed he was going to the loo. Then just at the door he stopped, made an inarticulate sound and fell to the floor. He had had a heart attack. An ambulance came quickly and we telephoned his girlfriend Judy Geeson, and his agent Patricia MacNaughton. At Bart's he had a stroke and lingered for a few days before he died. He had helped start the Mermaid, helped give it its special identity. And despite a sometimes abrupt manner he loved both the theatre and Bernard. It took Bernard some time to recover from this blow.

Sean died just as rehearsals were about to start for his production (first seen in Canada) of *Juno and the Paycock*. Bernard asked the great Irish actress Siobhan McKenna who was playing Mrs. Boyle (Juno) to supervise the production and she was helped by a recent recruit to the Mermaid – Andrew Hilton, like Jonathan James-Moore and me was a Jonathan Miller protégé – who quickly adapted and was of immeasurable help to Siobhan. The production carried no trace of its trouble, received excellent reviews and was much appreciated by full houses.

Another 20th century classic also came up strong in Bernard's production of J.B. Priestley's *An Inspector Calls*. With a cleverly-angled design by Sue Ayers (who also painted most the Mermaid's sets) he was not likely to provide the kind of deconstruction job such as Stephen Daldry's at the National Theatre later, but it was a good example of Bernard at his best as a director – meticulous, paced exactly right and trusting the play, with an unsettling Philip Stone as Inspector Goole. It, too, did excellent business.

Then – disaster. Bernard became determined to programme a new play by director Ronald Eyre, a fine director and maker of television programmes, but when Bernard asked me to read *Something's Burning* I was very dubious. It seemed to me that, dangerous for any audience what was billed as "a comedy" simply was not very funny. A curious affair set in a police station it moved into somewhat apocalyptic territory. Corinne Rodriguez and Andrew Hilton thought the same as I but Bernard was obdurate. And then we began to think we must all be wrong when Ron, also directing, cast Bill Fraser, Roger Rees, Penelope Wilton and other top-flight actors. I watched a late rehearsal – it was very smooth but I still could not see why Bernard felt so passionate about it. Previews were passable but there were virtually no laughs. The opening night too was perfectly professional but as arid as the previews. And the notices were poor – so terrible as to be newsworthy, featured on radio and television programmes. Joan Robinson said she was finding it difficult even to give tickets away. The production closed early, a sad occasion with so much talent involved.

A new play which came to me from the author's American agent intrigued me and Bernard liked it too – although I suspect that a simple set and a cast of only four were inducements too. By a young M.I.T. professor, *Children* was an early play by A.R. Gurney who also wrote fiction. His special field was the WASP world of the Eastern seaboard, its foibles, snobberies and traditions. Taking place over a Thanksgiving weekend, a recently-widowed mother has unexpected problems with her children, not all of whom share her values and sense of tradition. Recently widowed herself after a long marriage to the playwright and Labour MP Benn Levy, this role was superbly played by Constance Cummings, who the previous year had won the Evening Standard Award for Best Performance by an Actress opposite Laurence Olivier in *Long Day's Journey into Night*. *Children* was altogether a quieter play but rippling with subterranean tensions. The notices were mixed – the WASP world is often misunderstood by British critics – although Irving Wardle in *The Times* described it as "the best new American play since Arthur Miller." Gurney went on to a distinguished New York career.

Another of what the Mermaid staff came to call "Bernard's follies" came along with another new play, *The Great Society* by Beverley Cross, playwright, librettist and adaptor. Joan Robinson's reaction to the news that the subject of the play involved the Peasants' Revolt was one of the heaviest sighs ever heard and the prediction it would be off very quickly. She was right but the real reason for this flop was less the play than a dreadful production, doomed from the outset by the set by Bernard, returning to design work. Everything seemed to be in grey – grey backing drapes, grey steps, grey costumes (Bernard played the itinerant preacher John Ball, previously tackled in a radio play by Jack Lindsay), with much backlighting and so despite committed and spirited performances from Pete Postlethwaite and Geoffrey Whitehead (Wat Tyler and Richard II) who had some meaty and well-written scenes, the evening was relentlessly monotonous visually. This, too, was one which had to close early.

Bernard had been much taken by a new theatre buzzword – "Marketing", now something of a growth industry. He shrewdly talent-spotted a young man, Graham Jenkins who proved a wizard at organising group bookings. But even he was unable to convince many theatregoers to book for productions like this.

The success of *Cowardy Custard* naturally had led Bernard to think of other potential musical revues and he jumped at my suggestion of one based on the words and music of Cole Porter. Luckily the music scholar Robert Kimball recently had edited *Cole*, a handsome publication with the lyrics of all Porter songs. I had one trip to New York to work in the Porter Archive in the offices of the law firm still headed by Porter's lawyer, John Wharton a remarkable man who had been much involved with the Playwrights' Company, very active on Broadway in the 30s and 40s who was unfailingly helpful. It was cast as soundly as *Cowardy Custard* with an elegant Art Deco-inspired set of many levels using projections to a degree unseen previously on the British stage. We rehearsed miles away in a spacious Clapham hall. Bernard and Josephine stayed mostly away but I was aware that there was much worry back at Puddle Dock about finances. Jonathan James-Moore came over on occasion; I saw through the bonhomie and enthusiasm and knew that he too was deeply anxious, knowing that should *Cole* flop, the theatre would have to close at least temporarily, a worry that only increased when we got into the theatre to find the old Mermaid switchboard was not going to cope with the demands of the show and another had to be hired at no small expense. Moving into the theatre was complex logistically – costumes late, arrangements by Ken Moule superb but often in need of revision (we were using no body-mics), projectors misbehaving, the performers panicking about the numbers of quick costume changes. We had only two previews but both were encouraging and it was clear thankfully that *Cole* needed no last-minute cutting or re-shaping. It was a magical first night with many outstanding moments – Una Stubbs in a minimal black and gold dress shimmering through '*Jazz Baby*' a seldom-heard extract from Porter's ballet *Within the Quota* written with his friend Gerald Murphy and wittily choreographed by David Toguri, Julia McKenzie out-Mermaning Merman with a defiant '*Down in the Depths on the Ninetieth Floor*', Angela Richards finding real pathos in '*Make it Another Old-Fashioned*' or Peter Gale's wry cynicism in '*I'm a Gigolo*'. Of course at that time we had no idea of the reviews' content until the next day although the audience reaction had been terrific.

The reason for Bernard's tension at that time became clear when he called me away from the theatre to his office. He told me that Jonathan had cracked up just as the show began. Bernard handled this with consummate tact, first bringing his doctor down to see Jonathan and then agreeing to take him to East London's German Hospital which looked after such nervous breakdowns. Jonathan was there for some time and was finally diagnosed as Bipolar. He did not return to the Mermaid but a job was found for him in BBC Radio (eventually he became Radio 4's head of comedy). Jonathan Miller pronounced that there were only two places ideal for people with such nervous complaints – the Mermaid or, even better, the BBC.

Bernard would have had trouble persuading the Arts Council to let him keep *Cole* running with no stop-date (eventually it ran for 400 performances) and so to follow he turned to the fail-safe of Shaw with a diamond-sharp production of *The Doctor's Dilemma* with an impressive list of senior British character-actors and a young Simon Callow as the clerk at the beginning. Once again Shaw bested Shakespeare – the following *Merry Wives of Windsor* was a mirth-free zone unfortunately and was whisked off early.

After the disappointment of this leaden *Merry Wives* Bernard – seemingly re-energised – gave the Mermaid one of its finest Shavian performances. *On the Rocks* had not been seen in London since 1933. One of those political comedies which always seem to have contemporary parallels, *On the Rocks's* themes included unemployment, a drifting government, racism, union power challenging a corrupt Labour movement, half-baked promises from upper-class young radicals etc. etc. J.W. Lambert in *The Sunday Times* described it as "an immensely exhilarating evening made out of nothing but the dance of the mind." And Bernard gave a sparkling performance as Mr. Hipney ("the old street-corner speaker – good old Hipney.") His clashes with the Prime Minister in Downing Street (the play is set throughout in the Cabinet Room) were comedy gold with Bernard well matched by a veteran Shavian, Stephen Murray, as the P.M. Sir Arthur Chavender, being constantly lectured by Hipney rousing the electorate:

"Give them a choice between qualified men… not windbags and movie stars and soldiers and rich swankers and lawyers on the make."

Lambert was only one of the critics to laud both production and Bernard's performance:

"he possesses all of the crinkled charm in the world, voice full of devious, caressing innocence."

Following the box-office success with the Mermaid's musical revues, Bernard turned to a long-nurtured plan to showcase Farjeon's work, collaborating on the script with veteran critic Jack Trewin and choreographer David Toguri, although nobody involved was in any doubt that Bernard had the upper hand. It developed into a fraught production with cricket imagery (Farjeon was cricket-mad) predominant in Peter Docherty's design, mostly green and white. It became somewhat charged with endless arguments about the running order of the material, to David Toguri's despair. But the sad fact was that Farjeon's revue material had dated badly, its humour out of sync with contemporary taste. The only item to come in for unanimous praise was one of Bernard's "Clod" sketches which delighted those who had never seen Bernard's solo act. Business was depressingly thin for *Farjeon Reviewed*.

A salutary lesson for Bernard was provided by a revival of *Gulliver's Travels*. He got his own way – finally – by insisting this version should use only Swift's first two books but he realised (too late) that he was wrong. The first two books still had the visual delights of Lilliput and Brobdingnag but the evening overall seemed skimpy, without the piercing insights of the Struldbrugs or Yahoos sequences.

At this time inevitably, amidst all the City redevelopment, questions were being asked about the progress confirming the ODP after five years. In the summer of 1974 Bernard approached the Department of Environment (taking over from the Board of Trade) asking for an amendment to the ODP allowing for 20,000 sq.ft. of office space.

Repeating points made previously he stressed:

"It is our understanding that the ODP was given specifically to ensure the future of the Mermaid… We would therefore ask for a clarification from the Department of their original intention in that regard. Was it not that planning again should provide the means to make the theatre viable?"

One very crucial amendment was mentioned. Under the original ODP the demolition of the current theatre and the building of a completely new one was allowed. But now:

"After careful reconsideration it is now felt very strongly that the current auditorium which has been so successful and which has become the model for new theatres throughout the world should be retained."

The architect Colonel Seifert added:

"This decision was to ensure that Bernard Miles's original idea is preserved for posterity."

But at a later meeting at the Department of the Environment he was told that an extended ODP was "unlikely to be achieved." So it was back to the drawing-board; Bernard never got his additional square footage. But crucially he did get a good deal of what he was requesting, including the design of a new theatre which would still incorporate his original conception. This new scheme would require a new planning permission and also a new ODP. This was not acquired until 1976. Bernard tried to force the City to put their cards on the table:

"Does the City really want the Mermaid Theatre? If so, the only way we can keep our own dignity is to be encouraged to develop both the theatre and it amenities by the careful incorporation of our ODP alongside a really non-penal ground rent otherwise I believe it would be honester to say 'We don't want the Mermaid in the City and you would be doing us a service to wind yourselves up, phase yourselves out within the next three or four years so that you are no longer a thorn in our flesh and the flesh of the RSC, the only organisation to inhabit the Barbican Theatre.'"

The last sentence reveals Bernard's long-held conviction that the Barbican housing the RSC represented a threat to the Mermaid. He suspected intense jealousy and wily doings. Quoting Alexander Pope:

"They bear, like the Turk, no brother near the throne."

Changes at Puddle Dock included the arrival of Vivian Cox as clerk to the Court of Governors, replacing Frank Gordon, and my departure. When he invited me to join the Mermaid staff he had vaguely suggested "a few weeks." It became over six years, one of the happiest periods of my career and in many ways a proper blooding in the ways of a producing theatre. I suspect I should have not subsequently managed over ten years as director of another London theatre (at Greenwich) without absorbing everything Bernard taught me directly or indirectly. Before long there would be no work at Puddle Dock during redevelopment. Also, although he had given me my first real break (I never did find out why) we both, I think, felt it was time to move on. I had turned down a few West End offers previously but then Michael Codron (another mentor figure) offered me the West End production of *A Family and a Fortune* with Alec Guinness and Margaret Leighton. I asked Bernard if I had his permission, to which he happily agreed. There was no rancour, and Bernard hinted that perhaps we could work together again after the redevelopment was finished. His goodbye gift was perhaps an unusual choice – a copy of Rilke's '*Letter to a Young Poet*' in exquisite binding.

Bernard strapped up his leg once again for a Christmas run of *Treasure Island* at the New London Theatre. He and Josephine had made a comfortable Yorkshire retreat of a small cottage at Pately Bridge. She drove Bernard up from London, laid on a full Christmas lunch for the family before going to bed, not surprisingly feeling "a bit washed out." She dropped Bernard off at the New London then drove on to the Mermaid. Corinne Rodriguez was at the theatre and was at once alarmed: "She was blue. It was obvious something was very wrong." Corinne telephoned for an ambulance to take her to the London Heart Hospital where it was clear she had had a heart attack. Then Corinne went to the New London between shows to break the news. She recalled when she told Bernard: "His legs gave way. He collapsed." He recovered sufficiently for the evening performance, after which he went immediately to see Josephine in hospital where she had considerably rallied. Coronary artery disease had been diagnosed, the first indication that Josephine had inherited her mother's heart disorder.

Luckily the immediate Mermaid workload was less strenuous at the beginning of 1976, the first show of which was co-produced with Michael Codron, who had been much impressed on reading the Northern comedy, Mike Stott's *Funny Peculiar*. Directed with sure-footed control by Alan Dossor, the production fused a blend of broad farce, even slapstick and touching pathos with ease. No scene was more hilarious than that between Pete Postlethwaite as a travelling food salesman and Richard Beckinsale in the central part of a young grocer, an escalating fight involving cream doughnuts and those Northern sweets called gobstoppers. Looking for a sex life more innovative than that with his quiet wife (Julie Walters), Beckinsale's adventures end with him in a hospital bed, all his limbs in traction. But some things are still possible; behind a screen his wife, led by the willing local woman with whom he has dallied, gives him a lesson in more sophisticated sexual practices (Codron says he had to explain to Bernard what was going on.) Beckinsale's face conveys his ecstasy during his session of oral sex.

Funny Peculiar ran for a packed three months at the Mermaid, launched several careers (Matthew Kelly included) and then transferred successfully to the West End.

There were, predictably, quite a few letters of the "Disgusteds of Beckenham" variety plus some from Bishops and judges. Bernard wrote a polite rebuttal to the nay-sayers:

"We all have, for better or worse, been gifted – or should I say burdened – with these extraordinary organs and what we do with them, and with other people, must of necessity be a matter of the strictest privacy. But I see no reason why a particularly creative and clearly satisfying routine should not be revealed in public particularly as it takes place within the framework of married life."

Bernard was still anxiously looking for a show to follow this hit when, working on another production in the West End, at lunchtime I bumped into an unusually morose Ned Sherrin, frustrated at not being able to find a London home for the musical revue *Side by Side by Sondheim*, involving only himself as anchorman, a pianist and three superb musical performers (Julia McKenzie,

Millicent Martin and David Kernan.) I had been at the Mermaid the previous evening, so could suggest he contact Bernard – following *Cowardy Custard* and *Cole* the Mermaid would be the ideal home for this kind of anthology-revue and I knew that *Funny Peculiar* would be closing fairly soon. Ned found a telephone box nearby and a home was found for *Side by Side*. Sondheim had not yet reached godlike status but the material was superbly performed ('*Broadway Baby*' reimagined by Julia McKenzie especially brilliant.) It was a revelatory opening night and another success, later transferring to the West End and Broadway.

Bernard had seen and admired Joseph Losey's film *Hamp* with Tom Courtenay as the naïf young man being tried during the First World War. He is accused of desertion in the face of the enemy although it is clear his accusers view him as a chance "pour Encourager les autres." Paul Copley, unsentimental and deeply moving, was a wonderful Hamp – the play, by John Wilson, was produced at the Mermaid under its original title of *For King and Country*. Ron Pember, directing, was unhappy with the design; supposedly set in the shell of a bombed French farmhouse which Ron felt was simply too elegant for the play. Late one night after a dress rehearsal Ron was joined in the auditorium by Bernard, in evening dress from a function. He agreed with Ron about the set and then took his dinner-jacket off and disappeared – returning with a wheelbarrow full of broken planks and rubble. Together they 'distressed' the set, with Bernard using a blowtorch to scorch key elements of the design. The designer's reaction is unknown, but the set had splendid notices.

Treasure Island needed a break and *Dick Turpin* was not likely to succeed commercially on a third showing. Quite late in 1976 Ron was in Connie's Bar when Bernard came in with a tall, large Nordic-looking man; this was Harry Nilsson, the American singer who wrote and sang such beautiful songs including the theme song for *Midnight Cowboy*. Bernard and Nilsson had an immediate rapport. Soon Bernard was mulling over whether it might be a good idea, suggested by Ron, to commission a full-length musical from Nilsson's 20-minute show, *The Point*, about a boy without a pointed head in a country where everybody has one. It had had several rejections but when thinking about casting the central boy, Oblio, Bernard at once said "Wayne Sleep" who accepted the part in the show which expanded from its first brief incarnation into an enchanting all-singing, all-dancing show. Bernard was in his element and adored playing the pointy-headed King. Children (and their parents) loved the colourful production (several reviews carried the same injunction: "Don't Miss the Point.") The atmosphere around the theatre seemed joyous once again.

But the tough world of finance still was relentless. At times Bernard must have wished he had never heard of the idea of an ODP. But now there was a group – supposedly to advise him – including James Woolgar, a partner of St. Quintin, Son and Stanley expert in the City's workings and the property market, as well as architect Richard Seifert and others.

"So we had a consortium of these high-grade operators putting their heads together to see what could be done to use this Office Development Permit."

Their proposal was clever – a 'package' in the form of an owner / occupier who would use the Mermaid's ODP to erect prestige offices for their own use and simultaneously renovate and improve the theatre then lease it back to the Trustees for a 'peppercorn rent.'

Woolgar had heard that the high-flying firm of finance managers Touche, Remnant & Co. had to leave their London Wall offices in 1981 and were interested in Puddle Dock as new premises. But negotiations with the City (who owned the site) were tough in the extreme. Lord Delfont (of EMI) took over as Chairman of the Mermaid's Board of Governors after the sudden death of Val Duncan. The minutes of a meeting held on 3rd June 1981 at EMI's Golden Square headquarters make it clear that there was no hope of reducing the proposed price of the freehold. Also – ominously – "There was already some City opposition to the project." Time now was vital. Delfont pronounced that he was happy to proceed "with caution and imagination" which could realise what he described as "this ambitious and highly desirable plan."

There were still triumphs to come in the 'old' Mermaid, although the planned sequel to *Cole*, with which I was not involved, rather whimsically titled *Oh, Mr. Porter!* was decidedly hampered by *Cole* having used virtually all the vintage Porter songs. Willy Russell's abrasive comedy, *Breezeblock Park*, set on a Liverpool estate with Julie Walters and Wendy Craig in the cast, did well enough to transfer to the West End. And other of the Mermaid's surprise successes followed; Vivian Cox's version of Henri de Montherlant's *La Ville Dont le Prince est un Infant*, translated as *The Fire That Consumes*, tightly directed by Bernard with Nigel Hawthorne as a tormented priest in a Catholic seminary. Dai Bradley impressed as the boy while Hawthorne had an almost frightening intensity when forced to confront his own disturbing jealousy and desire.

The Point returned for another sell-out season over Christmas 1977-8 and then the Mermaid struck gold with a new play, co-produced with West End impresario Donald Albery. It sounded to most an unlikely commercial success – a complex set, a large cast and with death at the centre of the story. But *Whose Life is it Anyway?* by Brian Clark, better known for his television writing, seemed to strike a major chord. The central performance by Tom Conti, immobile in a hospital bed and unable to use much beyond his eyes, was highly praised as a man determined to control his permanently-damaged body and choose his own death. This later transferred to the West End and to Broadway.

A Mermaid favourite returned with another unexpected success with Alec McCowen's solo play of *St. Mark's Gospel*. Rather as *Hadrian VII* had come along at what McCowen felt was a low point in his career, so his idea of a solo show, finally fixing on the Bible, and the Gospel of St. Mark which he found to be "remarkably dramatic in structure" with even some ironic comedy was a providential idea at a point when his career seemed stalled. He did a few try-out performances, including some at the Riverside Studios and word began to spread about this extraordinary event; the Riverside was programmed for some time ahead at which point McCowen contacted Bernard:

> "Typically he was on the phone at nine o'clock the next day, full of enthusiasm for the idea and chiding me for not coming to him first. He threatened to empty St. Paul's Cathedral and fill the Mermaid with the devout. He envisaged brass bands playing hymns and massed choirs crying Hallelujah! We made a provisional date in April for me to give three performances a week for a two-month season."

Ten years after opening *Hadrian VII* Alec opened in *St. Mark's Gospel* at Puddle Dock. After the first performance Bernard gave an anniversary *Hadrian* party on stage, a happy reunion for Peter Dews and Peter Luke plus many actors who had appeared in it. Bernard had sent out 3,000 leaflets advertising *St. Mark* to London churches and Christian magazines: "We expect the buggers to come in large numbers," he told Alec. They did. Soon, with Alec running alongside *Whose Life is it Anyway?* in repertory, the Mermaid was doing what the showbusiness paper Variety described as "boffo biz." For Bernard, of all the productions he had steered *St. Mark* was one of which he was most proud, even if it had not been his idea. For him its assertion of faith, its humanity touched with humour made it near-perfect theatre. He also hugely admired Alec's performance – its hold over an audience, its matchless vocal variety and its unshowy panache moved him deeply.

The Mermaid was on a roll as it approached redevelopment time and the final production in the old building was typically ambitious. Nevertheless in 1977 the Arts Council described Bernard as "erratic"; this really stung and he wrote a long rebuttal to the Finance Director:

"The word 'erratic' is based upon the word 'error' and that is really at the root of my reiterated objection and feeling of wounded pride. For 'erratic' suggests, indeed means, wandering mindlessly off course, without settled aim or purpose. But when you come to analyse the reasons why Mermaid policy may from time to time appeared to be what you call 'erratic', it boils down to a very simple answer, the answer you know all too well – the age-old question of L.S.D. If you have enough subsidy or anything approaching enough, you can plunge for a settled policy, announce a year or two's programme and stick to it come hell or high water… But we have all too often found ourselves overhanging a precipice and had to rescue ourselves by moves which invite the word 'erratic' but which all here in the heat of battle would call brave, adventurous, varied, wide-ranging, constantly creative and more than once inspired."

It certainly was adventurous to present *Every Good Boy Deserves Favour*. Its progress to the Mermaid began when Bernard Levin, often a stern critic but equally often an admirer of Bernard and the Mermaid was given lunch ("a sparing lunch") at the theatre during which he asked if Bernard had seen the RSC's staging of *EGBDF* at the Festival Hall. This had a text by Tom Stoppard and a score from André Previn, a daring piece about Soviet dissidents and the attempts to break the chains in which so many Soviet liberals had to live. Levin told Bernard it had a relatively small cast (eight). And ninety-plus musicians.

The last gave Bernard only momentary pause. Immediately after that lunch he telephoned Stoppard to establish whether the RSC had extended its option on the piece. They had not. When Bernard asked if Stoppard and Previn would consider a Mermaid production Previn was just then with Stoppard, who said they would drive to Puddle Dock at once. Negotiating in the dark, as it were,

Bernard had to face the fact that an A-List team such as Previn and Stoppard would expect handsome terms including an option which could be as much as £5,000. Stoppard said they would ask for £5 between them. "Suits me," said Previn. Royalties? Bernard anticipated they might ask for up to 15%. But the duo seemed happy to ask for 6% - 3% each. On to a major issue – the size of the orchestra. Could this be reduced? "By how many?" asked Previn. Bernard did some rapid thinking. "I knew I wouldn't disgrace myself if I jumped for Mozart or Handel." The Handelian orchestra was 34. "Suits me," said Previn again. This was going almost too well. Bernard thought and he still had one problem, possibly an expensive one. How would they get the score re-orchestrated for a smaller ensemble? It so happened that Previn was flying to Pittsburgh for a concert the next day. He would work on it on the flight and then give it to a colleague, the leading orchestrator Al Woodby who lived in San Francisco. "How much will that cost?" Previn thought then said "About $3,500 but I will give you that provided I can have copies of the score afterwards."

As Bernard said: "Two acts of sublime beneficence in a very, very tough world."

A bonus was that the shortish piece (70 minutes) could be performed twice nightly. Working patterns in the City had changed of course, with the digital age abolishing the old 9-to-5 routine and business for *EGBDF* held up strongly. Since May 1959 the Mermaid had staged 150 productions. Not long after the original building closed Bernard prepared a chart recording "Twenty Years of Housekeeping", revealing two low points – March 1966 when the accumulated deficit stood at £62,946 and March 1978 when it reached £139,717. But he pointed out that over 20 years, overall the Mermaid showed an accumulated deficit of only £5.042. No wonder he reacted so strongly to the Arts Council's accusation of being "erratic", saying that "it doesn't quite know where the Mermaid fits in with the scheme of things." He pointed out that unremitting economy and the devoted work of "a very small crew" had kept the ship afloat and helped it to struggle into harbour for a refit and a fresh voyage.

During the latter part of *EGBDF*'s run I had visited Bernard at the theatre where he proudly showed me his model of the redeveloped theatre, about which he had said little previously. I was not surprised by the exterior, now linked into the transformed 'Blade Runner' kind of architecture, all very 1970s and soulless. But I had not anticipated how the internal changes to the auditorium would affect the building. Now it seemed to me to lack the character of the original but, more troubling, I deeply disliked the widening of the auditorium at the front, knocking down sections of the old brick to fan out the front of the auditorium to create 100 extra seats. At a stroke it utterly destroyed the old theatre's priceless asset – the unbroken continuity of stage and auditorium walls, a theatre which had happily accommodated musicals, Shakespeare and the classics, Brecht, Shaw and so many others. Bernard seemed delighted ("It's going to be one of Europe's most beautiful theatres and a permanency for the next 300 years.") I had not the heart to say what I really thought and could not help feeling that the whole design might have been different had Sean Kenny lived, but I felt decidedly depressed on leaving Puddle Dock.

Bernard had another fillip just before Christmas 1978. He was browsing in a bookshop on Ludgate Hill when his secretary brought him a letter from Downing Street offering him a peerage, only the second such theatrical honour. The first, Olivier, wrote from Hollywood:

"I cannot say that I am a socialist but I will say that in this respect Jim Callaghan has been inspired in picking the right person."

Bernard was delighted and spent many happy hours discussing his robes and the design of his coat of arms; it brightened a dismal period, the notorious 'winter of discontent' with public service unions waging a war to smash the government's 5% pay policy. Rubbish piled up in the streets, gravediggers created 'a burial crisis' and cancer patients had to be turned away at hospitals. Bernard could only laugh despairingly on hearing Food Minister John Silkin claim "There has been an improvement in the deterioration." The General Election on 3rd May saw Margaret Thatcher lead the Tories into power; at Puddle Dock things were moving more quickly. The neighbouring Telecommunications Building had been most accommodating, providing office space for two years, but now needed its space back. With the developers still in the Mermaid offices and the lower restaurant being used as a store for building materials, tempers on occasion frayed. Josephine was appalled by the delay in getting the Box Office properly functioning, with no doors on the North End, wet cement with customers having to negotiate planks across the Foyer. Even on Friday 26th June, on the eve of the first public performance, parts of the building were still cordoned off while the concrete was still wet and the restaurant remained unfinished.

Sunday saw a gala show "in aid of the Mermaid Appeal" (well-short still of its £1million target), directed and compered by Jane Asher with much help from Ron Pember. There were seven days of reduced-price previews and then the opening. The first programme leaflet for the redeveloped building was ambitious – six plays, each allotted a six or seven week run. Opening with a new musical, it went on to include a recent Broadway hit, versions of *Julius Caesar* and *Antony and Cleopatra* together under the title *Shakespeare's Rome*, an 11-week revival of *Lock Up Your Daughters* in repertory with *Treasure Island* at Christmas and, finally, the much-anticipated London production of Sondheim's latest musical, *Pacific Overtures*. Prices were still pegged as low as possible even at a time of galloping inflation (£6, £4, £2).

Finally on 7th July 1981 the refurbished Mermaid opened its doors. Unlike the ballyhoo and buzz of the 1959 opening, the new building had comparatively little fuss for its opening – a hastily-rehearsed woodwind fanfare and a hesitant short speech by Sir Ralph Richardson sufficed. There had been endless discussion about the opening production with Bernard opposed to reviving *Lock Up* as an opener, although he did want some nudge towards the theatre's past. Eventually he plumped for a personal favourite – a revival of *Eastward Ho!*, seen at the Royal Exchange and the original theatre, but now as a musical. Nothing necessarily wrong with that idea but, fatally, most of the creative team had had no or little experience with musicals. The director, Robert Chetwyn, had never directed one. Howard Schumann, his lyricist had written sharp lyrics for the TV series *Rock Follies* and the score was by a clever but relatively inexperienced Nick Bicât. The cast had some fine musical talent – Anita Dobson ("a Jacobean Bette Midler" according to Sheridan Morley) the wonderfully miserly Clive Merrison as Security and, making an early London appearance, Mark Rylance as Slitgut, gleefully murderous. The set had one visual delight when the intricate wooden timber construction opened up to reveal the Thames and its boats, but otherwise gave no impression of the goldsmith's workshop in which most of the action takes place. Overall the show never seemed to make up its mind what kind of musical it aimed to be. Francis King in *The Sunday Telegraph* described it as "enthusiastically amateurish", reflecting the general reaction to a show which never took flight. Business was depressingly poor; a City comedy of chancers and scammers must then have seemed an appropriate choice but little about this *Eastward Ho!* was a cheering experience. It was an uneasy first night with the spacious new Mermaid bars virtually deserted post-performance.

If the reviews were harsh for the show they were only marginally less so for the refurbishment which throughout had a nautical theme – the upper restaurant was now named "The Fo'c'sle" while the lower was "The Galley", all part of what *The Daily Telegraph* described as "the jolly nautical atmosphere." I did not care much for the whole refurbishment, with the public areas, with much pale wood, seeming like a branch of some popular eatery. Irving Wardle in *The Times* summed it up concisely:

"Those who remember Sir Bernard Miles's playhouse as a proud free-standing building will now have to seek it out in the bowels of the Touche-Remnant office blocks… another polished granite block of Seifert commercialism."

Wardle also had reservations about the internal changes:

"The Mermaid used to be a combined playhouse and pub. Now it is a theatre with two interval bars and the atmosphere of a long-established restaurant that has fallen into the hands of a chain."

He too had a crucial criticism of the auditorium and the fanning-out of the front rows together with the loss of much of the front side walls resulting in the theatre losing "its one-room character."

Mark Redhead in the *Middlesex Advertiser*, and others echoed Wardle:

"What it lacks is the charm of the old building, faintly chaotic but with an atmosphere of spontaneity and improvisation. The new Mermaid seems to blend in rather too well with the palaces of the money men."

Undaunted, Bernard publicly defended the new theatre against such criticisms; bubbling with ideas for the future. But in private he could be uncharacteristically disconsolate, even admitting that *Eastward Ho!* was a mistake. An expensive one, playing to audiences of around 30% and, given its large cast and musicians, it lost a great deal of money (£80,000). Moreover, both restaurants suffered from delays and building problems while the IM appeal had raised just half that amount.

Some relief came with the second production, the Broadway success of *Children of a Lesser God*, co-produced with Ray Cooney and Ian Albery, revolving around the battle of wills and eventual love story between a famous speech therapist and a non-speaking, non-hearing student, locked in her silent world. Starring Trevor Eve and Elizabeth Quinn, this was a runaway hit and after eight Mermaid weeks continued its success in the West End.

Its success only marginally eased concerns over the finances. This was against a background of now acute recession. Unemployment touched nearly three million in July 1981 and a stock market crash in late September brought unwelcome rumours of soaring interest rates. In this financial climate theatres struggled to survive – in the West End that autumn for a time ten theatres went dark. Some drastic action was needed at Puddle Dock. The upcoming revival of *Lock Up* was cancelled (involving over £10,000 as compensation for contracted actors) as was *Pacific Overtures*, a costly enterprise. Both *Shakespeare's Rome* and *Treasure Island* (with the box-office insurance of television's Doctor Who, Tom Baker) remained as programmed.

Anne Rawsthorne, an experienced hand who had worked for Donald Albery, had been drafted in as the Mermaid's manager. Unsurprisingly she was aghast at the financial situation and also worried that Bernard "had gone a bit wayward." Bernard and a frail Julius, to whom Bernard was always loyal, had arranged *Shakespeare's Rome* as a single evening which involved some major cuts to *Julius Caesar* and *Antony and Cleopatra*. She asked Ron Pember for help – his first task was to clarify the muddles over designers and actors – Bernard had simultaneously offered the design job to two different designers while two Antonys were offered the part. Ron somehow managed to sort out that ticklish problem. Not without some qualms he also agreed to co-direct with Bernard and Julius, not an ideal solution, although after all his time at Puddle Dock Ron knew the score:

> "I would feel as though I was on the top diving board about to do a double-twist dive and just as I was going to dive there would be no water in the pool, but like an idiot I'd jump off anyway."

Rehearsals – with a scaled-down cast, could be tricky with long ruminative silences from Julius and frequent changes of mind from Bernard. There were some pluses – both Timothy Dalton, who had played Antony previously, and Carmen du Sautoy had no small amount of vigour and sensuality (their scenes together were the highlights of a long evening.) But the cutting reduced most characters to ciphers while too many scenes, all against a monolithic columned set, were lost while banners were endlessly whirled about. Bernard in a programme note claimed that "two for the price of one can't be bad", but the press largely disagreed:

> "Oh, but it can" wrote John Barber in *The Daily Telegraph*, "if one is offered bleeding gobbets of the plays rather than the plays themselves. I came away feeling I had been short-changed."

This critical reception could only add to the gloom from the opening night's *Evening Standard* headline – MERMAID ON BRINK OF GOING BROKE.

In a letter to Walter Hodges, Bernard conceded he had made mistakes but his old enthusiasm was back when he wrote excitedly about the venture to follow *Treasure Island*. A typically "adventurey" production – his idea – with all the flair and imagination of the very best Mermaid productions, which saw some major talents working there. Bernard had been knocked out on reading George Steiner's book, '*The Portage to San Cristobal of A H*' which had created quite a stir on publication. Now Bernard believed a very good play might be adapted from it.

The theatre was now run by a Management Committee of Governors which had been set up by Sir David Steel (Chairman of BP) chaired by accountant Michael Jordan plus Bernard and Josephine, Eddie Kulukundis, the executive director of the Bank of England as well as a lawyer, David Freeman. After a meeting on 10th December the stress was very much on maximising income, such as exploiting the auditorium for conferences and seminars. Anne Rawsthorne was quoted in the press as saying:

> "This is not merely a theatre but a whole complex, housing quite separate commercial functions. Each of these must be exploited."

Bernard had always liked Anne and initially they had worked happily together; now he felt her loyalties were much more to the Governors than to him and Josephine. Nevertheless he was full of energy as he steered *The Portage* to the stage. Bernard had suggested a dramatized reading of the novel and Steiner was then "summoned" ("the only right word, I think") to Bernard's office to be asked "with a wonderfully imperative informality" why he had not thought of the idea himself? Steiner pointed out that the contents – the events surrounding the capture by a "strictly unofficial" Jewish search-party deep in the Amazonian jungle of the ninety-year-old cadaverous hermit that was Adolf Hitler had provoked a storm of outrage. But as Steiner said: "My objection seemed to strike Bernard as faint-hearted and, finally, irrelevant… Here, he felt, was a serious piece of work, an allegorical fable or argument at once subversive and worth hearing. Audiences should be treated as adults, and if there was going to be trouble, so be it! At this last point the eyes behind the glasses positively danced."

Christopher Hampton recalled being telephoned "out of the blue" by Bernard with a view to abridging it for a solo performer. Hampton, who had already read the book, said it might work better as a full dramatisation than as yet another solo show:

"Most managements would have hesitated at this point or at least drawn my attention to the fact that my proposal would cost a good fifty times as much as the original notion. Bernard, however, agreed at once."

Bernard asked John Dexter to direct ("we're both working-class boys. That's probably why we get on together.") Jocelyn Herbert, Dexter's regular designer, and lighting designer Andy Phillips were also on board and to Bernard's delight, Alec McCowen signed to play Hitler, with little to say in the early sections, an omnipresent, ominous presence who finally erupts into a long speech of self-justification which froze audiences in a rictus of horror as Hitler points out that the inspiration for his ideology lay in his days among the destitute, befriended by Jews in 1910 Vienna:

"It was there I first understood your secret power. Your teaching. A chosen people. Chosen by God for His own. The only race on Earth chosen, exalted, made single among Mankind."

This long tirade, powered by McCowen, climaxed a fascinating, challenging evening. Critical opinion was polarised (as expected) and some audience reactions were strong. Bernard's loyalty to the production never wavered ("not even when pickets gathered outside," said Steiner.) This was the final production at the Mermaid in which Bernard had any input. Steiner gave a vivid picture of Bernard as they left the theatre after the final performance which had been especially stormy. Pickets were gathered in some numbers outside the theatre and Bernard turned to Steiner, his eyes glinting again, saying, "It's been fun, hasn't it?"

There was no production scheduled to follow. The Mermaid was dark from the spring through to late September although Bernard wrote to Derek Glynne that summer when Glynne was in Australia, with the news that there were still financial troubles but "the theatre comes to light again, albeit it's an outside let, with *Trafford Tanzi*, all about a girl who becomes a successful all-in wrestler" set in a wrestling ring ending with an all-out match. Clare Luckham wrote this play, presented by a feminist company. It was a major success and ran for nearly a year. The theatre received a decent rent but nowhere near enough to reduce its debt significantly. At least the doors remained open.

On the surface nearly always buoyant, Bernard was finding the situation at Puddle Dock increasingly intolerable. In October 1982 he wrote to the Trust Charman, David Steel in some distress:

"I believed the Trustees would naturally wish to be on the side of the two progenitors of the theatre but gradually discovered five of them were only active in the capacity of watchdogs."

He went on to list "disloyalty compounding disloyalty":

"Josephine and I have had the unique experience of the treatment meted out to insolvents… the process of subverting Anne's loyalty to me and Josephine has been one of the most unpleasant experiences of my life."

He detailed what he called "professional monitoring":

"My mail opened, my secretary persuaded to report my every move, my diary examined, my filing cabinet probed, outgoing letters read over my secretary's shoulder then as she was typing them."

These final Mermaid years were not happy for him, now without most of his old staff, and uncomfortable in the building where the atmosphere was both uncertain and uneasy. His friendly assistant, Jacki Harding, did her best to support him ("he was treated very badly.") She more enjoyed times when he would pick up a portable typewriter and they got into a taxi to the House of Lords.

"He marched in, opening doors to find a place to set up his office – "Ah, here we are. This will do." "But Bernard, this is the Bishops' robing room, it says so on the door." "Well, they can share. It won't bother us – we're used to dressing rooms and people taking their clothes off." And off he went, leaving me to the typing! No bishop ever turned up!"

More bitterly Bernard now found the attitude of Sir Kenneth Cork, a recent Lord Mayor and someone he had seen as a supportive friend of the Mermaid – although his sole official connection was as one of the six Vice-Presidents of the Molecule Club – decidedly patronising. He was also one of those most involved with the Barbican Arts Centre project; he seemed busiest liquidating companies on a daily basis. Cork now had most of the Cork Gully's directorate among the Mermaid's Court of Governors. He brusquely brushed aside Bernard's concerns, sharply reminding him that he had "a lot of very important City people doing their desperate best to help the Mermaid."

This was not the view of those working at the Mermaid although some loyal staff had left. Bernard saw these "important City people" as "a shabby little group of frightened men, darting glances this way and that to seek a scapegoat."

The remaining staff felt the same – Derek Glynne, as Bernard's long-time friend and agent, was well aware of his client's volatile temperament but at this time he became appalled at the lack of support from the Governors. He remembered many visits by Michael Jordan and David Freeman to his office, now in Panton Street. They said things like "maybe the whole thing should close as soon as possible" and were surprised when Glynne strongly disagreed. He found Cork unpleasant:

"He was in my office on more than one occasion. I thought he was the most ghastly kind of man because he had no respect for the theatre. He was gunning for Bernard. I must say I found that period quite awful because they were in authority and yet they were ghastly people. I couldn't understand why Bernard should be treated in this way."

I knew Glynne well and grasped how concerned he was about the Mermaid situation. I saw Bernard one afternoon at that time; although he put on a brave front I could see how distressed he was.

At a Governor's Meeting in December held in Cork Gully's Boardroom, matters came to a head. Steel reported that enquiries had been made both about turning some of the space into more offices and creating an audio-visual leisure centre. Bernard kept calm, politely reminding the meeting that their original ODP had been granted in order to provide the Mermaid with financial security. No response is recorded in the minutes of this meeting. Bernard was only reinforcing what he had said previously to Cork when the Audio-Visual House was proposed:

"The Mermaid Theatre belongs to the public at large, who purchased it lock, stock and barrel with solid cash, leaving it to me and Josephine to gather a group of friends and well-wishers of unquestionable integrity to hold it in trust and operate it for them... we have too much regard for the responsibility, placed in us by the people to whom it morally belongs to ever let it slide into such a sorry state as is now envisaged."

He knew that help from the City was unlikely, given that all its efforts then were concentrated on opening the Barbican Arts Centre at a cost of some £200million (the City's contribution to the Mermaid's refurbishment appeal amounted to a princely £5,000).

In a note in his files Bernard noted that the forthcoming Lord Mayor, Sir Anthony Joliffe, offered no support:

"The richest square mile in the world and it cannot stand by one of it most precious children when it finds itself in trouble. They have for 20 years wanted us out of the way. The opportunity suddenly arose when, for the first time, we fell off the high wire."

In some ways Bernard was something of an innocent. He believed that by and large people behaved well to each other. Always busy looking to the future at the theatre, he momentarily took his eye off the ball without having properly noticed that the City was now ruled by a breed utterly removed from the values of 1959. It was a much more venal world, tougher and less sympathetic to the sight of even a small amount of red on a balance sheet.

Bernard and Josephine tried hard to negotiate with a major American Video company with a view to clearing the Mermaid's accumulated deficit and taking the theatre on a long-term contract to present live productions and then pass them on to the video market. But the Governors were, it seemed, in no mood to wait.

The following day was one of the saddest in the Mermaid's history. A meeting was held – for some reason at the offices of Laurence Harbottle, a powerful and expensive theatrical lawyer. Derek Glynne, suspecting that Bernard's fears that the Governors wished to get rid of him and Josephine were true, made himself available to attend. Glynne recalled his embarrassment when he, Bernard and Josephine were kept waiting in a side room while the Governors conferred with Harbottle. They called Bernard and Josephine in briefly – Glynne was told simply to wait, "irked by the general incivility." Bernard was able to tell Glynne that his and Josephine's contracts were secure although they could both give six months' notice at the end of June, according to the contractual terms. Bernard was now utterly worn down by this war of attrition with the City. He wrote to Steel on 11th April:

"For all our sakes I think it is time to put an end to this miserable charade."

Now events limped towards their inevitable conclusion. *Trafford Tanzi* was still running but the Management Committee was soon to advertise the lease in order to clear the accumulated deficit (£650,000). However, finally the Trust dispensed with advertising altogether, although it took two months for this to reach the press.

In the meantime there were some occasions to lift Bernard's spirits. His Maiden speech in the House of Lords was a genuine high-spot. People had expected an Arts-oriented speech but it was lucid and fascinating, arresting from the opening when he quoted the American scientist Vannevar Bush, a member of President Roosevelt's 'Think Tank' who had a few years ago hailed the advent of a new way of living due to science. He produced – with flair – a five-ounce piece of silicon ("from this piece about 30,000 chips can be cut.") The speech broadened into a passionate rallying call for the Government to embrace wholeheartedly and with urgency the digital revolution. In closing he thanked his fellow peers for such an attentive hearing:

"I only once met an audience fuller than this – it was more solid and as representative and gracious – and that was some 15 years ago. I ventured to give a performance to a misguided but very gifted audience in Wormwood Scrubs."

He used time when the theatre was dark to finish some writing with two well-received children's books – '*Robin Hood*' and '*Favourite Tales from Shakespeare*' – and appearing in various TV series including Agatha Christie's *Why Didn't They Ask Evans?* Then he began work, in collaboration with J.C. Trewin on a theatrical anthology, '*Curtain Calls*'. He and Josephine had never owned a London property but continued to rent, now moving from their London Bridge apartment to a terraced house in Alwyne Villas, Islington. He made regular visits to the Lords, much appreciating its library.

Then his old colleague Lindsay Anderson raised his spirits by casting him as Firs, the aged family retainer in *The Cherry Orchard* for a short tour prior to a season at the Haymarket Theatre. Always fond of Bernard, Anderson recalled his arrival for the first rehearsal, alongside Joan Plowright and Frank Finlay, keenly displaying several prosthetics including an elaborately misshapen nose, which he had had made. However;

"he didn't resist at all when I suggested he abandoned the make-up and performed much more simply himself. The result was a beautiful piece of unadorned naturalistic acting."

It was a very touching performance, fussing over his charge, Gayev (Leslie Phillips, splendid) and, at the close when the household has gone, closing up the house and leaving him alone inside, ineffably moving.

He thoroughly enjoyed being back on the stage; Anderson remembers him holding court, particularly charming to the younger actors:

"He enjoyed being naughty as well as being awfully good. It was a joy to have him there, carefully respectful with that touch of irony that communicated always a healthy disrespect. There has always been something naughty about Bernard. Perhaps that is one of his secrets."

During the run he received the first letter for 35 years from Joan Waterhouse, now contemplating a big life-change by leaving her old life even in late middle age. Bernard was happy to encourage her – "Yes, take a new motto for the rest of your life!" Perhaps he felt that, after two decades with the Mermaid which was now ending so sadly, it might be better to take risks.

Then, finally the press broke the story of the Mermaid with *The Stage*'s headline:

"REVEALED! BID TO SELL AILING MERMAID"
Amid a shroud of scenery, trustees of the Mermaid are trying to sell the
building and repay its debt."

This was despite staff denials. The asking price was said to be £1million.
The Trust spokesman denied that there had been vigorous attempts to keep
the sale secret. Even Michael Jordan, Chairman of the Trust's Management
Committee admitted that "someone is trying to cloak it in secrecy" although
he denied any involvement. Not many of Bernard's staff remained and more
left when it was announced, in September, that the Mermaid would be sold
to Abdul Shamji, one of the Ugandan Asians expelled by Idi Amin, who
had built a company, Gomba Holdings, a private and acquisitive industrial
and trading conglomerate in a cash deal of £675,000 which would clear the
theatre's debts. Gomba's interests stretched from military hardware, a stake in
Wembley Stadium and, recently, an interest in two West End theatres. Shamji,
an exuberant character, was described regularly as "one of Mrs. Thatcher's
favourite businessmen." There had been other interested parties – a group of
trade union leaders contemplated a bid of £650,000 to turn the theatre into
"a cultural and arts centre" led by union leader Ray Buckton. The Manchester
Royal Exchange also expressed interest in using the Mermaid as a venue for
their London transfers. But on 24th October the Trustees sent a circular letter
notifying creditors of the exchange of contracts with Gomba.

It marked the end of the story of the Mileses and the Mermaid:

"For Lord Miles and his wife the sale ends more than 30 years of devotion
to the Mermaid," wrote *The Stage*.

It was sad to see Bernard at this time when he seemed, despite all
reassurances to the contrary, to feel he had failed ("Thirty years of work down
the drain!") The theatrical profession was sad that the Trust sold the 97 years
remaining of a 99-year lease (rent-free) of a virtually brand new theatre which
had cost £3million (including fittings) for little over half a million. In the City
there was some glee but just as much regret with whispers of both corruption
and cupidity. Spike Milligan amused Bernard with a copy of his letter to David
Freeman who had asked Spike for his resignation as a governor saying that
actors were not needed (and by implication not wanted) at Puddle Dock but

businessmen were, to which Spike retorted "well, your prediction appears to have gone wrong."

This gloomy period was compounded by the death of Julius Gellner, long-time friend and ally, described by Bernard in a *Times* obituary as "a loyal, much-loved and deeply knowledgeable member of the Mermaid's artistic development." Also he and Josephine were having to come to terms with Sally's illness; she had been diagnosed with motor neurone disease and was now confined to a wheelchair, partly cared for by her devoted family. Then Bernard's brother Leonard died at 81.

Under the Gomba banner, managements brought plays to the Mermaid: Glenda Jackson in *Mother Courage*, an RSC season in collaboration with a West End management and Alec McCowen in a solo Kipling show by Brian Clark, a fine evening. Alec wrote to Bernard to say he was happy to be back at the Mermaid, but added "The heart is missing. You provided that." With some reluctance I directed one production there – a transfer from Greenwich Theatre which I was now running, of Tennessee Williams's *A Streetcar Named Desire*. The play continued its Greenwich success but I thought the theatre poorly run; during one of the gentlest passages, regularly beer barrels very noisily were shifted across the foyer – nobody seemed to care among the front-of-house or management staff. I was very touched that Bernard and Josephine came to see it. I was opening a play in the West End that night so couldn't be there but they wrote a lovely letter saying how much they had enjoyed it. As a postscript Bernard had added Joe Gargery's phrase from '*Great Expectations*' we often used: "Wot larks!"

Over and over in his mind Bernard retraced the 'puzzling events' of his last period at the theatre, writing copious notes, usually on various scraps of paper in an increasingly shaky hand, often berating himself:

"I had no hand in these later negotiations – was considered not sufficiently experienced and was advised to leave it to 'the professionals' which I dutifully but mistakenly did."

Increasingly he came to believe that the Trust passed the benefit attached to what was supposed to be the Mermaid's 'magic stone', its ODP, to Touche Remnant who seemed the most successful lot financially of the whole story.

His belief was that the City – a club of which he never had fully-fledged membership – had played an adroit but shady hand in the later years of the

Mermaid. And it was true that in the theatre's earlier days quite a few friendly City figures – in the days when it was less ruthless – gave him warnings: "The City will try to get that land back one way or another." Or "Many feel you tricked them out of a part of the City's heritage."

He planned to write the whole saga into a paper – one scrap of paper is headed "Rough notes for a paper to be read to the Critics' Circle or The Royal Society of Arts." It would seem he was bought off. The Trust owed Bernard and Josephine £22,000 as creditors but shamefully offered them only £15,000 ("ex gratia") but on condition that they must see a copy. He never finished this as far as can be established but the notion of it seems to have given the Trust pause. Certainly they came back with the £22,000 smartish. Also Josephine wanted an end to any haggling – not just for peace of mind but continued wrangling might damage the ongoing work of the Molecule Club.

They may have lost the Mermaid but they still had the Molecule Club, dear to both but especially to Josephine who would fight like a tigress to stop the Governors from attempting to seize its assets. The minutes of the Trust meeting on 16th December recorded that the Molecule assets should be considered part of the assets of the Mermaid Theatre Trust. Luckily there was in existence a separate Molecule Trust Deed and the enterprise, called now the Molecule Theatre of Science for Children – using as its logo the original heraldic Walter Hodges Mermaid - left its Puddle Dock home for the Bloomsbury Theatre.

Josephine remained artistic director with much help from Andrew Hilton. With great energy and flair they gave the Molecule organisation a new name but also a new lease of life. Andrew wrote several plays for the enterprise, most imaginatively with *The Snatch*, based on the theories of mechanics and with some clever on-stage illustrations of the basic principles but never over-didactic (*The Snatch* was cast to a degree in the style of a Victorian melodrama, very amusingly.) Andrew also wrote *Fire Island*, just as environmental issues were rearing their heads; he also directed this innovative piece. However after the deaths of both Josephine and Bernard in the early 1990s, the ties between Molecule and industry were fundamentally weakened and the Molecule adventure – a unique success story despite its financial pressures – finally ended at the very end of 1994. Andrew Hilton went on to mastermind, very successfully, Bristol's Tobacco Factory operation. Bernard had remained a Molecule Governor along with Jane Asher and Spike Milligan with Geoffrey Sneed of the Science Museum and Colin Ronan. With Government funding from the Department of Education the Company was now able to tour a remarkably varied repertoire of plays to over 30 theatres a year.

So Bernard still had much to do despite the loss of the Mermaid. TV work included the BBC series *Oscar*. With his old colleague Laurie Johnson he worked on a sound picture of the *Battle of Waterloo* with a text from Herbert Kretzmer and, also with Johnson, recorded two further collections of his own dialect Bible stories.

But he went into a perceptible decline in December when Sally died. She was multi-talented – actress (featuring strongly in the suffragette series *Shoulder to Shoulder* on TV), director, singer – but with a restless nature which led to an often stormy relationship with Bernard. The discovery of Buddhism saw her become a member of the Nichirin Shoku, the UK end of the worldwide Buddhist movement of peace through culture and education (*The Guardian* unfairly labelled it loftily as "the new trendy people's religion.") In the weeks prior to her death she kept working, directing a vast undertaking of a musical version of Lewis Carroll. *Alice* had four charity performances at the Hammersmith Odeon (featuring an amateur Buddhist cast of over 300). She was still adjusting the production until the night before her death. She had always shared her parents' work ethic and total commitment to the causes in which she believed. Her death was a devastating blow to Bernard and Josephine; despite their often heated clashes he truly loved Sally and admired her. He managed one last film – the cameo role of a judge in a television movie adapted from Barbara Cartland based on *The Lady and the Highwayman* with a cast including John Mills, Hugh Grant and Michael York.

Early in 1989 the Mileses moved from the house in Alwyne Villas to a ground floor flat ("very small," said Bernard) in nearby Prior Bolton Street. Geoffrey Sneed noticed how quickly he had aged following Sally's death and how he fretted over money – the lion's share of film fees and royalties were always ploughed into the Mermaid – although he finally received a pension of £30 p.w. from the Civil List. Just before Christmas that year Bernard fell at the flat and broke his leg. After an operation and physiotherapy he was back home, walking using a stick. But when he insisted on accompanying Josephine to the pharmacist, entering the shop he tripped and broke his other leg which became a much-embellished story. Sneed visited him in the Homerton Hospital several times ("He seemed lost without Josephine.") Back home when he was stronger he managed to record three radio programmes on the Mermaid for Jonathan James-Moore, to be broadcast on Radio 4.

Then Josephine became ill with severe chest pains and was admitted to the Whittington Hospital on Highgate Hill, worried more about Bernard than herself. She had nursed him with a broken femur and then a broken hip for ten months – it was hardly surprising that she had a heart attack. Luckily, the Actors' Benevolent Fund was able to find room for him in the Actors' Home, Denville Hall in Northwood, not far from the Uxbridge of his childhood. Bernard occasionally wrote to Josephine in hospital calling her "Dearest Girl" and sounding fairly chipper ("Food is Excellent – I have all I could wish for.") He did not mix much with fellow residents, although he knew quite a few. He enjoyed remembering:

> "When I look back over my little life I am aware how much I have been blessed with exceptional parents, both sisters, schoolteachers, Pembroke College, Tom Hopkinson, Baliol Holloway and others. Our three children and their marriages and the little tribe of young. How much we learned from each other. Dear Doris Paul and her hunger for love. And all we managed to do together. And dear Julius. I live with all this in mind and thank you from a very full heart – endlessly love and gratitude."

He added down the length of a margin: "And most of all Kirsten, to whom you loaned me for a while."

Biddy recalled taking him in his wheelchair from Denville Hall to visit Josephine:

> "She was in bed when he arrived but got up, combed his hair. And he asked if she had enough money."

Soon afterward she wrote to him: "The next step – for me to come to you is very near!" The staff at Denville remember him as very excited at the prospect of her joining him.

It never happened. Her consultant at the Whittington stated: "She had recurrent episodes of angina and developed congestive cardiac failure" and on 5th November she had "a stroke followed by a cardiac arrest from which she could not be resuscitated." John took his father to see her for the last time. He did not weep as he kissed her and said "I love you." He was, said John, "very stoic, very strong." Josephine was cremated at the North London Crematorium on 10th November 1990.

For the next few months Bernard remained at Denville Hall. Geoffrey Sneed visited him and noted that his room was unusually devoid of mementos or photographs. I visited him twice – on the first occasion he was very tired and slept most of the time. On the second he was much brighter – he seemed not to want to talk of the Mermaid or the past, much more interested in what I was doing and how the new play I was working on was going. I knew he would not want any effusive thanks but I wanted in some way for him to know how grateful I was to him for taking me on at Puddle Dock when I was very green. And how much I admired his achievements with the Mermaid. He tried to wave away my thanks but he finally smiled, his eyes glinting behind the glasses and said "We did have fun, didn't we?"

I saw him for the last time when he was able, a short time later on 3rd March, to attend a "Celebration for Lord Bernard Miles" at the Mermaid. He was in his wheelchair but mostly alert and attentive. Ron Pember had put together a programme which was directed by Nicola McAuliffe with excerpts from *Lock Up*, *Cowardy Custard*, *Cole*, *The Wakefield Mystery Plays* and other productions, with a contribution from the Molecule Club and a glorious recording of Flagstad singing '*Dido's Lament*'. Bernard even managed, rather deaf now, to give some pieces from *On the Wagon*. The event raised £16,000 which at Bernard's request was given as a Bursary for a science student at Pembroke College, Oxford.

Two weeks later he had yet another fall and had to be taken back to hospital. Then he was taken by ambulance to Yorkshire and admitted to the Thistlehill Nursing Home near Knaresborough. His final weeks were spent there with Biddy and Roy nearby at Pately Bridge in their cottage. Roy was still sculpting while Biddy taught art at a Harrogate school. For the last few days Biddy described him as "floating." She thought he might like some music and at first thought of some Kirsten recordings. But then she thought "No. Nellie wouldn't like that. Beethoven." So she bought a few tapes and a little Walkman. Bernard died on a summer's day (14th June 1991) with The Pastoral Symphony softly playing.

There was a funeral service at the North London Crematorium with only the immediate family and some friends. It was a simple but deeply moving occasion with the service including Kirsten singing '*Om Kvallen*' and – so appropriately – the congregation joining for '*Jesus Bids Us Shine*'.

Bernard's death coincided with that of Dame Peggy Ashcroft and so the following day's obituaries tended to give her the lion's share of space and his tended to be somewhat bland, although all paid due recognition to the extraordinary achievement that was the Mermaid.

The ashes of both Bernard and Josephine were scattered close to their Pately Bridge cottage. In remembrance two trees were planted – a walnut for Bernard, a beech for Josephine. Both thrived.

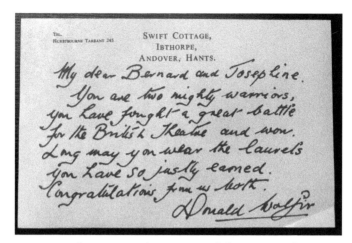

a. Letter of support at the opening of the Mermaid Theatre from Donald Wolfit.

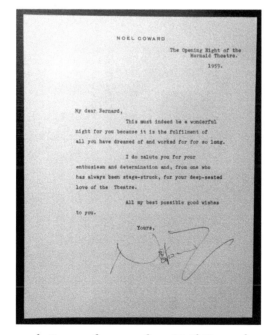

b. Letter of support from Noël Coward.

JOHN GIELGUD

161 E 80 7th Street
New York City

April 13, 1959

My dear Bernard,

I salute the courage of your vision and enterprise
in conceiving and carrying through your imaginative
scheme of a new Theatre in the City of London.

The doubts and fears and difficulties you must have
encountered on the way must have been phenomenal,
and I know of no one but yourself who could have
surmounted them. So, by way of Acacia Road and the
Royal Exchange, you emerge a full flown butterfly
with your own building and project achieved.

It must be a very proud and thrilling occasion
for you and I wish you the greatest possible success
and happiness in furthering it to a permanent and
lasting life.

Good luck to you and your company always.

Ever yours,

John Gielgud

Mr. Bernard Miles
Mermaid Theatre Trust
Puddle Dock Blackfriars
London EC4, England

*c. letter of support from
John Gielgud.*

Doris Day

April 2, 1959

My dear Bernard,

Marty and I are so thrilled with the opening of
your new theatre. We know this must be the
happiest day of your life.

We have been following with great interest
your untiring work on this project and share
with you the joy that comes with this wonderful accomplishment.

Our best to you always.

Doris and Marty Melcher

Mr. Bernard Miles
Mermaid Theatre Trust
Puddle Dock Blackfriars
London EC 4, England

*d. letter of support from
Doris Day.*

VIVIEN LEIGH

February 2th
1959.

My dear Bernard.

My warmest Congratulations
on this great occasion.
The opening of the Mermaid
Theatre is a wonderful achievement
on your part—I do hope your
faith will be matched by the
enthusiasm of the audiences, + that
we shall see your Mermaid grow
into a seasoned + better
madame!
All my best wishes to you.
Yours ever. Vivien.

e. Letter of support from Vivien Leigh.

April 14 1959.   Annaghmakerrig
                                 Doohat
                                 Nounaghau
                                 Ireland.

Dear Bernard,
Congratulations; and may
God bless the Mermaid
of Puddle Dock!
Yours ever,
Tyrone Guthrie

f. Letter of support from Tyrone Guthrie.

My dear Bernard,
So the "mermaid" gets her scales wet for the first time tonight! It must be a wonderful feeling to see all your efforts and dreams at last fulfilled. May the "Mermaid" swim merrily along for many, many years to come.
God Bless,
Harry

g. Letter of support from Harry Secombe.

Peter Sellers 37, Panton St. S.W.1
9/4/59

My dear Bernard,
It is difficult to express the deep admiration which all lovers of the theatre have for you and your achievements. But as a member of the younger generation of actors I can testify to the glorious infection of your persistence and enthusiasm. The Mermaid Theatre is not only a splendid conception by itself, but it is surely the only monument ever erected to symbolize our faith in the future of our profession.
God speed
Peter Sellers

h. Letter of support from Peter Sellers.

JOHN OSBORNE

My dear Bernard —
You have
done a wonderful Thing —
to start a new theatre in this
strange, apathetic London we
work in. It is tremendous.
May the whole venture be
successful, as well as exciting
and courage.
My very best wishes
John Osborne

*i. Letter of support
from John Osborne.*

*j. Letter of support
from Burl Ives.*

k. Letter of support from Diana Dors.

l. Letter of support from Teddy Knox (The Crazy Gang).

Epilogue

THE HISTORY OF the Mermaid after the ousting of Bernard and Josephine makes for melancholy reading. Audiences still came; Glenda Jackson's *Mother Courage* did strong business as did the solo play *Kipling* with Alec McCowen. The RSC in partnership with producers Frank and Woji Gero played a long Puddle Dock season; some productions, including *The Rover* with Jeremy Irons attracted big audiences while others struggled at the box-office. But before long it became clear that Shamji was not much interested in the fabric of the building and was also, to say the least, cavalier in the theatre's financial dealings. The public areas of the building became neglected and bills went unpaid. Possibly looking to improve the Mermaid's image after Shamji's prison sentence (15 months) in 1989 for perjury in lying to the Official Receiver about the extent of his losses, actor-producer Mark Sinden was brought on board as the outfit's artistic director. He was soon frustrated, having looked forward to a challenge, by the Shamji modus operandi. Regularly Sinden would suggest productions and budget them but then nothing would be done to progress them, and before long Sinden became deeply suspicious about Gomba's handling of finances which often looked shifty, even possibly illegal. The whole Shamji concern was, in fact, based on debt. Sinden had to cope with regular bailiffs' visits, basic utility bills and cheques for staff salaries often bounced and his suspicions increased when the City of London police contacted him to warn him to be wary of the Shamji outfit. The police had been quietly pursuing them for some time. Moreover despite Sinden's pleas for cash to address the upkeep of the building the Mermaid was in a sorry state – there were buckets to catch drips from leaking ceilings, light bulbs were missing, auditorium seats broken. The City, obviously, had washed its hands of the Mermaid, left stranded between the two rising giants of the Barbican and the National Theatre.

After the first financial trouble at Puddle Dock under the Shamjis, when the debts amounted to over a quarter of a million pounds, the theatre went dark until November 1987. The Shamjis then simply re-opened under yet another company, called Comfortcall; its two directors were Shamji's two older sons. The theatre, although shamefully decrepit, was still clearly viable but decay was visible (torn carpet unrepaired or held together by gaffer tape.) Surprise, surprise – in December 1992 Comfortcall followed its predecessor into liquidation. Nobody anywhere in the City would seem to have done due diligence into the true nature of those businesses run by Mrs. Thatcher's pet tycoon. Comfortcall's debts touched another quarter of a million. As with the Shamjis' previous Mermaid Theatre Company, Comfortcall had no assets because the building belonged to Gomba, the parent company.

Yet another company, Quorum Quest Ltd., took over the theatre, run now by Abdul Shamji's youngest son, just down from Cambridge. Ambitiously he produced a special event, *Ali*, for which Muhammed Ali and his entourage were flown from the USA with a fat fee awaiting the legendary boxer. He was one of the few to be paid.

By the summer of 1994 Quorum Quest had also collapsed (debts on this occasion only £180,000.) Yet again the theatre went dark. Mark Sinden sensed that the atmosphere around the Mermaid seemed somewhat sinister. The City of London police suggested that perhaps he should, after he quit the Mermaid, keep a low profile for a while.

There had been efforts to keep the theatre afloat – brave attempts by actor-director Roy Marsden and his producing partner Vanessa Ford (their productions included *Vivat! Vivat Regina!* and *A Christmas Carol*) and also Stephen Berkoff. But, as ever, the problem was financial; the Mermaid now needed significant sums spent on the building after its years of Shamji neglect, not to mention the spiralling costs of mounting productions.

Many in the theatrical profession had been appalled by events at Puddle Dock. There had been some resistance, however, not least a continuing campaign led by an intrepid and fearless woman, "La Passionaria of Puddle Dock", Maggie Sutton who had worked in the Mermaid's Accounts Department. So saddened and angered by what was going on as the City prepared to sell the theatre, now in deep danger, she tirelessly organised marches, leaflets and media publicity. The public response was impressive and the then Mayor of London, Ken Livingstone, rescinded the order to demolish the building and redevelop the site. Maggie might have achieved much more but she became gravely ill and died in 2020.

With the theatre dark after the sad saga of the Gomba era, yet another deal – not exactly transparently – saw the Mermaid up for sale again. There was no long queue of interested buyers. Bernard hoped that something might come of the idea of a major redevelopment especially after the City granted a certificate. Behind the scenes, as it were, quietly negotiations were going on and the Mermaid was sold for much less than might have been expected to a property developer, Blackfriars PD Ltd., who had grandiose plans for a major redevelopment of a certificate which removed the theatre status of the building. So – for an undisclosed sum – Blackfriars PD Ltd. was not obliged to follow the terms in the lease under which the building had to be run as a theatre.

Now it has been scrubbed up and makes for a handsome conference and events venue. I was in the building once not so long ago. It was busy with smart-suited, name-tagged captains of industry. But nowhere in the building could I see any reference – not even a photograph – to Bernard and Josephine.

That night I picked up the book, Rilke's '*Letters to a Young Poet*' which Bernard had given me when I left Puddle Dock back in 1975. He had lightly pencilled down a particular page, which clearly was a passage to take particular note of, Rilke's hopes for the younger writer:

"That you may find in yourself enough patience to endure and enough simplicity to have faith; that you may gain more and more confidence in what is difficult and in your solitude among other people… And as for the rest, let life happen to you. Believe me, life is in the right, always."

Endnotes

Gerald Frow's book remained unrevised and no critical apparatus was found. He relied very much on conversations and interviews with family and friends, especially in the earlier chapters together with the sadly few pages which Bernard wrote about his own life. Also sadly, most of the correspondence between Josephine and Bernard when they were parted by work have not survived. Nor have the letters between Bernard and Kirsten Flagstad. Of course all the relatives and colleagues who supplied Gerald with so much of his material have died, although their testimony has the stamp of truth. Much of his Variety material is available on CD. Also a few books written after Bernard's death have useful insights:

Material covering film work with Michael Powell comes from Powell's autobiography, '*A Life in Movies*' (p194).

Anna Massey's description of Powell at work is in her autobiography, '*Telling Some Tales*' (p.76)

On Powell's suggestion of co-directing Bernard's planned battledress version of *Henry V* from '*My Life in Movies*' (p.48),

On *In Which We Serve*, John Mills wrote in his autobiography '*Up in the Clouds, Gentlemen, Please*' (p254)

In his autobiography, Kenneth More wrote of *Chance of a Lifetime* ("an extremely happy picture") in his autobiography '*More or Less*' (p.75)

An evocative account of the first season at Acacia Road was written many years later by Terry Wale who played Ariel in *The Tempest* and who became incurably stage-struck, even volunteering to work the thunder-sheet in the wings for the storm in *The Tempest* as well as playing Ariel; it is in his autobiography '*Pretending to be Somebody Else*' (pp12-13)

Ned Sherrin's much-repeated tale of Bernard and his megaphone is told in his autobiography '*A Small Thing, Like an Earthquake*' (p107)

Joss Ackland's description of Bernard at the Mermaid is from his autobiography '*I Must be in There Somewhere*' (p107)

Alec McCowen wrote illuminatingly of Bernard and the Mermaid and of *Hadrian VII* and *St Mark's Gospel* in '*Double Bill*' (p.167)

For the later years of the Mermaid after the Miles' departure much valuable detail was provided by the late Derek Glynne, Jacki Harding, Marc Sinden and the late Maggie Sutton. I am grateful to all of them.

INDEX